DIRECTING THE WRITING WORKSHOP

Directing
the Writing Workshop

An Elementary Teacher's Handbook

❑❑❑❑❑❑❑

Jean Wallace Gillet
Lynn Beverly

❑❑❑❑❑❑❑

THE GUILFORD PRESS
New York   London

© 2001 The Guilford Press
A Division of Guilford Publications, Inc.
72 Spring Street, New York, NY 10012
www.guilford.com

Printed in the United States of America

This book is printed on acid-free paper.

Last digit is print number: 9 8 7 6 5 4 3 2 1

Library of Congress Cataloging-in-Publication Data

Gillet, Jean Wallace.
    Directing the writing workshop : an elementary teacher's handbook /
Jean Wallace Gillet, Lynn Beverly.
        p. cm.
    Includes bibliographical references (p.) and index.
    ISBN 1-57230-655-6 (hardcover)—ISBN 1-57230-656-4 (pbk.)
    1. English language—Composition and exercises—Study and teaching
(Elementary) I. Beverly, Lynn. II. Title.

LB1576 .G4514 2001
372.62´3´044—dc21

                                                        2001040112

About the Authors

Jean Wallace Gillet, EdD, is a reading specialist in Orange County, Virginia. A former classroom teacher of English, social studies, and language arts, and a teacher educator at the university level, she is the author of several books on reading and spelling, including *Understanding Reading Problems: Assessment and Instruction*, with Charles Temple, and *Teaching Kids to Spell*, with J. Richard Gentry. Dr. Gillet is a frequent contributor to professional journals, has presented extensively at state and national reading conferences, and is a senior author of the basal reading series *SRA Spelling*. She also consults with publishers on a variety of school materials, provides staff development to school divisions, and is a member of the National Advisory Committee on the ETS Praxis Reading Specialist Test. She lives in Charlottesville, Virginia.

Lynn Beverly has taught first and third grades, and researched and piloted a multi-age primary school program. She has conducted staff development workshops on various aspects of language arts, including literacy centers, thematic development, and using literature to enhance writing instruction, and has instructed language arts classes at the college level. She is currently an educational consultant and tutor in Charlottesville, Virginia, where she lives with her husband, Bo, and their two daughters, Alexa and Shaye.

Preface

Teaching writing has never been more important, or more challenging, than it is today. Writing instruction has enjoyed a renaissance in recent years, but today's students still struggle to write clearly, precisely, and powerfully. The need for high-quality writing instruction has never been greater.

We wrote this book for elementary classroom teachers who want to utilize a workshop approach to teaching writing, or who want to build on the strengths of their writing programs. The book grew from our experience as classroom teachers and from our genuine love for teaching young writers. We have tried and used everything in this book; many ideas are our own inventions, while others we learned from colleagues, or from studying and reading about composition instruction. We have adapted all these ideas as necessary to fit the needs and abilities of our students, and we know you'll do the same with the ones you find useful.

We've based the organization of the book on the stages in the writing process, from the earliest stage of deciding to write something to the final stage of producing a "finished" product. As we pondered the many ways of organizing the book, we asked ourselves repeatedly, "What would a teacher need to know at this point in order to teach tomorrow?" The results are the seven chapters that follow.

Chapter 1 describes in detail the fundamentals of the *process writing approach*—which, as its name suggests, emphasizes the process the writer utilizes, as well as the outcome or product of writing. The process approach, in other words, values the journey as much as the arrival. The stages through which the writer must progress in the journey from first ideas to final copy; common stumbling blocks along the way that can trip up young writers; and ways to organize time, space, and materials to maximize efficiency are detailed in this chapter.

Chapter 2 describes how children develop as writers, from the first marks they make as toddlers to their arrival in mid-childhood as full-fledged writers. The concepts children need to develop about writing, and the experiences they must have with it in order to develop, are demonstrated; many examples of early writing attempts are provided. How children learn to spell, which is similar in many ways to how they learn to talk, is detailed in its developmental progression. The predictable spelling strategies and errors of young children, and the ways that writing and spelling develop in tandem, are also described here. Our discussion is based on an extensive body of research in spelling and phonology.

Chapter 3 introduces the beginning of the writing process. How writers develop authentic reasons to write, how they formulate and organize their first thoughts on a chosen topic, and how we can help them find topics are the bases of this chapter. Sample mini-lessons, lists, and other ways of helping students think of topics and avoid the "blank-page barrier" are featured in this chapter.

Chapter 4 deals with the next stage in the writing process, that of revision. The emphasis here is on improving the quality of the writing by making it clearer, more precise, more detailed, and more tightly organized. Writers learn how to give and get feedback from other writers on the clarity of their message. Teachers learn how to conduct conferences with writers, from individuals to groups, in order to foster independence and resourcefulness. Sample mini-lessons help teachers see how a single revision topic can be presented quickly and clearly.

Chapter 5 demonstrates how to help students move through the editing stage, in which writers polish their work by correcting errors and making improvements in sentence and paragraph structure, formatting, grammar and usage, spelling, punctuation, and other surface features. Writers learn to assist each other and engage in "peer editing," but learning to edit their own work is emphasized. Several different activities and mini-lessons, editing aids and checklists, and similar features help young writers master these necessary operations.

Chapter 6 deals with the final stage in the writing process—publishing or otherwise sharing the completed writing. Numerous ways students can share their writing with each other, from the simplest oral reading of a finished piece to the most elaborate publishing effort or young writers' conference, are included. Helpful hints for informal sharing, displaying written work, and book making abound.

Finally, Chapter 7 details the special demands and rewards of nonfiction writing, including various kinds of journals, letters, reports, and informational writing. This chapter explicitly connects writing throughout the curriculum, and includes multiple connections to the subject areas of math, science, social studies, and so forth.

Throughout the book we have included numerous vignettes of actual students and teachers (with identifying details changed or omitted), as well as samples of actual student work that colorfully illustrate the points being made and allow you to see how other teachers handle a particular lesson or concept. Where we've listed steps, sequences, points to remember, and so forth, we've summarized them in highlighted boxes to help you find and remember them. Throughout, we've also provided brief "Teacher's Tips" that condense a particular point to remember. Two appendices at the end of the book give lists of resources (both children's literature and professional works) for teaching mini-lessons and for facilitating journal writing, respectively.

It has been our privilege to share with you, teacher to teacher, the best practices we have found in writing instruction. But, like you, we don't have all (or even *most*) of the answers. We continue to grow and learn, to modify and adapt strategies and procedures, and to wrestle with the never-ending needs of our students. We try to "stop and smell the roses" a bit each day; to recognize and appreciate signs of progress, no matter how small; and to remain open to the wonder and transforming power of children's writing.

In these pages, we invite you to sit beside us in classrooms, to look over our shoulders and read our students' words, and to reflect on the meaning of learning to write.

Contents

CHAPTER 1

■□

Essentials of the Writing Workshop

WRITING INSTRUCTION THEN

What was learning to write like for you? We often begin writing classes or workshops by asking participants to reflect on their school writing experiences. Their recollections, and yours, can be illuminating.

Many teachers can remember little about writing instruction before high school; some can only remember *handwriting* instruction, not composition. Most of what teachers remember about learning to write took place in junior high, high school, or college. More often than not, these recollections are negative. We have listened to voices describing a writing experience, trembling with decades-old anger.

Descriptions of nearly silent classrooms, where the only sounds are the scratching pencils of those writing and the heavy breathing of those who can't think of anything to write, often elicit rueful chuckles. Teachers describe seemingly endless minutes spent staring at blank paper, afraid to begin. They recall looking furtively at others' papers to see how much they'd written, and being foiled by their neighbors' forearms curled around to hide their work.

They recall their teachers admonishing them, "Do your own work, keep your eyes on your own paper, and no talking!" They remember with often painful clarity getting papers back with numerous errors circled in red, and finding cryptic comments like "Disorganized!," "You can do better," or "Awkward!" scrawled across the top. (We share the memory of getting a paper back in a graduate school class, unmarked except for the terrifying command "See me!" written at the top.)

Teachers often recall diagramming sentences; cutting apart duplicated paragraphs and gluing the sentences in the correct order; and writing formulaic paragraphs consisting of a topic sentence, three supporting sentences, and a concluding sentence that restated the topic. They recall contrived topics, timed writing, red pens, recopying in ink, having their moms or big sisters proofread their work at home, trying to figure out what the teacher would like, and using words they could spell instead of words they meant.

Sometimes teachers describe having a love of writing, a need to write, that transcended the way they were taught. These writers recall writing neat, mechanically perfect, lifeless little pieces like "Why I Want to Be a Cheerleader," "Our Greatest President," and "A Visit to Venus" for their English teachers, while simultaneously filling volume after volume of notebooks and diaries with their original fiction, plays, cartoons, and movie scripts. Mostly, they were "underground" writers; their teachers often had no idea they even liked to write, much less that they wrote outside of school. Their school writing was formulaic, teacher-driven, confined, and safe, while their personal writing was free-flowing, deeply personal, and wildly experimental.

But too many of yesterday's students—today's and tomorrow's teachers—never cared for writing, and the ways they were taught to write never changed that. They wrote what their teachers wanted, wrote it over when they were told to, and threw it away when it was handed back. When a teacher in a graduate language arts class confessed, "I decided to become a teacher even though I *hated* to write; I thought I could figure out how to teach it somehow when the time came," many of her classmates nodded in silent agreement.

WRITING INSTRUCTION NOW

The picture is quite different in many classrooms today. Of course, we still struggle with reluctant writers, outdated writing curricula, and inauthentic assessment requirements. Many of yesterday's issues continue to be issues today. But fewer and fewer classrooms today represent the kind of sterile, constrained, teacher-centered writing instruction many of us endured. The boxed "Let's Visit" vignettes in this chapter show real classrooms in several very different schools. (The classrooms, people, and events are real, but the names of schools, students, and teachers are pseudonyms.)

LET'S VISIT: Brightwood Elementary, First Grade

At Brightwood Elementary, a rural school, first-grade teachers have worked together to develop and refine their program for beginning writers. Students write daily, in journals they make with primary paper pages and construction paper or wallpaper covers. They generally choose their own topics, frequently referring to class lists of possible topics that are prominently displayed. For prereaders, the teacher has thoughtfully labeled many of the class topic lists with small pictures or drawings (a house, a dog and cat, young children who might be siblings, a family, an elderly person reading to a child, etc.). Students are encouraged to refer to these lists, to reread old journal entries, and to ask each other for help when they can't think of a topic.

Within a few weeks, the children are "regulars" at helping each other. When Matt moans that he can't think of anything to write about, Patty tells him to look back in his journal for a topic he wrote about before, while Juan suggests he look around the room for something to write about. Although Matt does neither, just getting some help seems to reassure him; in any event, after another moment or two, he begins writing about playing with his brother.

Many children draw in their journals before they write, and the teachers encourage this, as they have found that drawing first helps writers stick to the topic. Of course, many would draw exclusively and never write if given the chance; limits on drawing time ("You may draw until you hear the timer ring; then you should begin writing about your drawing,") and supportive direction ("It's time to put down the crayons and write something about your picture. You may finish coloring *after* you write") help move reluctant writers forward.

(cont.)

All writing is not self-selected. These teachers regularly assign general topics, knowing that in subsequent grades students will have to be able to do assigned writing. When students share writing on the same topic, the teachers point out that even though the topic is the same, each writer produces something different and unique. Assigned writing topics usually feature informational and personal writing and are often outcomes of thematic units, or of field trips and other special events.

Student writing is shared in a variety of ways. A few volunteers read their work daily from the Author's Chair, a fixture in many classrooms. Before the selected students read their finished work today, the others are reminded of the rules for good listening: sitting on bottoms, hands in laps, eyes on the writer, ears listening, mouths quiet.

Individual pieces are displayed both inside and outside the classroom, and each student has work displayed at some time. Writing is often polished, decorated, and given as gifts for holidays and special occasions. Pieces on a common topic may be edited, illustrated, and collected in group and classroom books displayed in the classroom library. Students enjoy publishing their work so much that next year, Brightwood teachers intend to gather writing from all classrooms for the school's first-ever literary magazine.

TRENDS IN WRITING INSTRUCTION TODAY

One important feature of contemporary writing instruction is *collaboration:* across grade levels, students are not only encouraged to help each other, but are directly taught how to be helpful to other writers. Another feature is an emphasis on the process of producing writing, not just on the final product; hence this approach is often referred to as a *process writing approach.* A third feature is that the writer, rather than the teacher, "owns" the writing in the sense of retaining control over many aspects of the topic, the voice used, the means selected to get help, and the ways in which the writing is revised and edited.

In general, writing instruction today tends to be more *differentiated*, more *writer-centered* than teacher-centered, and more *authentic* than the traditional writing instruction of the past. Features of the process writing approach are explained more fully in the next section.

AN OVERVIEW OF PROCESS WRITING

The traditional writing instruction of the past, which you may have experienced as a student, was often based on these beliefs:

- Students need topics given to them.
- Letting students choose their own topics is a risky business.
- Students need to complete writing exercises before they can write.
- The teacher is the best (or only) audience and judge of student writing.
- Good writing is formulaic.
- *Really* good writing is mechanically perfect.
- Writing is a solitary activity; if students work together, they will copy.

A process approach to writing instruction challenges each of these tenets. As its name implies, the emphasis is on the *process* of writing, not on the final *product*. Students learn to write not from exercises and textbooks, but by actually writing. Direct instruction occurs frequently if not daily, but is based on the issues students are struggling with, not on the scope and sequence of a composition text.

The vehicle for direct instruction is most often the *mini-lesson*—a short, focused lesson wherein one skill, point, or procedure is explained and modeled or demonstrated, and then students who need it seek to implement it in their writing. Often mini-lessons are directed toward a group of students who need help in that skill, rather than to everyone in the class regardless of whether they need it or not. Mini-lessons are active and hands-on; groups are most often flexible, temporary, and needs-based.

Instead of silent writing classrooms where students cover their work to keep others from "stealing" it, in process writing students are encouraged and expected to collaborate with each other, and are systematically taught how to do so successfully. A topic belongs not just to the one who thought of it, but to anyone who wants to use it. Ideas are not owned, but shared. What students "own" is their own work. They also decide when they need help; seek help from others, including, but not limited to, the teacher; and decide what suggestions they will implement. Teachers may critique work, but rarely collect it to mark the errors.

BOX 1.1. Basic Tenets of Process Writing

- Emphasis is on the process, not the product, of writing.
- Children learn to write by writing.
- Mini-lessons are the major vehicles of direct instruction.
- Instruction is based on what students need to learn at the time.
- Instructional groups are temporary and needs-based.
- Collaboration is encouraged.
- Writing is shared with a wide audience.

Most often students write on their own self-selected topics. When everyone writes on the same topic, options are available so that students can use different writing forms or "voices," and retain ownership of the work. Students collaborate with partners; seek help from each other privately or in group conferences; implement the suggestions that make the most sense to them; and experiment freely with styles, voices and topics.

Teachers show students how to break the task of writing into several manageable parts: preparing and organizing ideas, writing a tentative draft, revising draft(s) to clarify meaning, editing work after revisions are complete, and producing a final copy to share with a wider audience. Rarely is the teacher the only audience for a work, or the only source of criticism or praise. Rarely is writing done solely to fulfill an assignment; for example, when they learn to write letters, students write real letters to real people, put stamps on the envelopes, and mail them.

Writing is shared frequently—with partners, groups, and the whole class. Writing is often given to others; students present each other with pieces they have written, and write poems and create books to give as gifts. Literature is used as a source of inspiration and modeling for young writers: Author studies, genre studies, and thematic units in literature segue smoothly into writing lessons on description, dialogue, suspense, character development, and researching topics.

The process writing approach has challenged much of what we were all taught about learning to write. Many of our most cherished beliefs about good writing may be shattered by what ordinary teachers and students are able to produce in this very different writing environment.

THE CRAFT OF WRITING

What causes a writer to sit staring at the blank page, unable to begin? Writers call this the "blank-page barrier," and its cause is fear. If they haven't written

---

BOX 1.2. Good Writers . . .

- Write a lot.
- Write about what they know.
- Use real writers as teachers.
- Help each other.
- Write for authentic purposes and audiences.
- Aren't afraid to "mess up."

LET'S VISIT: Rosa Parks Elementary, Third Grade

At Rosa Parks Elementary, an urban school, third-grade students have a 45-minute writing period daily. Their writing period begins with a group or whole-class mini-lesson. This is followed by a brief portion of quiet time for reflection and writing, and then by a somewhat longer phase in which students can collaborate, work on group projects, and confer with peers or the teacher. The writing period concludes with sharing time.

On a typical day, we would see the teacher deliver a mini-lesson on a particular skill or operation the students need to practice. Today she reads examples of dialogue aloud from several trade books, and students discuss what makes dialogue sound real and natural. Students are encouraged to try adding dialogue to something they are writing, or to try to improve dialogues they have written already, when they begin today's work.

Ten minutes of quiet writing time follow, during which the teacher unobtrusively circulates to observe what students are working on, to exchange whispered comments with a few individuals, and to jot notes of her observations on each student. These provide documentation of student progress, difficulties, and behaviors, which she will use when conferring with parents and evaluating student progress.

During the 15- to 20-minute collaboration phase that follows, these third-grade writers work together in a variety of ways. Ashley and Stephanie are collaborating on a story, but have gotten stuck on the next part of the plot. They ask Cecily to help them get "unstuck," and Cecily listens to the story and makes several suggestions. Ashley jots them on a scrap of paper; later she and Stephanie will decide which, if any, they might try.

A few minutes later Raye asks Ashley to help her think of a way to put a character's name into a story without writing "His name was _____." Ashley suggests adding dialogue: "Have somebody come up to him in the story and say, 'Hi, Whatever!' "The teacher mentally notes that Ashley has just applied today's mini-lesson skill to help Raye.

Maurice has just finished a revised draft of a vacation story he's been working on for almost two weeks. Beginning as a factual travelogue, it has evolved into a work of fiction in which the heroic Maurice saves his cousin from a fire. Maurice rereads his draft, then throws himself back in his chair with a huge sigh of satisfaction. Soon he'll look for a partner to read it to; for now, he's savoring a delicious moment all writers understand.

anything, they haven't messed up yet, remember? Writing anything is seen as the biggest risk, and many students try to avoid as many risks as possible, at least in their schoolwork. This blank page barrier arises from the conception that writing is like sculpting in stone. It's like in the cartoons when a man is going to cut a diamond. He holds the hammer over a big rock, and the hammer just hangs there for the longest time. He gets ready, he aims, and finally he brings the hammer down. *Bam*! The diamond shatters into a million pieces. It's ruined.

The hardest part of writing is often starting out. The beginning seems somehow to cast the die for the rest of the piece. "I agonize over the first sentences," a middle schooler told us. "If I have a weak beginning, the whole piece will be nothing. I have to find just the right beginning before I can go on." This writer looks at her writing as an uncut diamond or a piece of marble. A slip of the wrist will ruin the whole piece. Beginning is a risk, but even with a strong beginning, the risk grows with each sentence, each word. No wonder so many students scrawl two or three sentences, then announce with relief, "I'm done!"

Students need to conceive of writing as working in soft clay, not hard stone. A marble sculptor who makes a mistake may crack the piece down the middle, or have to change the design to cover up the flaw; however, a potter doesn't throw away the misshapen clay, or roll it into a ball and begin again. Instead, the potter continues to reshape the wet clay, for it is malleable. Not until it is finished, glazed, and fired does it assume its permanent form. This is the analogy we continually make to young writers. We have even taken classes to the art room so the art teacher can demonstrate how to rework clay. When frustrated writers announce, "I messed up!" and throw down their pencils, we remind them, "It's clay, remember? Whatever is wrong can be fixed up."

TEACHER'S TIP: Post signs in your writing center with thoughts like these:
"Writing is more like working with soft clay than hard stone."
"Good writing doesn't just happen."
"Good writers are made, not born."

In the same way, we try to help students realize that good writers are made, not born. Good writing is not the result of being gifted or having a "natural talent" for writing, although surely some people are more strongly drawn to the written word than others. But people are not born good writers, we remind our students, the way they are born brown-eyed or left-handed. Good writing is the result of work and effort. Everyone can produce good writing by working at it.

Students often think that good writing just *happens*. This myth is a prevalent one. Students earnestly ask visiting authors, "Were you a great writer when you were a little kid?" The authors invariably laugh. "Of course not!" they answer. "I was just like you!" Kids rarely believe this. Good writing is thought to pour out in finished form, like turning on a faucet.

When writers appear as characters in TV shows or movies, we see them busily tapping away at a keyboard; they rarely pause for more than a few moments, and the lines roll forth majestically. A popular TV series that featured a grandmotherly writer/detective opened each episode with the heroine typing furiously, a satisfied smile on her lips; when she withdrew each page from the typewriter, it appeared as a finished copy, which she placed between the covers of a book. Conversely, what is the universal symbol of the frustrated (or failed) writer? A brimming wastebasket surrounded by balled-up pages that have missed the target.

Images like these reinforce the notion that writing is an all-or-nothing proposition. Either the words are pent up inside waiting to be released, pouring forth in orderly ranks of sentences, pages, and chapters as fast as the writer can push the pen or hit the keys; or the well is dry, and the writer sits in despair, head in hands. Donald Graves (1983) referred to this myth when he wrote, "Like the Tablets, words are dictated to us from on high; we only hold the pen and a mysterious force dictates stories, poems and letters. The better the writer, the less the struggle" (p. 43). We come to believe, wrongly, that "good" writing emerges nearly effortlessly, or at least without much struggle, and in finished or nearly finished form, needing only to be copied over in ink. We come to think that "bad" writing has to be hacked at, fought, vanquished, cut apart and re-fashioned, scratched out and erased, perhaps finally even thrown away and be-gun anew.

□□

TEACHER'S TIP: Nobody is born a good writer. Good writing is a result of effort and practice.

□□

All of these notions and ideas about "good" versus "bad" writing are more than just wrong; they are very harmful to young or developing writers. Every writer struggles, and there is no way around this. If young writers believe that struggling with a piece means it must be bad, or that struggling means they are bad writers, or that doing something over means it was wrong in the first place, then they will never develop the patience, persistence, and tolerance they need for putting in long periods of hard work over a piece of writing.

Writing is a craft like any other—like pottery, to return to our earlier analogy. Throwing pots and writing both require sets of skills that can be learned and that must be practiced over and over again. Mistakes occur, but mistakes can be fixed. Writing can be reworked over and over until the writer is satisfied. Writers work at their craft.

WHAT WRITERS NEED

Young writers can learn a great deal about being a writer from real writers. Au-thor studies, or units on the life and work of particular authors, are very beneficial. There are many kinds of materials available that help students learn what published authors go through as they write—articles, books, videos, and so forth. Through the words of published authors, young writers can learn what writers need in order to grow.

1. *Writers need authentic reasons to write*. Writing is a form of communication. If it is authentic, it is created to express something to others, and its message is received by others. If it is inauthentic, it is produced not to communicate, but to get a grade or complete an assignment. It is written to someone else's specifications, not to convey a message, or it is received by someone other than the one for whom it was intended.

2. *Writers need lots of time to write*. Almost all published authors agree that writing is a job—one they pursue systematically. A best-selling author describes in a magazine profile how he routinely puts in six to eight hours a day at the keyboard. An award-winning poet gets up several hours before her family rises, and works for four hours a day on three poems simultaneously, in addition to full-time university teaching. A writer of popular horror books for children writes eight hours a day five days a week, and finishes a book every four weeks, like clockwork.

3. *Writers need a predictable time each day to do their writing*. When they know that each day at a particular time they will write, they can begin to make plans for their writing at other times during the day. When good ideas occur to them, they know when they will be able to write about them. They know they won't have to wait until the next rainy recess, or next month for the "creative writing unit," or Friday afternoon if there isn't an assembly. They will be writing that day.

4. *Writers need colleagues*. Most crafters choose to work at least part of the time in the company of others who share their interests and skills. For hundreds of years, artisans have gathered together in guilds; artists have gathered in art colonies; artists and crafters have formed studios to share space, materials, and ideas. After materials, artists and crafters need colleagues to share their ideas, inspire them, and keep them company as they practice their art. Creation, after all, is a lonely process; creators seek the company of other creators who know what they are experiencing and can support and help each other. Writing is a creative act, and the writer's medium is words. Words exist only to communicate. Writers need other writers to communicate with, to share ideas with, to celebrate and commiserate with. The classroom is the ideal place to establish a community of writers.

5. *Writers need assistance*. Even professional writers join writers' groups, manuscript exchanges, and classes to get help and support from other writers. Young writers need a tremendous amount of support and help as they develop skills and try new things. In the past, the teacher was expected to be the sole provider of such help. Pity the poor teacher who was unskilled in writing or in

LET'S VISIT: Mountain View Middle School, Sixth Grade

Sixth graders at suburban Mountain View Middle School have a 90-minute language arts period daily, but teachers still struggle to get in all the reading, writing, grammar, spelling, and other subjects they need to teach.

One team opts for daily writing, concerned that students will not progress in writing without daily practice. Another team utilizes a longer sustained writing period two or three times weekly, finding that the longer writing provides more continuity, allows for longer or more detailed lessons, and gives students time to write longer drafts and confer more effectively. However, some students are having more difficulty remembering what they were doing from one writing period to the next, and reluctant writers who are easily frustrated may give up sooner when they are faced with a longer instructional period. Clearly, there are no easy or clear-cut answers to these scheduling issues.

Sixth graders are able to do much more revising and editing than younger writers, and much of their instruction focuses on revising to make writing stronger and more effective. Skills lessons frequently focus on revision issues, such as clear organization, constructing effective leads and conclusions, creating variety in sentence length and complexity, using transitional phrases effectively, and selecting vivid vocabulary. Because sixth graders are still quite concrete learners, their teachers use models from literature, examples of student writing from other classes, and their own writing to illustrate their points. Teachers use a structured lesson format, featuring introduction of the skill, direct teacher modeling, guided practice in applying the skill (often with a partner or group of three), and independent application of the skill in one's own writing. Such *scaffolding* provides support for less able writers, while it avoids subjecting more advanced students to repeated practice or review.

Today students learn a new way of *webbing* a topic prior to writing a first draft. After making a list of as many topics as they can think of that relate to a recent school vacation, students work in small groups to color-code related topics with colored pencils and identify what relates all the items in a category. Back together as a large group, each student identifies one of the color-coded categories from his or her list. Listening to others' categories helps several struggling students understand the task.

Tomorrow the students will label the center of a web worksheet with their selected category, then fill in the surrounding web segments with the individual items that share the same color code. In subsequent sessions they will use their webs as outlines for writing personal narratives about the recent vacation. Their teachers hope that by practicing different ways to construct and use webs, the students will learn to use this technique independently when they must complete quarterly writing assessments.

teaching it! And pity the poor teacher with 100 or more students, as was (and still is) common in middle and high school English. The expectation that teachers can provide all the help writers need is nonsense. Peers can provide more support, encouragement, and real help than even the most involved teachers can. Peers are right there at hand when writers need them; if one is busy, someone else can be consulted. If peers don't understand something, or if they do, they will say so. Sometimes all that's needed is somebody to listen.

6. *Writers need a predictable place for all their "stuff."* For many writers, this is the writer's notebook—the physical storehouse for all their ideas, reminders, bits of dialogue, and other scraps that have possibilities. For others, it is the writing folder—the place where they keep their topic lists, first and subsequent drafts, and parts that have been deleted from a piece but might be salvageable for another piece. Teachers and students adapt different ways to meet these needs; some use hanging files, pocket portfolios, notebooks with pockets and dividers, and so forth. As in any craft, a writer needs a place to keep all his or her writing-related stuff. (You will learn more about writing notebooks, and other ways to organize, in Chapters 2 and 3.)

CREATING AND CRITICIZING: OPPOSING FORCES

During writing, two forces are acting upon the writer: the *creating force* and the *criticizing force*. These two forces constantly oppose each other. Think about when you yourself are writing. A part of your mind comes up with great ideas, and another part of your mind casts doubt upon them. It's as if you heard two voices in your ears that no one else heard; one says, "Try this!" and the other says, "That's a terrible idea!"

BOX 1.3. Does Your Writing Program Provide . . .

_____ Authentic reasons to write?

_____ Plenty of time to write?

_____ A predictable time each day to write?

_____ An atmosphere of helpful collaboration?

_____ Instructions for peers to support each other?

_____ Support from the teacher when problems arise?

_____ A predictable place for necessary materials?

What needs to be changed in order for these criteria to be present?

The inner voice that comes up with ideas is the Creator—the one that tells writers, "That's a terrific idea! Put that in!" The inner voice that discourages those ideas is the Critic—the one who urges caution, who throws a wet blanket on each idea, who says, "But what if the teacher doesn't like it? That's a dumb idea!" Unfortunately, most of us listen to our Critic's inner voice altogether too much! At least, we listen to our Critic when it's harmful to do so: when we are beginning to write or constructing early drafts.

Of course, the voice of the Critic has its place; writing or any other creative endeavor only works when there is balance between these two forces. Without the Creator, nobody would ever have an original idea in writing. And without the Critic, nobody's writing would ever be considered objectively, shaped, or corrected. But when one voice outshouts the other, imbalance results. The goal is not to try to muffle one or the other, but to have each one exert its rightful authority at the right place and time in the writing.

Breaking the process of writing into separate steps helps young writers find the right balance between their Creators and Critics. At the beginning of a piece, when writers are coming up with ideas, experimenting with styles and voices, and trying to cast their meanings in words, the Creator should be allowed full rein and the Critic muffled.

We tell young writers to put a mental hand over the Critic's mouth and to refuse to listen to the Critic saying things like, "That's a dumb idea!" or "Take that out!" At this stage, the Critic is not helpful; its voice will only prevent a writer from coming up with all the raw material necessary to eventually create a finished work.

In the middle of the writing process, when writers are revising their pieces, the Creator and Critic both have a role. Here writers are clarifying what they have written, adding and deleting, moving parts around, still working with content rather than mechanics or appearance. This requires a step away from the material; a writer's own Critic is needed here—in a subordinate role—as well as input from other writers, to help the writer discern what works and what doesn't. The Creator is still necessary, as writers at the drafting or revising stage still need to come up with new ideas, fresh approaches, and original thinking. At this stage, the two forces must work in harmony (or at least alternately!).

⊡⊞⊞⊡

TEACHER'S TIP: Keep the Critic in a subordinate role until the
Creator is done.

⊡⊞⊞⊡

The final stage before completion, when writers are editing and polishing their work, is the real domain of the Critic. Here the Critic wields its figurative red pencil with authority. No longer is the writer concerned with developing new ideas or fresh approaches; these were the objectives of the revising stage. Now that the final draft has been created, and its ideas, images, and information are satisfactory to the writer, the real work of the Critic begins. The Critic helps the writer find misspelled words and makes sure that subjects and verbs agree, sentences are complete, proper nouns are capitalized, paragraphs are complete and indented, events follow one another in logical order, dialogue makes sense, characters behave in believable ways, and so forth. The Critic helps the writer polish the work and achieve the physical correctness that it deserves.

The steps in the writing cycle, which help writers separate the very different functions of the Creator and Critic, are shown in Figure 1.1. Discussing such a scheme with writers may help them understand that each step in the writing process has a different function, and that separating the process into stages helps them gain control of each function.

ESTABLISHING A WORKSHOP CLIMATE

You watch your students enter the classroom on the first day of school, or any time in the first weeks of the year, and all you see are individuals. Each student has his or her own learning agenda; each has very different and personal prior experiences, at home and at school; each contains the essence of what prior teachers have taught him or her; each one has very different social and emotional needs. They all want what they want *first*: They all want to talk first, line up first, get everyone else's attention first, and hold it as long as possible. Each one has needs, and has a strong drive to get those needs met one way or another. And your job, so your supervisors tell you, is to create a "community of learners" out of this group of diverse individuals!

It may seem unlikely in the first days—even impossible—but it happens. A classroom *is* a community; individuals *do* come together as a team. But this

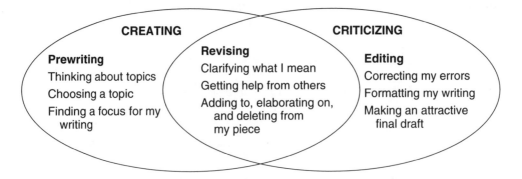

FIGURE 1.1. The writing process: Opposing forces.

rarely happens spontaneously. Instead, it takes consistent effort on everyone's part, as well as systematic instruction on how to work together productively.

Workshop Rules and Procedures

Students learn how to behave in writing workshops (1) by what you *teach* them directly, and (2) by how you *model* for them.

▢▢

TEACHER'S TIP: How you respond to writers is as important
as what you teach.

▢▢

Many teachers begin the first day of writing workshop by going over a lot of rules for what to do and not to do. This is one way to begin. However, we prefer to get students started brainstorming and choosing topics, and beginning to write first drafts, on the very first day. We avoid giving topics the first days and then easing into having students generate topics; in our experience, the student who is given a topic today will expect one tomorrow or next week, and this only prolongs the difficulty. We like to get students started writing right away, so that they will see themselves as writers right from the start.

We also want to teach an important point right away: *Topics are not owned, but shared by all.* So we begin by modeling starting a topic list and doing a first freewrite, then sharing it. During this first day or two, we model exactly what we want students to do, including how we want them to respond to each other. You will learn more about topic selection mini-lessons in Chapter 3.

After the first couple of days, we start introducing rules and procedures. They are tailored to the grade level of the students, but they are generally like this:

- "Keep all your writing materials in your folder (or notebook). Don't throw anything away!"
- "Instead of waiting for me to come to you, you may ask classmates for help when you need it. But ask politely! Someone may be busy working and not able to help you."
- "When someone asks you for help, make suggestions in a helpful, not bossy, way. It's up to the writer to take your suggestions or try something else."
- "Don't take someone's paper and write on it. Papers belong to the person who wrote them."

LET'S VISIT: Robert F. Kennedy Middle School, Eighth Grade

At Kennedy Middle School, eighth-grade teachers help students prepare for the required statewide writing assessment in the spring of eighth grade. Instruction at this level includes emphasis on the types of writing required by the state assessment and on the criteria used to evaluate them. Students complete trial runs for the spring writing assessment at least quarterly; they are given a topic and an uninterrupted 90-minute writing period in which to produce a complete composition entirely without assistance. Students are to use prewriting techniques, such as brainstorming and webbing; create a first draft; revise the draft for quality; edit the revised draft for correctness; and produce a correct, polished final draft, which is to be no longer than two handwritten pages in length.

Today all eighth graders will spend their 90-minute language arts block in a writing workshop, which occurs once weekly. Students retrieve their writing notebooks or folders when they come in, and settle into individual desks and around tables. Each teacher presents a mini-lesson based on skills being taught and reinforced during the grammar and usage lessons. For example, today Mr. Hancock's mini-lesson focuses on checking for complete sentences, while Mrs. Morris reviews pronoun and referent agreement. After working through an example together, students edit a short sample piece individually and compare their findings, then check their own work for similar problems. Following the mini-lesson, all students work independently on a current piece. While some think and write quietly, others confer with peers, read their drafts to partners, or help each other with editing. At a central table, teachers meet with individual writers to go over a recently graded piece, pointing out strengths and weaknesses in each paper and reviewing or demonstrating particular operations. Each individual conference lasts five to ten minutes, and is the teacher's best opportunity to observe the writer's progress, provide individualized instruction, and engage in a focused dialogue with the writer about the piece.

While Kennedy teachers acknowledge the necessity of teaching their students how to pass these mandatory, high-stakes assessments, they also chafe at the ways they think state requirements dominate the instructional program. English teachers feel strongly that such assessments do not adequately assess students' writing ability, and strive to enrich their writing instruction by including thematic units, author studies, and other projects (such as poetry writing, plays, and writing for research). They keep portfolios of student work and help students self-evaluate, but they know that the bottom line is this: How well can their students produce a polished composition on a random topic, no longer than two handwritten pages, without assistance and in a single 90-minute sitting?

In the first few days we circulate freely, visiting with each writer as soon as possible. We model how we want students to respond to each other by making positive comments, finding something good to say to each student, asking questions, and refraining from telling students how to solve their problems. We do, however, suggest ways writers can get help: looking in a story, asking another student for help, looking in a resource book, and so forth. We're careful to make suggestions, not to give orders.

After a few days, a mini-lesson on good ways to respond to others' writing is appropriate. With prior permission from several students, we conduct two or three brief "public" conferences with everyone else watching and listening. We direct students to do particular things—for example, "Ask the writer a question about the topic," or "Identify a part you liked and tell why you liked it." Then writers pair up and follow the same procedure, taking turns. Afterward we discuss positive comments and negative or unhelpful comments.

In a subsequent lesson, these may turn into student-generated rules or guidelines, which may be posted conspicuously. Middle graders especially love to make rules. If given the opportunity, they will make dozens of rules prohibiting just about everything! Avoid this by encouraging them to make just a few (say, five or fewer) "biggie" rules.

A few procedural reminders will be needed at frequent intervals about materials. Students should learn right from the beginning to save everything, and never to throw out drafts they don't like. They might like them later, or might find just the right sentence, idea or image in a discarded draft for a later piece. Have students give everything at least a tentative title, and date it at the top. Older students who write numerous drafts can mark them "Draft 1," "Draft 2," and so forth. Related papers can be paper-clipped together. Writers should use only one side of the paper (so they can cut and paste later) and skip lines (for ease in inserting corrections and additions).

As time goes on, you will discover what issues need to be discussed and what rules or procedures need to be formalized. If your students have difficulty keeping materials organized, mini-lessons on care of materials may help. Some students may have more difficulty than others cooperating rather than competing, or some may have difficulty offering suggestions instead of "bossing" or taking over. These issues can be dealt with in class meetings or in whole-class or group mini-lessons.

The Importance of Predictability

Consistency and predictability are key ingredients in a successful writing workshop. As mentioned previously, when writers know they will write every day at a particular time, they begin to plan for that; they begin to "think like writers" at other times of the day. Routines are also important because they allow students to take control of their own actions; we teachers don't have to constantly direct the action. When routines change frequently, students' focus tends to be on the "frame"—the time and duration, rather than the content, of the lesson. When we establish consistent routines for the writing workshop, we allow students to focus on the writing and take control of some of their behavior.

Predictable routines may include when mini-lessons usually occur (*before writing? during the writing?*), when and where students will gather together to share (*at desks? on the rug? in a circle? at the end of the workshop? after lunch?*), how many and which students will share each time (*sign up? ask the teacher? race each other to the Author's Chair?*), and so forth.

You can answer some of these questions before the year begins. We ourselves like to conduct mini-lessons at the beginning when everyone is paying attention; we like students to come physically together in one place rather than sitting at their desks to share; and we *never* allow students to race to the Author's Chair! Some routines, however, must be established after students have become individuals to each other, and the group has begun to reveal its own unique chemistry.

THE MINI-LESSON: THE VEHICLE OF INSTRUCTION

The major vehicle for delivering instruction in writing workshops is *the mini-lesson*—a short, focused lesson in which the teacher raises an issue, demonstrates a method, focuses attention on an author's technique, or reinforces a strategy. Mini-lessons often occur at the beginning of the workshop, but not necessarily; many teachers prefer to move among writers at work for a while, noting strengths and problems, and then call together a group (or the whole class) during or after the workshop to deal with the issue at hand.

How do mini-lessons differ from the usual beginning-of-instruction lessons you experienced as a developing writer? Lucy McCormick Calkins (1994) has described it this way:

> The difference can be summed up in a single word: *context*. In mini-lessons, we teach *into* our students' intentions. Our students are first deeply engaged in their self-sponsored work, and then we bring them together to learn what they need to know in order to do that work. This way, they stand a chance of being active meaning-makers, even during this bit of formal instruction. First our students are engaged in their own important work. Then we ask ourselves, "What is the one thing I can suggest or demonstrate that might help the most?" (pp. 193–194; emphasis in original)

Mini-lessons represent *needs-based instruction*—that is, teaching what students need to know at a given moment in order to get on with their work successfully. As such, they do not follow a structured scope and sequence, like those

---

BOX 1.4. Mini-Lessons . . .

- Are short.
- Focus on one topic or strategy.
- Can occur before, during, or after the writing workshop.
- Are based on what writers need to learn today.
- Require systematic monitoring of students' needs.

---

of a composition text or program. This requires that we teachers constantly monitor what students are doing and what they are struggling with.

The only ways we can do this are to *read what students are writing, and talk with them as they write*. That's why some teachers keep index cards in their pockets, and jot notes about what particular students are doing. Other teachers have other ways of doing this. One jots notes in the margins of her plan book; another keeps long narrow sheets of paper tucked into the edges of her blotter and jots notes to herself during breaks. Figure 1.2 shows a sample mini-lesson planning sheet we use to keep track of our notes and ideas. However you work this out, you need to read your students' work and talk with each one at least once a week. Otherwise you won't know what they need to learn, practice, or be reminded of.

The Content of Mini-Lessons

Whether they occur at the beginning of the workshop or at a predictable time during it, mini-lessons need to be *short*. Many workshops break down because teachers forget this; they try to do too many things at once, or forget how to teach quickly. An effective mini-lesson should only cover one tip, strategy, or procedure. It should be explained concisely and, if necessary, demonstrated briefly. Students then proceed with their writing, using the strategy or procedure if it serves them.

Mini-lessons often turn into "maxi-lessons" because many of us were taught that instead of lecturing to students, we should pepper our teaching with questions. Although most of us use this question-and-answer technique often, we also know how cumbersome it can be. The student we call on wasn't listening, so we have to call on someone else; one waves a hand enthusiastically, but wants to ask a different question rather than answer ours; by the time we get the answer, half the students are no longer paying attention.

In an effective mini-lesson, the teacher clearly and quickly tells the students

Mini-Lesson Idea

Materials

Have: **Need:**

Possible Resources

Lesson Plan

Children's Books:

Professional Resources:

People:

FIGURE 1.2. Mini-lesson planning sheet.

what he or she wants them to consider, think about, or try, such as *one* of the following: "Read your whole piece to yourself before you start revising," "Find all the places where someone is talking and put quotation marks around that person's exact words," "Think of at least three new titles for your piece and decide which one you like best," and so forth. No question-and-answer exchange, no students volunteering; just a quick strategy with a well-selected example or two, and off they go.

TEACHER'S TIP: Don't let mini-lessons become maxi-lessons.

Not all students will implement the lesson that day. Think of teaching a mini-lesson as adding some bit of information to the pot. Those who need it right then will have it available; those who don't need it right away will have it introduced to them, and very probably will be reminded of it again when they need it. Those who use it will have it available to share with others as they seek help from each other.

Mini-Lessons in Action: A Series of Lessons on Dialogue

Many of the most effective mini-lessons center around the use of literature as a model. We've enjoyed observing a colleague who is particularly skilled at them. In these brief lessons she reads aloud a portion of a story, or the whole story if it's short, and shares the illustrations. (Whenever she can, she uses a big-book version of the story, so that everyone can clearly see the print and illustrations.) She and the students then explore an issue she wants them to be aware of and try.

For example, when she felt that many students could benefit from using dialogue rather than straight narrative description, she chose several books that contained extensive dialogue. For one lesson, she created two transparencies conveying the same information: One was a narrative description that she had written, and the other was a page of dialogue from the story. Students read both versions and then compared their effectiveness. The narrative, they decided, sounded like a book; the dialogue sounded like "real people" and sounded more immediate.

After finding specific lines of dialogue that showed the reader what was happening, students were sent to their writing with the reminder that they could make characters talk as well as act. In the days that followed, the teacher reinforced this notion by choosing several other stories to read that contained lots of dialogue, and drawing attention to it.

Sure enough, a number of students began inserting dialogue in their narratives right away, and some others followed. When she conferred with students, the teacher was careful to respond to their attempts by saying things like "You're beginning to make your characters talk! Dialogue makes stories more interesting to read," or "When So-and-So said that, I could just *hear* her! You've made her sound like a real person."

But many students' dialogue sounded stiff and phony. Another mini-lesson followed, in which two books' use of dialogue were compared. In one, the characters sounded real, lifelike, and human; in the other, the characters spoke in long, stuffy sentences. Students were encouraged to begin listening carefully to the ways people talk around them, and to use small notebooks to write down bits of "talk" that sounded interesting, colorful, or even mysterious.

The next two days were given over to comparing these notes and figuring out what makes dialogue sound natural. Students figured out, for example, that people often didn't finish sentences; used a lot of exclamations; used slang and nicknames; and often used words that sounded different than they would be spelled, like "Wouldja?," "Wuzzat?," and "wanna." They also interrupted each other a lot and often finished each other's sentences. Kids sounded different from adults, and teenagers sounded different from everybody! Friends' talk was more casual, slangy, and frequently interrupted than strangers'. These observations, coupled with continued attention to dialogue in books, helped students begin to construct more natural-sounding dialogue.

Other issues soon surfaced. Some writers used quotation marks eccentrically, many not at all. Readers began to express confusion: "Who's talking here? The character or you?" Some writers remembered to use the first half of a pair of quotation marks, but omitted them at the end of the utterance: "Is she still talking? Where does he stop?" readers asked. And many writers ran two or more characters' dialogue together, often without benefit of punctuation, like this:

Do you want to go to the park? All right but I have to get my brother Ronny we're going to the park OK let me get my shoes on. Come on we're going all right all right!

"Wait! Who's saying this? How many people are there talking here?" readers asked in bewilderment. Obviously there was more to this dialogue business than met the eye!

Further mini-lessons on the correct use of quotation marks were clearly called for. One strategy was to create two copies of story dialogue, one without quotation marks; students read the text and tried to figure out just where the characters' exact words were. Their attempts were then compared to the text with quotation marks in place.

Another strategy consisted of having pairs of students stand up and read aloud a few specially prepared sentences to each other as if they were having a conversation: "Did you do your homework last night?" "No, I had to go to my cousin's." "Does your cousin live in town?" "No, she lives out in the country."

After a speaker read his or her line, students dictated to the teacher how the related sentence would read in text, and where the quotation marks should be placed. Here is an example:

Shaina asked, "Did you do your homework last night?"
"No, I had to go to my cousin's," Cecily said.

A third strategy consisted of having students work in groups to rewrite play scripts into narrative. For example, this is a portion of a children's play by Valerie Tripp (1994), *Actions Speak Louder Than Words*:

SAMANTHA: All right, Nellie, here are seven beans and here are five. Now, if you add them together—
NELLIE: Twelve.
SAMANTHA: Good! How about fourteen and nine?
NELLIE: (*without counting*) Twenty-three.
SAMANTHA: (*surprised*) Seventeen and fifteen?
NELLIE: Thirty-two.
SAMANTHA: Jiminy! You're quick as lightning! Where did you learn arithmetic? (pp. 16–17)

Here is how the script was rewritten as narrative text by students, using quotation marks to show each speaker's exact words:

Samantha said, "All right Nellie, here are seven beans and here are five. Now, if you add them together—" "Twelve," Nellie interrupted. Samantha said, "Good! How about fourteen and nine?" "Twenty-three," said Nellie. She didn't even have to count the beans. Samantha was surprised. She said, "Seventeen and fifteen?" Nellie answered, "Thirty-two." Samantha yelled, "Jiminy! You're quick as lightning! Where did you learn arithmetic?"

These students clearly got the point about placement of quotation marks. With a little polishing on starting a new paragraph with each speaker change and commas in dialogue, they would have it down pat. At this point in their writing, however, it was most important for them to be able to use quotation marks correctly, because these marks signal to readers who is talking and who said what. They were now ready to make necessary changes in their own pieces to clarify the dialogue they were including.

Mini-Lessons Using Literature to Study the Writer's Craft

Teachers frequently use literature to provide models and examples. In Appendix A of this book, you'll find lists of books that we think are particularly good examples of different writing features, such as dialogue or description. In addition, *Craft Lessons: Teaching Writing K–8*, by Ralph Fletcher and Joann Portalupi (1998), is a very useful resource for planning literature-related writing mini-lessons.

There are countless ways good literature can be used to inspire writers to consider or try something new. Very young and beginning writers respond well to books with a picture and one word of text on each page, like those of Tana Hoban, Richard Scarry, and many others. They enjoy drawing and labeling. They can be moved toward a picture-and-sentence format by exposure to books that have one sentence of text under each picture, like Eric Hill's *Spot* books. An effective mini-lesson can involve young students' sharing a picture they have drawn and telling what they would write or plan to write about the picture. Such sharing inevitably inspires the ones who are temporarily stuck. Much the same thing can be done by having young students quickly share their topics.

▣▣▣

TEACHER'S TIP: Use high-quality literature as models as often as possible, so writers can learn from experts.

▣▣▣

With writers of any age, being introduced to high-quality literature of different genres and topics, or different writing and illustrating styles, adds to their repertoire and inspires them to try something new. Just as the teacher in the previous example used stories featuring dialogue to help her students learn to write dialogue effectively, we often use literature to introduce other features of books. Students interested in embellishing their finished drafts study the illustrating styles of different writers and illustrators. Jan Brett's intricate borders, for example, were closely examined by one class, and students noted how Brett works elements of the story into the borders. Many then experimented with creating borders for their finished pages.

Another way that we use literature is to help students remember that common objects, everyday events and the ordinary people in our families are the stuff of stories too. It's too easy for children to create fanciful, even far-fetched stories like Chris Van Allsburg's *Jumanji*, in which children discover a dangerously magical board game that fills their house with rampaging animals. These are fun to read and to write, but many children come to think that good stories have to be superexciting, or filled with writing's equivalent of "special effects."

We want students to realize that some of our best, most wonderful stories come from the realities of our own lives and the lives of our loved ones. So we use books like Montzalee Miller's *My Mother's Cookie Jar*, Ron Brooks's *Timothy and Gramps*, Camille Yarborough's *Cornrows*, Ina Friedman's *How My Parents Learned to Eat*, Barbara Williams's *Jeremy Isn't Hungry*, and Cynthia Rylant's *When I Was Young in the Mountains*. Books like these help children value their own stories and those of their families, and enjoy writing about them.

Mini-lessons are major vehicles for delivering direct instruction to groups of writers or the whole class. There is no limit to what topics or procedures can or should be taught. Anything that your students need to learn, experience, or try can be the topic of one or many mini-lessons. Figure 1.3 provides an extensive list of useful mini-lesson topics, many of which are based on Nancie Atwell's (1987) work at the Center for Teaching and Learning, Edgecomb, Maine. Important things to remember are that mini-lessons are typically short, they are focused, they model what writers should do, and they are based on what writers themselves are trying to do or struggling with, rather than on a predetermined sequence of skills.

ORGANIZING THE WRITING ENVIRONMENT

We can learn a lot about organizing our classrooms for writing by thinking about how professional artists and writers organize their work environments. They are predictable, consistent, and organized in such a way that real work can proceed. Supplies are at hand; useful resources are readily available; and the person working knows where things are, so that little time is wasted searching and gathering necessary materials.

Scheduling and Duration

Most writers find they need blocks of time in which to write. Regie Routman (1994) noted, "I cannot write anything meaningful in a half hour. I need long, quiet periods of time" (p. 165).

Time must be organized so that writers have an extended chunk of time daily in which to write. Good writing takes time—time to think, to experiment, to daydream a little, to confer, to look something up, to write again. In most classrooms, time is the ultimate luxury, but we need to decide what our priorities are.

When the writing period is short, much time is spent in getting started and then putting things away. Reluctant or lazy writers can spend just about the whole time getting out their things, sharpening a pencil, finding their place in their notebook, arranging their papers just so, and then putting it all away again. For those who enjoy writing, one of the most frustrating things is getting to "the good part" and then hearing that it's time to put the writing folders away.

□□

TEACHER'S TIP: Most students need to write daily, or nearly so. It's hard for them to invest much in a piece of writing that they start today and won't get to again for days.

□□

Workshop Procedures

Rules for writing workshop
Writing program expectations
Room organization and location of
    materials/supplies
Quiet writing time and collaborative
    time
Writing resources (dictionaries, editing
    tools, paper, etc.)
Purposes and organization of the
    writing folder and/or notebook
Why we confer about writing
How, where, and when to confer with
    peers
Conferring with the teacher
Group sharing procedures
Self-evaluating procedures
Setting goals for your writing
Getting topics from others
Keeping a writing portfolio
What to do when you're "finished"
How to use the editing center
Ways writing can be shared/published

The Craft of Writing

Stages in the writing process
The Creator and the Critic
Where writing ideas come from
Keeping a topic list
What writers do when they get ready to
    write, create a first draft, revise, edit,
    and share
Genres: Many types of writing
Writing effective leads
Writing effective dialogue
Creating suspense
What to do when you're stuck
Character development

Naming characters
Writing good descriptions
Using vivid words
Figurative language
Writing good titles
"Thoughtshots" and "snapshots"
Flashbacks and flashforwards
Information: Too much, too little, out of
    order
Effective conclusions
Dedications, prologues, epilogues

Strategies for Correcting and Polishing

How editing and proofreading are
    different from revising
Using the dictionary, thesaurus, spell-
    check, rhyming dictionary, and other
    resources
Passive and active voice
Apostrophes in possessives and
    contractions
Paragraphing narrative and dialogue
Spelling demons and frequently
    confused words
Formatting of business and friendly
    letters
Using parentheses
Writing numbers as words and
    numerals
Dividing words at the end of a line
Pronouns and agreement issues
Capitalization of titles, dialogue, and so
    forth
Use and misuse of dashes, colons,
    exclamation marks
Poetic devices (line breaks, margins,
    capitalization, etc.)

FIGURE 1.3. Mini-lessons for writing workshops.

Consider your own writing as an example: If it's been several days since you worked on a piece, it's hard to remember what your next great idea was, or where you were going with the piece next, or what somebody suggested to you in a conference. Instead, it's a whole lot easier just to begin a new piece. Similarly, when students write only a few times a week, they spend most of their time starting new pieces, or writing very short pieces that can be "finished" in a single period. Neither strategy builds good writing.

Teachers in the lower elementary grades may have somewhat more flexibility in planning their schedules than those in the upper elementary grades or middle school. In the lower grades, teachers typically decide for themselves, or as a team or grade level, how much of the day will be devoted to reading instruction, to writing, and to math, which are still considered the curricular "big dogs." We recommend 30 minutes a day for kindergarten and first grade, 45 minutes for second grade, and an hour for third grade and above.

Teachers in the upper elementary grades and middle school may have less flexibility in scheduling time for writing. Block scheduling allows for fewer, longer class periods, but usually comes at a price: Either teachers have to teach a lot more content in longer periods, or the same class doesn't meet every day. There are several ways to organize time, and unfortunately none of them are perfect. Some teachers schedule writing time every day, but the periods are often not long enough for sustained work. Others schedule longer writing periods several times a week, or even an entire period once or twice a week, but they find that it's difficult to carry over a piece from one day or week to another. Still others plan extended writing units, doing continuous writing workshops for several weeks, with reading and English put off for the time being. This is probably the least popular and least effective organizational scheme, but it works for some teachers in upper grades. The point is that there are no easy answers to the problem of how often and how long students should write, especially beyond the early or middle grades.

Organizing Space and Materials

Organizing space requires thinking first about what a group of writers will need to do. It is comforting to know that in order to teach writing effectively, you do not need to have special furnishings or equipment, or set up your classroom any differently than you typically would for teaching the other subjects in your day.

Students will need to meet together, so a carpeted space on the floor is ideal, but anywhere they can all gather is fine. This space will also be used for group sharing, class meetings, and many other group functions. They will need to look things up and browse through books before and during their writing, so a classroom library area is necessary. They need to confer and work together at times, so a table that accommodates four to six is helpful, with chairs so that they don't have to drag their chairs around with them. Of course, this table will also be used for reading and math groups and the like, so this will be a multipurpose piece of furniture. Students also need to write and think quietly, away from others, and a few individual desks or a table with a divider that separates it into four "carrels" may be a good investment of space. An overhead projector and screen for projecting transparencies are useful for mini-lessons.

Writing materials need to be stored in an organized fashion. Stackable plastic boxes or hanging file holders are efficient ways to store them. Probably each student will have a writing folder or a notebook as well as other writing materials that should be kept together in one place. (You will learn more about writing folders and notebooks in Chapters 2 and 3.) Materials needed for editing and publishing—such as correction tape and liquid, markers, paper of different types and sizes, posterboard and other cover materials, staplers, scissors, glue, and so forth—can be organized in boxes or trays and placed on shelves or in centers for these purposes.

Having to search all over the room for a dictionary or tape is frustrating to the writer and disruptive to everyone else. It's impossible for writers to concentrate on their words when their train of thought is broken by having to search for something they need. Make a consistent place for everything, and teach your students how to put things back when they are done with them. Arrange traffic lanes so that students going to the editing center don't have to walk between the desks where students are working alone, or someone who needs to sharpen a pencil doesn't have to ask the group conferring together to move aside.

Computers

Computers are common in most classrooms, and teaching word-processing skills is a routine part of most students' technology education. Whatever grade you teach, if you have a computer and printer in your room (or access to a computer bank or lab), start using them right away. Students should be taught how to type or use a keyboard as early as possible, and by third grade they should be able to use different fingers and both hands, rather than the "hunt-and-peck" method.

We have students start off writing their first drafts in handwriting, then putting their drafts on a disk for editing. Some teachers prefer to have students begin right at the keyboard. It depends very much on the age and proficiency of the students, and on how many computers are available and for how long a period of time. If your class has an hour of computer lab time three days a week, and each student has access to a computer, then they can all complete a piece from first draft through revision and editing, and can publish the piece from the computer without ever putting pencil to paper.

If, however, you are limited to one or two computers on rolling carts, and you share them with other classes, chances are that your students' time on the computers will be extremely limited. They might better use their time, then, editing their final drafts and producing finished copies. Students will need their own personal disks; assign each student a number and write the number, rather than the student's name, on the disk. This discourages students from getting into and reading (or changing!) others' disks.

There are also inexpensive, easily portable keyboards that are ideal for classroom use. They consist of a small keyboard and screen (battery-operated with AC adapters), and diskless memory storage for eight or more documents. Students can type their drafts right at their desks and store them in the keyboard's memory. Later when they have access to the regular computer, they unplug the computer's keyboard, plug in the portable keyboard, bring a story up onto the computer screen, and perform all of their editing functions. They then save the document on a disk and print it out as usual. Personal keyboards make it possible for a number of students to type and save their drafts for later revision and printing. Since they cost about 10% of what a computer costs, they are a good investment for schools with a limited number of computers available to students.

Use of computers for writing is a basic skill everyone needs, and certainly must learn in school. Mini-lessons may center around basic word-processing functions, such as changing the font and size of type, single- and double-spacing, scrolling to a particular part of the text or to the beginning or end, highlighting part of the text, and moving parts of text from one place to another. When students are familiar with these basic functions, revision and editing become much easier.

Another important thing the computer can do is check spelling. Most students love to use the spell-check function! Unfortunately, they sometimes think that spell-check is like a computerized teacher who can find each and every error. Of course this is untrue. We explain to students that the computer has a tiny dictionary inside its "brain." It very quickly looks up each word in a story in its dictionary. If it finds the word, it presumes that the word is spelled right. It has no capacity for figuring out whether that word has been used correctly.

For example, the sentence *My brother in me can't go which you* would be considered correct by spell-checking alone, since *in* and *which* are both in the computer's dictionary, although the writer meant to use *and* and *with*. Any error that is a real word will not be caught. Those tricky homophones and easily confused words (*there* and *their*, *its* and *it's*, *his* and *he's*, *to* and *too*, etc.) are all equally correct to spell-check. Spell-check can help students by finding the really big spelling errors, as well as common typos like *hte* for *the*, but it can't find all the mistakes they might make. You have to make sure that students understand what spell-check can and can't do, and emphasize that they must not overdepend on it to correct their work. We'll return to this topic in Chapter 5, when we take a close look at editing and how to help students learn to find and correct their own errors.

In Chapter 2 we look at how young children develop concepts about print, stories, and writing that are necessary for learning to write and spell, and what influences children's growth toward writing and spelling in the early years. We examine samples of young children's writing and spelling, and attempt to figure out how each sample represents what each young writer already knew or was familiar with. Finally, we look at the organization of effective writing and spelling workshops in the primary grades.

REFERENCES

Atwell, Nancie. *In the Middle: Writing, Reading, and Learning with Adolescents.* Portsmouth, NH: Heinemann, 1987.

Calkins, Lucy McCormick. *The Art of Teaching Writing* (new ed.). Portsmouth, NH: Heinemann, 1994.

Fletcher, Ralph J., and Joann Portalupi. *Craft Lessons: Teaching Writing K–8.* NY: Stenhouse, 1998.

Graves, Donald. *Writing: Teachers and Children at Work.* Portsmouth, NH: Heinemann, 1983.

Routman, Regie. *Invitations: Changing as Teachers and Learners K–12* (rev. ed.). Portsmouth, NH: Heinemann, 1994.

Tripp, Valerie. *Actions Speak Louder Than Words: A Play about Samantha*, eds. Tamara England and Jeanne Thieme. Middletown, WI: Pleasant, 1994.

CHAPTER 2

▫▫▫

The Foundations of Writing and Spelling in Young Children

When Jenny was only a baby, she could hold up her end of a conversation pretty well. That is, when Jean, her mom, talked to her as she sat in her baby seat on the table or counter, Jenny would babble back. If Jean asked, "Are you a good baby?", Jenny would babble back something that had a rising inflection on the end, just like Jean's question. When Jean announced, "*What* a good baby!", Jenny would crow something like "*Ba*babababa," in imitation. At other times Jenny seemed to be carrying on a monologue, especially before she fell asleep, when she would run through much of her repertoire of speech sounds and other nonspeech "mouth sounds."

Although Jenny's babbling was clearly not yet speech, and her "conversations" were not much more than attempts to imitate her mom's intonation patterns, nobody had any doubt that her attempts were intentional, or that they would soon evolve into speech. As such, they were responded to *as though* they were meaningful. Lucy McCormick Calkins (1994) wrote:

> When we ask a baby, "Are you hungry?" or "How's your day been?" we don't check to be sure the baby has the necessary skills to answer us. . . . We ask these questions fully expecting that the baby will participate in the conversation as best she can. We know that by speaking with the baby as if she *can* carry on her half of the conversation, we teach her to do just that. (1994, pp. 61–62)

Likewise, well before her first birthday, Jenny began marking things. She scribbled on just about every surface with anything that would make a mark, from crayons and chalk to a wet paintbrush or a stick. At first little more than random marks (see Figure 2.1), these early attempts soon matured into more controlled scribbles, then into wavy lines, then into horizontal lines of repeating marks. Like her babbling, some of her early "writing" was clearly intentional and meaningful; she produced pages of wavy lines to be included in a letter to Grandma, wrote a line of random letters on the bottom of birthday cards, and made pretend shopping lists that she carried around the grocery store. Other attempts were simply playful, like "writing" on a steamy window, the damp sand of the sandbox, or a smooth asphalt driveway. As with her babbling, nobody worried that her marks were unreadable, her "letters" idiosyncratic, or her lines crooked. Early writings were responded to enthusiastically, with the assumption that they would mature into readable marks, as indeed they did.

Learning to write is a lot like learning to talk. Children's early attempts don't look much like their later writing, nor does their babbling sound much like their later speech. But just as babbling has intonation patterns like speech, and seems to be a combination of invention and imitation, children's early writing attempts combine their own invented marks with what they have figured out about writing from their environments. Both babbling and marking seem to be spontaneous behaviors that appear as soon as the mouth can produce several different sounds and the fingers can grasp and direct a tool like a pencil, crayon, or stick (Trawick-Smith, 1997). Neither has to be

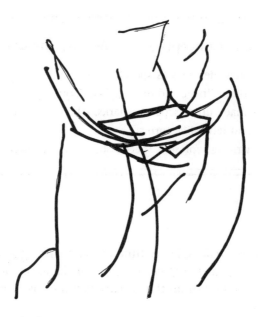

FIGURE 2.1. First writing attempt by Lexi Beverly, age 20 months.

taught; all we have to do is talk to babies and give them something to mark with, and away they go.

In the sections that follow, we trace some of the developmental benchmarks of early, or *emergent*, literacy, and describe the influences that children need in their early years in order to become readers and writers.

CHILDREN'S EARLY CONCEPTS ABOUT WRITING

Just as they figure out the complex phonology, grammar, and vocabulary of spoken English by about the age of five, children figure out much of what writing is and how it works entirely by experiences with it, in about the same time frame. But the big difference between figuring out how speech works and how writing works is that in nearly every family people use speech all the time, but in many families little writing is in evidence. While children hear people talking all day, everywhere they go, they don't necessarily see people reading and writing nearly as frequently. We have to make much more deliberate attempts to get writing into the environment than we do speech.

In literate homes and child care settings, young children see people using writing purposefully in many forms. From this adult modeling, and from their own experiments with writing, they figure out for themselves many of the basic concepts that they will need later as real readers and writers.

Perhaps the first concept about writing children develop is that *writing car-*

BOX 2.1. Concepts about Writing Include . . .

- Writing carries messages as speech does.
- Writing is often linear and arranged horizontally.
- Writing is made up of separate marks, which may be letters, numbers, and letter-like forms.
- Letters in writing represent speech sounds (*phonemes*).

---

ries messages, just as speech does. Every time we read writing aloud—whether it be a storybook or greeting card, a street sign or can label, a shopping list or telephone message—we demonstrate that it carries a message, which can be transformed into speech.

"Mom, did you put shampoo on the shopping list?" Big Sister yells from the bathroom. "Somebody from the bank called, and his name and number are by the phone," the babysitter tells us. "Aunt Laurie says she's getting a new puppy," Mom announces as she reads a letter. "Is Dr. Wolfe under 'Dentists' or 'Orthodontists'?" Dad asks as he thumbs through the Yellow Pages. From such everyday occurrences, young children deduce that writing is meaningful and related to speech.

Since young children are great imitators, they begin to play at reading and writing just as the older siblings and adults around them do. As shown in Figure 2.2, Jenny's two-and-a-half-year-old sister, Leslie, wrote a message on a greeting card for Grandma. She confidently "read" her message aloud to several family members; each time, what she "read" was a different message.

Probably next comes the discovery that *writing is linear.* From looking at books and being read to, children discover that writing is often arranged in horizontal lines. So, it is no accident that they begin to arrange their writing horizontally. Figure 2.3 shows an example of two-year-old Leslie's wave-like writing. At the top and bottom of the sample, Leslie wrote her name. She did so with using two lowercase *e*'s, lowercase *l* and *i*, and two upside-down capital *L*'s—features she knew were in her written name.

Similarly, Figure 2.4 shows three-year-old Susan's shopping list, with her name written at the bottom, and Mom's translation of Susan's list. Both girls were aware that their names were made up of letters written in a particular way and a particular order; yet neither girl was using letters or letter-like characters in her writing yet. Other than their names, words were written as wavy lines, which were pretty much what they saw when they looked at lines of print in their storybooks. What they had intuited so far is that writing is linear and that it conveys a message (Clay, 1975).

FIGURE 2.2. Scribbled message and letter-like forms by Leslie, age two years, six months.

This figure originally appeared in *Teaching Kids to Spell* (p. 8), by J. Richard Gentry and Jean Wallace Gillet, published by Heinemann, a division of Reed Elsevier Inc., Portsmouth, NH. Copyright 1993 by J. Richard Gentry and Jean Wallace Gillet.

TEACHER'S TIP: Children's earliest attempts to write are intended to convey a message, not to represent speech sounds.

Further experience with looking at familiar books, signs, and labels leads children to the discovery that, rather than lines of wavy marks, *writing is made up of separate marks*. At first they don't discern that the marks are members of a finite set, each of which must be made in a particular way. They may use letters, unique letter-like characters, stars, numbers, squiggles, and other idiosyncratic marks. As depicted in Figure 2.5a, three-year-old Jenny wrote a story about a little bus, in which both recognizable letters and letter-like characters were used; she also experimented with the spelling of her name. At about the same time, she created a sign (Figure 2.5b) for her pretend nursery school; in the fourth line, she incorporated the numerals in her phone number (some written backward) as letters. In her mind, numbers were just another kind of letter.

This stage doesn't last very long, and many children skip it altogether. Their writing quickly evolves into linear strings of letters, although they may not all be correctly formed. As shown in Figure 2.6a, three-year-old Leslie used only letters, principally *E*, *I*, *L*, *B*, *D*, *R*, *M*, and *N*, to write a descriptive caption for her picture of butterflies; as depicted in Figure 2.5b, Phillip, a kindergartner, used only letters to write a story about flowers.

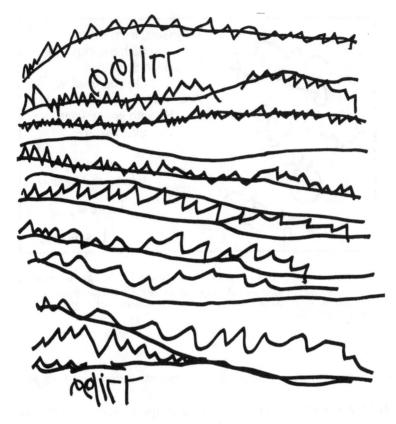

FIGURE 2.3. Wave-like prewriting by Leslie, age two.
From Temple and Gillet (1996, p. 320). Copyright 1996. Reprinted by permission of Allyn & Bacon.

At this stage children often produce pages of lines of letters, and enjoy reading their messages to anyone who will stand still for them, even the dog. Each time they read their writing, however, the message is different. They have not yet figured out that what is written down stays the same—that it says the same thing each time. Writing is made up of linearly arranged random letters, which stand for a message but not yet for anything else.

▫▫

TEACHER'S TIP: Respond to the message behind young children's writing,
not to its appearance.

▫▫

What they have not yet discovered, of course, is that *letters represent speech sounds*—what is called *letter–sound correspondence,* or the *alphabetic prin-*

FIGURE 2.4. Wave-like prewriting shopping list by Susan, age three, with her mother's translation of the list at left.

ciple. That's why spelling experts refer to this kind of writing as *prephonemic*; the letters aren't yet used to stand for phonemes. Just a little more book experience (especially exposure to ABC books of the "*A* is for apple, *B* is for bear" type) and coaching from an adult or older sibling (e.g., "That says McDonald's; see the *M*? MmmmmmmmmcDonald's"), and the connection is made. The penny drops: "Oh! I can make this sound when I see this letter!" And, of course, what quickly follows is "I can write this word with this letter!" *Voilà!* Children start using letters to represent sounds. Readable writing, and spelling, are born.

THE DEVELOPMENTAL PROCESS OF LEARNING TO SPELL

Research has demonstrated that most children's learning to spell in systematic, predictable ways follows an orderly developmental sequence. In the sections

FIGURE 2.5. (a) A story about a little bus by Jenny, age three. (b) Jenny's nursery school sign.

Figure 2.5b is from Temple and Gillet (1996, p. 322). Copyright 1996. Reprinted by permission of Allyn & Bacon.

that follow we describe some of the most common, easily observed features of children's spelling as it matures from the earliest real spellings (in which only one or two letters are used to represent sounds) to the later developmental stages (in which children represent all or nearly all of the sounds they hear in words, and invent ingenious strategies for spelling unfamiliar words). Although our primary focus in this chapter is on the development of young children, we include descriptions of the later spelling stages as well, so that you can see where our youngest writers are headed.

FIGURE 2.6. (a) Description of a flock of butterflies by Leslie, age three. (b) A story about flowers by Phillip, a kindergartner.

Figure 2.6a is from Temple and Gillet (1996, p. 322). Copyright 1996. Reprinted by permission of Allyn & Bacon.

> ## BOX 2.2. Prephonemic Spelling . . .
>
> - Is made up of letters and letter-like forms, including numerals and incorrectly formed or invented letters.
> - Is unreadable; letters are used randomly, not to represent sounds.
> - Is usually arranged in horizontal lines.
> - May be arranged in continuous lines or have spaces between groups of letters.
> - Shows that the child knows writing is made up of letters and is linear.
> - Is typical of prereaders.

Early Spelling Attempts:
Segmenting and Representing Phonemes

When letters begin to appear that stand for letter sounds, syllables, or even whole words, a young child's writing takes a huge leap forward. Now, with effort, others can read the writer's message; even more important, the writer can read the same message the same way time after time. Writing gives words permanence.

This leap forward usually accompanies the child's advance from emergent to beginning reader. Beginning readers are very much occupied with matching the letter names (which they largely already know) to their sounds (which are often new information, especially the vowels). For this reason, beginners typically start using one or a few consonants (which have quite regular and predictable sounds) and long vowels (which are also predictable, because they "say their names"), and either add other random letters or use only the letters for the sounds they can represent. This kind of early spelling is sometimes called *semiphonemic*, because only a few of the phonemes are represented (Gentry and Gillet, 1993). Although these spellings are very incomplete, they mark the transition into "real" spelling.

TEACHER'S TIP: Semiphonemic spellings, though incomplete and hard to read, demonstrate the child's discovery that letters stand for sounds.

In the example shown in Figure 2.7, Brian, age six, used only one letter for each word except *mother,* which he represented with the initial and final

FIGURE 2.7. Semiphonemic spelling by Brian, age six.
From Temple and Gillet (1996, p. 324). Copyright 1996. Reprinted by permission of Allyn & Bacon.

sounds, possibly because it was the only two-syllable word in his piece. As depicted in Figure 2.8, Leslie, now age five, wrote "Ideas of Quilts" using the long vowel *I*, the letter *D* for the second syllable in *ideas*, and consonants for other very salient sounds. She also made her first try on a short vowel sound, writing *AV* for *of*. As shown in Figure 2.9, she used only consonants, the names of which can represent whole syllables, in writing "Humpty Dumpty."

Once children discover that when they use a few letters their writing can be read by others (albeit with effort), they seem to redouble their efforts to repre-

---

BOX 2.3. Semiphonemic Spelling . . .

- Is made up exclusively of letters, usually in short strings of one to four letters; a single letter may represent a whole word.
- Represents the child's discovery of the *alphabetic principle*: Letters are used to represent the most salient sounds in words.
- Commonly features consonants to represent initial sounds; sometimes final or medial sounds are represented, but spellings are very incomplete.
- Demonstrates the beginning of phonemic segmentation.
- Is typical of emergent and beginning readers.

FIGURE 2.8. Semiphonemic spelling ("Ideas of Quilts") by Leslie, age five.

This figure originally appeared in *Teaching Kids to Spell* (p. 28), by J. Richard Gentry and Jean Wallace Gillet, published by Heinemann, a division of Reed Elsevier Inc., Portsmouth, NH. Copyright 1993 by J. Richard Gentry and Jean Wallace Gillet.

sent even more sounds in the words they want to write. They really *work* at this! What they are doing is quite complex, and it pushes their writing and spelling further ahead quickly.

The process of representing more of the sounds requires children to *segment*, or separate, the phonemes in words; moreover, they have to hold onto each phoneme while they search their memories for a letter that can represent the sound. At the same time, they have to remember the rest of the word they're spelling, or they will forget what their message is. This happens quite frequently to beginners; it accounts in part for their very incomplete spellings, and for the missing words and incomplete thoughts that sometimes pepper their writings.

If we could listen in on a youngster trying to proceed through a word in this way, it might sound something like this: "Let's see, *kitten*. K-k-k-k-k-kitten. K-k-*kay*. [Writes *K*.] K-itten, ih-ih-itten. Ih-ih-*eee*. [Writes *E*.] Kit-t-t-t-ten. Kit-ten. *Tee*. [Writes *T*.] Kit-ten-n-n-n-n-n-n, *en*. [Writes *N*.] *Kitten, K-E-T-N*."

This youngster is actually quite good at this complex process of *phonemic segmentation*, or breaking words into their component phonemes and matching

FIGURE 2.9. "Humpty Dumpty" picture by Leslie, age six.

This figure originally appeared in *Teaching Kids to Spell* by J. Richard Gentry and Jean Wallace Gillet, published by Heinemann, a division of Reed Elsevier Inc., Portsmouth, NH. Copyright 1993 by J. Richard Gentry and Jean Wallace Gillet.

them with letters. She is able to segment and match four of the five phonemes in *kitten*, including a short vowel sound. The only phoneme she doesn't represent is the *schwa*, or reduced vowel, sound in the second syllable. The reduced vowel between the /t/ and /n/ sounds in *kitten* is so reduced that a phonetician might say it is nonexistent; however, our spelling system requires a vowel letter in every syllable, no matter how reduced the sound is. Besides, the letter name *N* contains the necessary vowel sound! The substitution of *E* for the short-*i* sound is developmentally appropriate, and is a sign that the child is moving into the next developmental stage.

TEACHER'S TIP: The ability to segment phonemes in words is critical to both decoding and spelling.

A child with less experience in phonemic segmentation would be able to represent fewer phonemes, as Brian did in the sample shown in Figure 2.7. Like many of his peers, Brian could only hold onto the word he was spelling long enough to represent the first sound, resulting in *L* for *love* and *M* for *my*. As his phonemic segmentation ability develops, he will represent more of the sounds in the words he writes.

Growing in Spelling: Building on Phonemic Awareness

This development—being able to represent more of the sounds in words—coincides with beginning to read. Beginning readers develop some whole words they can read and write automatically, and begin to learn decoding strategies. As children learn to decode more sounds in written words, they concurrently learn to encode more sounds in their writing. Their spellings become increasingly complete, at least from a phonemic standpoint, although their spellings are often far from correct.

These more complete, although still incorrect, spellings are called *phonemic*, because the sounds in words drive writers at this stage. Their spellings become more and more readable. No longer do they have to read their writing to someone for their messages to be received. They can write and expect others to read what they have written, with less effort than their earlier attempts required.

When these young spellers discover that they can represent any word they can say with letters, and that others can read their writing as well, they typically become prolific writers. They also become proficient at inventing spellings for the words they want to write. Their spelling strategies are ingenious and systematic; they use everything they already know about letter sounds, letter names, and words they know how to read, and they "spell what they hear" (Temple and Gillet, 1996, p. 324).

□□

TEACHER'S TIP: When children discover that they can represent the sounds in words with letters, and that others can read their writing, they usually begin to write prolifically.

□□

Spellings that are fueled by children's growing mastery of the names and sounds of letters are often called *letter–name spellings* (Ehri, 1992; Ganske, 2000; Gentry and Gillet, 1993). Young spellers often use the name of certain letters to represent both individual letter sounds and whole syllables in words.

For example, a speller using a letter–name strategy may use the letter S to spell the first syllable of a word like *escape* (*SKAP*), as well as the beginning sound of a word like *snake* (*SNAK*). Likewise, the name of the letter *H* ("aitch") is often used by letter–name spellers to stand for the /ch/ sound, as in *church* (*HRH*) or *witch* (*WIH* or *WEH*); and the name of the letter *Y* ("wy") is often used to represent the /w/ sound, as in the beginning of *whale* (*YAL*) and *once* (*YNS*).

Spellers using a letter–name strategy typically represent long vowel sounds correctly, as these letters "say their names," so to speak. They figure out ingenious ways to deal with the ambiguities of short vowel sounds, which do not correspond with their letter names directly as long vowels do. Short vowel sounds are typically spelled using the vowel letter name that most closely approximates the sound in the word; that is, letter–name spellers use the vowel letter name that is formed at the same, or nearly the same, place in the mouth (the "point of articulation") as the short vowel sound. Referred to as *vowel substitution*, this strategy of using vowel letter names to represent short vowel sounds is one of the hallmarks of this developmental stage.

For example, the short vowel sound in *bat* is most often spelled correctly with *A*, because the vowel sound /a/ and the letter name *A* are formed in the same place in the mouth. But so is the short vowel sound /e/ (as in *bet*), so letter–name spellers often represent /e/ with *A* as well. The short vowel sound /i/ (as in *pig*) most closely corresponds to the letter name *E*, so letter–name spellers are apt to invent spellings like *PEG* for *pig*. The short vowel sound /o/ (as in *hot*) most closely corresponds to the letter name *I*, so a typical letter–name spelling of a word like *hot* would likely be *HIT*. Finally, the short vowel sound /u/ (as in *hug*) most closely corresponds to the pronunciation of the letter name *O*, so a typical spelling of *hug* would be *HOG*. The letter name *U* is mostly used for the vowel sound we spell *oo* (as in *school*, often misspelled as *SKUL*).

A number of other phonemic features are spelled by letter–name spellers in typical ways, such as past tense endings, digraph and blend sounds like *ch*, *th*,

---

BOX 2.4. Phonemic/Letter–Name Spelling . . .

- Shows the child's firm understanding that letters represent sounds in writing.
- Is based entirely on how words sound; for example, silent letters are omitted.
- Is still incomplete, but more phonemes are represented than in semiphonemic spellings.
- Is more easily read than previous spellings.
- Shows use of letter names as well as letter sounds as a spelling strategy.
- Is typical of beginning readers who need support and are not yet reading independently.

dr, and *tr,* and the sounds of *M* and *N* before other consonants as in words like *jump* and *hand.*

Figures 2.10 and 2.11 show two such phonemic pieces by Leslie, written as a first grader. They show her growing grasp of letter–sound correspondences, as well as her growing repertoire of strategies for spelling sounds that don't have a one-to-one correspondence with letters.

In the example shown in Figure 2.10, she used *T* for /th/, and *C* and *CH* for /ch/. She represented most short vowel sounds with vowel letters, but not the ones we would use. She wrote some words from memory (*AND, MOM*), and other words as one configuration, as they sound when one says them ("hope you" / *HEPUOU*). And she was experimenting with ways to show word boundaries, including using dashes between words.

By the time Leslie wrote the sample shown in Figure 2.11, she had learned how to represented /th/ correctly, and was adding to her collection of known words (*is, was, not, we, she, love, by*). She represented long vowels correctly, without "silent letter" markers, and put a vowel in most syllables.

The Transition to More Mature Spelling

As success begets success, more readable written messages beget even more readable spellings. Concurrently, children learn to read more words, decode more ef-

FIGURE 2.10. Phonemic spelling by Leslie as a first grader. Translation: "This is a picture for Mom. I hope you like this picture of Donald Duck and Daisy Duck."

FIGURE 2.11. More phonemic spelling by Leslie as a first grader. Translation: (a) "This is Tiger. When we got Sunflower Tiger was not born. I love Tiger." (b) "This is Sunflower. He was very nice. I loved Sunflower." (c) "This is Rainbow. She was very nice. I loved Rainbow."

From Temple and Gillet (1996). Copyright 1996. Reprinted by permission of Allyn & Bacon.

ficiently, spell more words automatically, and invent more complete spellings. By the end of the primary grades, most children are producing very readable pieces. These may be studded with misspellings, but they show the use of a variety of strategies for writing unfamiliar words.

□□

TEACHER'S TIP: Spelling progress is shown not necessarily by fewer errors, but by errors that show more complex strategies.

□□

The appearance of these strategies marks the transition into ore mature spelling; for this reason, such spellings have been called *transitional* (Gentry and Gillet, 1993; Temple and Gillet, 1996). Within this broad category, spelling researchers have identified several characteristic stages—including the predictable ways writers deal with more complex vowel sounds and patterns, and the spelling patterns most often found in words with more than one syllable. These stages, referred to as *within-word* and *syllable juncture* stages, are most typical of writers in second or third grade and beyond who are becoming independent readers (Ganske, 2000). However, younger children who are advanced readers, and older students who lag behind in reading and writing development, exhibit the strategies typical of these developmental stages.

Figure 2.12 shows an example of a second grader's within-word spelling. Here Josiah used many strategies for spelling both long and short vowel sounds, including correct but inappropriately used vowel marking (*MATEERIAL*, *NEADLES*) and the use of known words as parts of other words (*SOING*, *MEATIUM*). While Josiah was struggling with complex vowel patterns and using a variety of strategies to represent them, his spelling also showed his growing

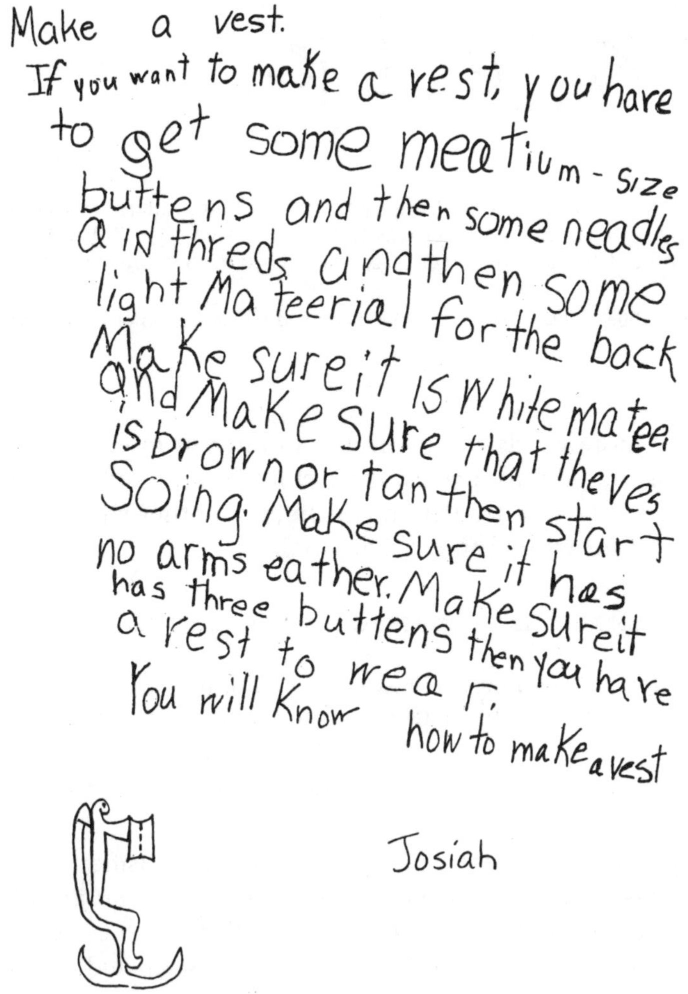
Make a vest.
If you want to make a rest, you have
to get some meatium-size
buttens and then some neadles
aid threds and then some
light Mateerial for the back
Make sure it is white matee
and Make Sure that theves
is brown or tan then start
Soing. Make sure it has
no arms eather. Make sure it
has three buttens then you have
a rest to wear.
You will know how to make a vest
Josiah

FIGURE 2.12. Transitional spelling by Josiah, a second grader.
From Temple and Gillet (1996, p. 331). Copyright 1996. Reprinted by permission of Allyn & Bacon.

mastery of spelling. He knew, for example, that all syllables have to have vowel letters in them, even if the vowels can't be "heard"; consequently, he included vowel letters in the final syllables of words like *material, buttons,* and *either.* He correctly spelled many words, and his misspellings were both readable and logical. These features are characteristic of transitional, or within-word and syllable juncture, spelling strategies.

EARLY CHILDHOOD INFLUENCES ON WRITING AND SPELLING

The foundations of literacy are laid in infancy and early childhood. We know that by the time they enter school, many children have had literacy-related experiences that give them an advantage over others in learning to read and write. We also know, however, that our job as educators is to level the playing field as much as we can—that is, to try to overcome the deficits some children suffer, as well as to challenge and encourage those whose progress is faster or easier. These lofty goals may seem overwhelming, but we get up, come to school, and try to achieve them each day anyway.

So what do young children need to do in order to become literate? And how can we make sure that, even if they haven't had these experiences at home and preschool, they will have them at school? We should address the following needs:

• *To hear stories, poems, and nonfiction books read aloud.* This helps children develop a "sense of story" (i.e., the sense that stories unfold in predict-

---

**BOX 2.5. Transitional/Within-Word
and Syllable Juncture Spelling . . .**

• Is nearly complete, with all phonemes represented, and is largely readable.
• Shows that the child is learning (but confuses) common spelling rules and patterns, especially vowel patterns, inflectional endings, silent letters, and consonant doubling.
• May show several different attempts at the same word or pattern; sometimes the correct spelling is abandoned for an incorrect spelling.
• Is typical of independent readers who still need some support, most often from late primary through middle elementary grades.

able ways), learn information about the world, develop familiarity with the language of books, and learn to love books.

• *To hear favorite stories read again and again,* until they are as familiar as their own names and faces. This feeds children's love of books, and helps them internalize language patterns.

• *To have picture books readily available to look at, and time set aside frequently to do so.* This enables children to examine features of illustrations and print, and to role-play being readers. They can pretend to read to themselves or others, and can practice turning pages, following lines of print, and so forth.

• *To see adults (and peers) reading* for enjoyment and information. This helps them see that adults (and peers) value and use reading, and makes them want to emulate other readers.

• *To have writing materials available for play.* Paper in different sizes and colors, notebooks and pads, pencils, felt-tip markers, crayons, pens, colored chalks, and chalkboards should be readily at hand.

• *To have their writing valued and responded to,* even if the message is not readable by others. This helps children see that they are writers and communicators.

• *To see adults using writing in spontaneous, authentic ways* that reflect the real-life uses of writing. Notes, letters, messages, lists, reminders, signs, memos . . . these are the kinds of daily writing most adults use and produce. As with reading, adult modeling helps children see that writing is a useful and enjoyable activity, and makes them want to engage in it.

• *To enjoy adults' approval of their efforts and progress* in becoming literate.

Skilled preschool and primary teachers integrate reading and writing into all activities every day. Writing and reading are seen as enjoyable, enriching, and useful activities in which everyone will naturally participate. Stories are read to individuals, small groups, and large groups at intervals throughout the

---

BOX 2.6. To Become Literate, Young Children Need . . .

- To hear stories, poetry, and nonfiction read aloud.
- To hear favorite stories read again and again.
- To have picture books to look at and time to do so.
- To see adults reading and writing.
- To play with writing and writing materials.
- To have their writing valued and responded to with enthusiasm.
- To enjoy adult approval of their efforts and progress.

day; poems are read and recited daily; books are available at all times for private enjoyment and sharing. Print fills the environment in the form of signs, lists, labels, reminders, directions, and so forth. Adults and children are given real reasons to read and write every day; materials for writing and drawing abound in quantity and variety; and children are regarded as literate long before they meet the technical criteria for literacy (Temple and Gillet, 1996).

▫▫

TEACHER'S TIP: Young children need to be surrounded with reading and writing all day.

▫▫

Opportunities for play should be structured so that writing and reading are a natural part of the play. If traditional "play centers" for activities like housekeeping and dress-up games exist, writing materials should be readily available so that shopping lists, menus, books for the dolls, and telephone messages can be written. Such "centers" may be deliberately generic—furnished with boxes, chairs, and tables, rather than cradles, stoves, and ironing boards—so that imaginative play can evolve in many directions. This way, children can create a bank, store, animal hospital, airplane, school, restaurant, and so on. Each different setting has its own requirements for print: A bank needs money, deposit slips, and checks; a store needs shopping lists, prices, and signs; a post office needs letters, postcards, stamps, and money; a restaurant needs menus, tablets for taking orders, signs, and so forth.

Classroom and school events often reappear in children's play as well. At our school, a Book Fair went on in the library for a week. Every day of that week, first graders in one class spontaneously played "Book Fair" after they'd finished lunch; they spread books out on a table, made signs, distributed play money, and bought and sold books. A kindergarten field trip to a grocery store led to the children's establishing a play store with shelves and empty food containers from home. Signs, shopping lists, and receipts were all necessary. A visit by animal shelter personnel resulted in a classroom animal shelter, with stuffed animals, signs, medical histories, and the like. All of these dramatic play activities, springing from real-life experiences, were enriched by providing writing materials and encouragement to write as part of the play.

▫▫

TEACHER'S TIP: Invite purposeful writing by including writing materials as props for any kind of imaginative play or role playing.

▫▫

It doesn't really matter whether or not others can read the signs, menus, and deposit slips; the communicative intent, and the functionality of writing, are the important things (as well as the children's construction of imaginary worlds, which will later feed their ability to compose stories). And if we respond to these attempts as though they were "real," not "pretend writing" or "scribbling" or any of the other patronizing ways children's early attempts have been characterized, then reading and writing will become connected to their lives almost effortlessly.

WRITING AND SPELLING IN PRIMARY GRADES

Creating a print-rich environment that invites children to write purposefully as an integral part of everyday activities, and treating children's writing efforts as we would like ours to be treated by others, leads naturally into the establishment of a workshop environment even in kindergarten and first grade.

We begin not with a curriculum guide, lesson plans, or even writing materials, but with a short list of beliefs that support our primary writing program:

• *Most children enter school believing they can already read and write.* Few need to be convinced that they can; the incongruence arises when they discover that what they think they are doing is not what their teachers want them to be doing.

• *Most children will naturally imitate what they see significant adults do.* They enjoy role-playing being adults! So we'll give them reading, writing adults as models to imitate.

• *Children learn to write and spell largely by trial and error,* just as they learned to talk, walk, eat, and so forth. They will make a zillion "mistakes" before they get it right. The only way to learn to do it is to do it.

• *Writing and spelling are natural everyday activities* that children will

---

BOX 2.7. Beliefs That Support a Primary Writing Program

• Most children believe they can already read and write.
• Children imitate what they see adults do.
• Children learn to write and spell by trial and error.
• Writing and spelling are natural everyday activities.
• A child's belief that "I can do this" is more than half of learning anything.

grow into in their own ways. They are not difficult, taxing, or tedious, and we should not teach as though they are.

• *A child's belief that "I can do this" is more than half of learning anything.* Success is more important than failure, and trying is more important than succeeding.

Getting Started Writing in Primary Grades

A journey of a thousand miles, they say, begins with a single step. A single act that shows children they can already write begins the day, whether it's the very first day of school or just the very first day of establishing a workshop climate in a primary classroom. We invite children to write something as soon as they enter the classroom, and we respond to whatever they produce as though it were entirely readable, regardless of its appearance.

TEACHER'S TIP: Show children that you see them as writers by inviting them to write from the very first day.

Some teachers invite children to "sign in" by writing their names on chart paper when they arrive. Others put writing paper and markers out on tables and encourage children to draw, then write about their drawings, and finally read what they wrote to the teacher. Still others provide baskets of small four- or six-page books, made from sheets of paper folded horizontally and stapled together, for children to draw and write about whatever they like. When a book is finished, the writer reads it to the class and shares it with friends. We give each student a journal to write in every day, and invite them to read parts to us, and to each other, frequently. We make sure paper and markers are in every center and strategically "salted" around the room, and we watch as the writing proliferates.

Responding to Early Writing

As we've already seen, most young children produce writing that no one else can read; often they can't read it themselves. How we teachers respond to these attempts is critical, not only for the individual writer but for the entire group or class. When we say, "Will you read it to me?", we tell the writer (and any listeners) that we presume this writing can be read and conveys a message, no matter what it looks like. When we comment, "What a writer you are!" or "Look at all the words [or letters] you've written!", we acknowledge the effort in spite of whatever might be lacking. When we say, "Why don't you hang up your grocery list on the refrigerator?" or "Where could you put your sign?", we show that writing *works*.

The ways we respond to each writer's efforts affects every other writer. One of the most potent forces that shape how children talk to each other is the way teachers talk to them. In our own classrooms and in others, everywhere we've gone, we've heard teachers' voices coming out of kids' mouths. (Sometimes that's scary!)

□□

> **TEACHER'S TIP:** How we respond to one student's writing affects every
> other writer in the room.

□□

In classrooms where teachers ask questions that encourage writers to think about and explain their writing, kids ask each other, "Where did you learn about that?" and "How did you figure that out?" In classrooms where teachers say, "Put this part here," or "You need to put in . . .", kids *tell* each other what to do rather than asking or suggesting.

In classrooms where teachers say, "You *know* how to spell that word," making the child who asked feel stupid, kids tell each other, "You don't know how to spell that? That's *easy*!" Where teachers tell writers what to do, kids tell each other what to do. But where teachers ask and listen, kids tend to ask and listen too—or at least they tone down their natural tendency to boss each other around.

Of course, responding sensitively to young writers is easier said than done. By the very nature of our jobs, we become accustomed to directing, assisting, and smoothing the way to ensure success, which we sometimes call "facilitating." We break down tasks into small parts, give directions over and over again, and check to see that students are doing just what we said. All of this can stifle young writers, discourage their creativity, and create hesitancy and dependence on the teacher.

Perhaps one of the most important ways we can respond to young writers is to forget (for the moment) what we're *supposed* to be doing as teachers, and just open our eyes and minds to what they're trying to do. Young children most often want us to respond with *delight*, and this we should be able to do more often.

□□

> **TEACHER'S TIP:** Respond to children's efforts with more delight and less
> correction.

□□

Connecting Writing and Drawing

At about age three, children begin to be able to distinguish between writing and drawing, and in their productions there appears a clear difference between their drawings and "writing." The drawings begin to be more picture-like, while their writing becomes less scribbled and more linear. From this point on, for the next several years at least, drawing and writing will be complementary processes that reinforce each other for the young writer.

If you give them writing paper and ask them to write something, many young children will say, "I can't write." But when they are given paper and markers or crayons, few will say, "I can't draw." Young children usually draw with abandon, although they lose this confidence by second or third grade. A good way to start is to give young children paper and drawing materials, let them draw whatever they want, and then encourage them to write about it.

TEACHER'S TIP: Drawing before writing helps children discover what they want to write about and what they have to say about it.

Just as they need to talk in order to think, young children generally *need* to draw before they write, to focus their thoughts and put them into words. The effort of thinking of a message, turning it into words, and then forming letters to represent those words is so great that without drawing, many youngsters lose their train of thought after just a couple of words. Drawing helps them discover what they want to write about and what they have to say about it.

Sometimes, of course, it's impossible for anyone else to know what the writer intended, as in Figure 2.6a (Leslie's story paired with her drawing of a flock of butterflies). In this case it only makes sense to have the writer tell about the picture and "read" the writing, while you write down what the child says.

Some teachers object to rewriting children's words on their papers; they say it sends a message to young writers that they have not written the message correctly. These teachers may be right, although we haven't had a problem with this. Our own experience has been that young children don't mind adults writing what it says on their papers. After all, they'll be the first to tell you that kids' writing is not like adults', and that adults have trouble reading it if they don't write it down.

We only do this with truly unreadable messages, and only when we have a clear purpose for writing the message in standard spelling, as when we want to preserve a particular piece as a writing sample. Then we are careful to place our writing unobtrusively, not right under or over the child's writing, so our writing doesn't visually detract from it.

□□□

TEACHER'S TIP: If you must write on a child's paper, do so selectively and unobtrusively.

□□□

When children write first, then draw about the writing, the words and pictures may not correspond very well. The illustration often conveys much more excitement and liveliness than the writing! Of course, you will also encounter children who will draw for hours rather than write a single sentence. This is particularly true of older, reluctant, or unconfident writers. Drawing is a good rehearsal for writing, but it can also be an effective delaying tactic. Be prepared to set guidelines about how much writing time can be used for drawing. We don't hesitate to tell children how long they can spend drawing before we expect them to begin to write—for example, "for five minutes," "until the big hand is on the 10," or "until the timer rings." Those who need more time to draw can return to it after they have made a good start on writing.

Lucy McCormick Calkins (1994, pp. 64–65) described helping a kindergartner make the transition from drawing to writing by placing her hand gently over the child's, bringing it away from the picture, and saying something like "Let's write something about your picture" in a gentle voice; she then fixed her eyes *on the child's paper*, waiting for her to begin. The little girl seemed surprised at first that she was actually expected to write something, but when Calkins continued to look at the paper instead of acknowledging the child's hesitation, the child shrugged to herself and began to write. "Often," Calkins wrote, "when children cannot engage my glance, they turn to the page and do whatever they can do" (p. 65).

If a child like the girl described by Calkins were unable to put down anything, we would encourage her to say aloud something she'd like to write. Then we'd repeat it very slowly, and say something like this: "What sound do you hear at the beginning of _____? What letter could that be?" Whatever the child produced (even if it wasn't the right letter), we'd say something encouraging like "I hear an *M* at the beginning of *my* too," "That's a smart guess," or even "You've gotten off to a good start; keep going!" and then move on. We try not to linger too long with a child who needs a great deal of encouragement; it seems as if the more time we spend with one, the more time he or she demands. And the next time, that same writer will expect us to stay right there beside him or her! Children only learn independence by experiencing it.

□□

TEACHER'S TIP: Staying too long with one writer, or scrutinizing the writing too closely, often encourages dependence on the teacher.

□□□

Encouraging Collaboration in Primary Grades

Young children are naturally egocentric. Still closer to infancy than to adulthood, they retain much of the self-centeredness of babyhood, and act as though each one were the center of the universe (which, of course, they are to themselves!). This early childhood egocentrism is not a character fault or willful lack of sensitivity, but rather the natural state of young children's cognitive and emotional development. How it is exhibited brings unique challenges to the development of writing workshops in the primary grades.

For example, two young children appear to be playing cooperatively together in the block area; they are seated side by side and taking blocks from a shared pile. But when we listen in, we find that each is building separately, and talking aloud to him- or herself rather than to the other child. Linguists call simultaneous conversations that look like real communication, but that take no account of the other person's words, *collective monologues:* Both talkers are listening only to themselves. This can create problems when we want young writers to share with each other. Typically, most young children are thinking about their own writing (or something else entirely) rather than listening to each other.

Likewise, young children find genuine cooperation difficult, especially for more than a few minutes. Cooperation requires a degree of other-centeredness that young children usually lack. What looks like cooperation is usually really *parallel play*—individuals working or playing amicably side by side, but each absorbed in his or her own efforts. This makes writing with a partner challenging. It also affects writers' ability to give and accept helpful criticism. Feedback from peers often takes the form of "bossing": "Take that out!" or "You should call it _____ instead." Asking for and receiving help from each other are learned behaviors, and they need to be modeled and practiced many times before they become second nature. Yet these are at the heart of a workshop environment for writers.

□□□

TEACHER'S TIP: Courteous active listening must be taught and practiced daily before it becomes second nature.

□□□

The goal in the early primary grades is to move students toward active listening and real collaboration, even if the results are less than ideal. We can structure both the physical environment and the workshop time to encourage collaboration, although young children will only approximate true collaboration much of the time. Creating ways for partners and small groups to share their work brings cooperative efforts to everyone's attention.

As teachers, we can encourage active listening and collaboration in these ways:

- Explicitly teach the behaviors we expect: "We listen with our eyes, our ears, and our undivided attention."
- Model what we expect our students to strive toward—for example, no marking papers while authors are sharing!
- Tell students specifically what they did right: "Charles, you gave Mark your undivided attention while he read his story."
- Make daily opportunities for students to practice the skills of active listening and collaborating.
- Arrange desks in groups, or invite writers to sit together at a writing table, so they can collaborate (or at least tell each other what they are doing).
- Set aside a few minutes at the end of the workshop to "show and share" with partners.

▫▫

TEACHER'S TIP: Structure the physical environment to foster collaboration.

▫▫

Of course, things may not be what they seem. Calkins (1994) described a "peer conference" between two first graders: They drew their chairs close together, read their work aloud to each other *simultaneously*, and then happily returned to their tables to continue their separate efforts! Neither child listened to the other, but they didn't seem to notice; at least they were *role-playing* sharing with a partner, and that was a step in the right direction. Working in parallel becomes real cooperation slowly, with time, practice, and maturation.

BOX 2.8. Ways to Encourage Young Children to Listen and Collaborate

- Explicitly teach what they are to do.
- Model active listening.
- Describe specifically what they do well or correctly.
- Create daily opportunities to practice active listening and collaborating.
- Arrange space so writers can sit together.
- Make time to "show and share" writing with others.

Writing Folders and Notebooks

Even very young writers need organization, a place to keep their work, and a place to store the "treasures" that might become writing (today, next week, or next month).

As the name implies, *writing folders* are folders with pockets in which writers can keep all their drafts, false starts, topic lists, and other writings. Folders will, of course, be messy, although children should go through them periodically— sorting, rank-ordering, or just straightening and putting items in order by date. They can also take home bunches of their writings periodically. But they should get used to the idea that *writers keep what they write* to work on another time or to give them new ideas. Dating papers is critical; even preschoolers can learn to write today's date on each sheet, or to use a date stamp.

Writing notebooks as conceived by Fletcher (1996a, 1996b) and others, by contrast, are places where writers can keep pictures, drawings, ticket stubs, pressed weeds, poems and jokes copied from books, and all sorts of other "stuff" as well as writings. They are more like treasure boxes than folders of papers. (You'll read more about writing folders and notebooks in Chapter 3.)

In practice, the distinction between folders and notebooks is blurry at best. Students often keep "stuff" in their folders (as well as in their portfolios, desks, and pockets!), and they often use their notebooks to record observations, write letters, and try their hands at stories and plays.

Some teachers encourage young writers to begin with folders, and some months later to examine what they have written about often, put those pieces together in piles, and create single-topic or related-topic notebooks from them. This process can help writers in several ways:

1. It shows them what it is that they write about over and over.
2. It helps them deepen their writing about favorite topics by collecting it all in one "anthology."
3. It encourages them to be aware of and try new topics and forms.

Where young writers keep their writing is less important than the facts that they need to write daily about things they know and care about, and that they need to share with and help each other.

Much of what we have said in this chapter about the language, writing, and spelling of young children spills over into what children do beyond the primary grades. Those who begin reading and writing significantly later than others often exhibit the typical behaviors and concepts of much younger children. Reluctant older writers often struggle with phonemic segmentation, letter–sound correspondences, and so forth, just as younger emergent writers do.

In this chapter we have attempted to give an overview of the beginnings of spelling and writing. In the following four chapters, we concentrate primarily on the craft of writing instruction, following the writing cycle from generating initial ideas through revising drafts, editing, and finally sharing finished products. We discuss spelling issues as they occur in the context of writing instruction within the writing cycle. Spelling takes a back seat temporarily in our discussion of finding topics and writing early drafts; it assumes greater importance as writers clarify their meaning in revision, and then correct and polish their work in the editing stage.

REFERENCES

Calkins, Lucy McCormick. *The Art of Teaching Writing* (new ed.). Portsmouth, NH: Heinemann, 1994.

Clay, Marie. *What Did I Write?* Portsmouth, NH: Heinemann, 1975.

Ehri, Linnea. "Review and Commentary: Stages of Spelling Development." In *Development of Orthographic Knowledge and the Foundations of Literacy*, eds. Shane Templeton and Donald Bear. Hillsdale, NJ: Erlbaum, 1992.

Fletcher, Ralph. *Breathing In, Breathing Out: Keeping a Writer's Notebook*. Portsmouth, NH: Heinemann, 1996a.

Fletcher, Ralph. *A Writer's Notebook: Unlocking the Writer within You*. Portsmouth, NH: Heinemann, 1996b.

Ganske, Kathy. *Word Journeys: Assessment-Guided Phonics, Spelling, and Vocabulary Instruction*. New York: Guilford Press, 2000.

Gentry, J. Richard, and Jean Wallace Gillet. *Teaching Kids to Spell*. Portsmouth, NH: Heinemann, 1993.

Temple, Charles, and Jean Wallace Gillet. *Language and Literacy*. New York: HarperCollins, 1996.

Temple, Charles, Ruth G. Nathan, and Nancy Burris. *The Beginnings of Writing*. Boston: Allyn & Bacon, 1982.

Trawick-Smith, Jeffrey. *Early Childhood Development: A Multicultural Perspective*. Columbus, OH: Merrill, 1997.

CHAPTER 3

■□

Beginning to Write

It's the beginning of writing time. You walk around the room, making sure everyone is busy with the task. But Jamie, his pencil tapping to the tune he must be hearing in his head, isn't writing. You're a great motivator, so you say, "What's wrong, Jamie? Why aren't you writing?" Jamie's surly response does not surprise you: "I got nuthin' to write about."

Of course, you know this is nonsense. Jamie is perfectly capable of turning ideas in his head into a topic for writing, so you respond accordingly: "Sure you do! You've got lots of things to write about!" But the cheerleader role does not appease Jamie, or send him off in a flash of pen movements and flying paper.

To help Jamie out a little, you ask, "Well, what did you do last night?" We can, however, predict his answer: "Nuthin'."

You won't stop there. You're on a mission! Trying to keep the irritation out of your voice, you urge, "You must have done *something*! Did you watch TV? Eat dinner? Talk to your family? Why don't you write about that?"

Embarrassed by all this time you've spent hovering over him, Jamie finally whimpers, "Okay," and begins writing.

What's wrong with this picture? We've all struggled with the child who just won't get on and stay on task, maybe in writing more than in any other subject. In the vignette above, Jamie does eventually get started writing something. So why does Jamie's exchange with you as his teacher seem unsatisfying? In part, the answer lies in how the student feels during that exchange. Read the vignette again, but this time imagine yourself as Jamie instead of the teacher.

It evokes many different emotions to take the role of the fledgling writer. When Jamie says he has "nuthin' to write about," what is he really saying? He is probably dominated by his internal Critic, as discussed in Chapter 1. He may not think that any of his ideas are worthy as a writing topic. He may also not even realize that *anything* can be written about in some way. So how do we overcome this "nuthin' to write about" obstacle?

FINDING TOPICS EVERYWHERE

Students may not understand that they can find topic ideas in all facets of their lives. We must teach them directly, over and over, how to find topics everywhere. Keeping a *topic list* is an important way to manage ideas. This list can be as simple as a blank sheet of paper stapled inside the cover of a writing notebook, or it can even serve as the first page. Or you can use a reproducible form, such as the one in Figure 3.1.

Students should be regularly encouraged to add to and refer to their topic lists. There is no "one-size-fits-all" method of topic selection. What serves as interesting material for one student may bore the life out of the next. Topic lists are designed by students according to their own needs and interests. They are not the places for teachers to display creativity and original thinking, but for *students* to do so.

_____ 's Topic List

_____   _____

_____   _____

_____   _____

_____   _____

_____   _____

_____   _____

_____   _____

_____   _____

_____   _____

_____   _____

_____   _____

_____   _____

_____   _____

_____   _____

_____   _____

_____   _____

_____   _____

_____   _____

FIGURE 3.1. Topic list.

▣▣

TEACHER'S TIP: Remind students frequently to read and add
to their topic lists.

▣▣

The next step is finding methods that will fill those topic lists with dozens of viable topics for each individual.

ACTIVITIES TO GENERATE TOPICS

We have used the following activities successfully, with necessary adaptations for younger and older writers, from first grade through middle school.

Free-Association Word List

A good early activity for students during the writing workshop is a form of free-association word list. They close their eyes and think of something, anything at all (a person, place, thing, action, etc.). As they call out their items, you make a list on a chart or the board.

We spend the next few minutes exploring the possibilities each topic holds. Something as trivial and unlikely as *watermelon* can spark ideas like these: "They could have a carving contest on the Fourth of July, like they do for pumpkins at Halloween!" and "It could be a kid's favorite food, so that all he'll eat is watermelon until he starts turning into one!" Play this activity up with comments like "If you had told me you could write a story about something as silly as watermelon and make it so interesting, I would have thought you were crazy! I can't believe you came up with so many great ideas!" Students tend to get very excited during this discussion.

We usually do two or three topics in this way as a whole class, then break into smaller collaborative groups. We'll give each group several topics from the list, plus a time limit in which to generate as many workable story ideas as possible. If each group writes the object at the top of a sheet of paper, and lists the story ideas related to it below, these sheets can be taped together to form a giant "story idea banner" that can be displayed and referred to any time someone needs an idea. Students can also jot down on their individual topic lists those they find most appealing.

Warning: This is not a quiet activity! Ideally, the excitement will be infectious and spread to each collaborative team. Furthermore, new topics will be generated through these small-group discussions. When this happens, point it out to the rest of the class. In this way, students model for each other how to explore and expand topics.

For example, you might announce, "I noticed that this team has come up with a new topic that we had not listed. As they were discussing the topic *my cousin*, they decided they could expand it to include other members of their family as well. Devonne immediately thought of how her sister in New York takes her shopping when she visits. Each person added a different member of his or her family. They took your ideas and added to them to make them their own."

□▣□

TEACHER'S TIP: Remind students frequently that they can "borrow" topics from each other and make them unique.

□▣□

Timelines

Another activity to generate topics is creating a *timeline*. To model the procedure for the students, create a timeline of your own lifetime or that of a well-known figure, of a historical period you may be studying, or of the events of the past year. Timelines are particularly well suited to biographical and autobiographical writing.

This is an activity that needs good teacher modeling. You'll have to think aloud about important or interesting things that have happened in your life, and think aloud as you construct a timeline for your life that can serve as a model. Draw a long line on the board. The far left-hand end marks your birth (you don't have to write the year!); the far right-hand end represents the present time. Make marks at intervals to show big events of your life, focusing especially on those events students might identify closely with: moving, birth of a sibling, death of a pet or special relative, and so forth. Tell a little about the events you're including, without being tedious. If you forgot some important event, add it where it belongs.

Lynn explains, "I might say to my class, 'I remember when I was seven and I had surgery to remove a birthmark. I was in the hospital, and I didn't know where my mom or dad were when the doctor came to remove this big bandage. It hurt like crazy! I was crying and screaming. That was pretty important, so I'll put that down.' And then I mark it accordingly, seven years after my birth. Next, I may skip back to a story my parents told about me when I was two. I was mad, and I slammed the door so hard that it bounced back. The doorknob gave me a black eye. I try to include both bad and good experiences that really did happen to me." Figure 3.2 shows an example of a timeline like this.

After you have modeled how you'd construct a timeline of your life, ask the students to begin timelines of their own. Depending on their ages, they may need help from family members.

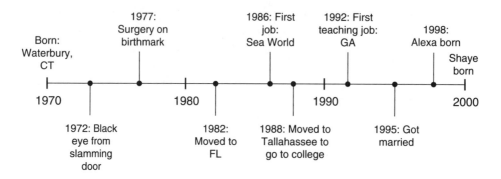

FIGURE 3.2. Sample timeline.

Another way to use timelines, and episodes from our lives, is to write real-life stories. These stories can be written factually, based on how we remember the event or on how it was told to us, or can be "fictionalized" by adding new elements that are made up. To demonstrate how a real-life event can be changed into an original story, we start with a story that is shared by a student, and invite others to suggest ways the basic event could be changed. For example, in one class Laura told about how she went roller skating and broke her wrist. Tamaine then suggested that we could say that a person was chasing her so she had to go fast to get away. Hans added that maybe the girl who was being chased wasn't very nice and had just made fun of the person chasing her. And on we went, manufacturing a new story based on a real event. Ideas from timelines are added to topic lists as students continue in this manner.

⬚⬚

TEACHER'S TIP: Events from students' own lives are perfect topics for
either factual or fictionalized stories.

⬚⬚

"Story Stew"

Discuss with students the various settings, physical descriptions and names of characters, and other story elements that occur in what they are reading. Encourage them to be "people watchers"—observers taking in every bit of detail about the people, places, and things around them. A whole story can grow from one particularly interesting place, character, or object.

Lists of these can be made, and then intriguing items can be selected to create a story of their own or add to a piece that's been started. An excerpt from one student's topic list after one such exercise looked like this:

- *Baltimore*
- *a really skinny kid whose nickname is "Stick"*
- *a round thing dug up out of the ground and nobody knows what it is*

In *What If?: Writing Exercises for Fiction Writers*, Anne Bernays and Pamela Painter (1990, pp. 128–129) recommend creating a list of "random elements," such as two characters, a place, two objects, an adjective, and an abstract noun—for example, *an unemployed bookkeeper, a skycap, an all-night diner, a tuna fish sandwich, a gardenia, shimmering*, and *infinity*. Then have students try to create a story in which each element in this list occurs in the first two pages. The idea is to help them practice "winging it" by letting story elements dictate to them the direction a piece will take. Although this exercise would be most appropriate for older writers, the idea can be adapted for younger or beginning writers.

We've had success (and a lot of fun) having students practice combining story elements in short pieces or story outlines. We've constructed a card file of story elements on different-colored file cards: Characters are on green cards, places are on blue cards, objects are on yellow ones, and so forth. We shuffle the cards and deal them out without looking at them. Sometimes we tell students what they'll get: "I'll give you two character cards and a place; try to figure out how these two characters got to this place, and why they're there." Other times we'll let them choose: "Choose three cards of different colors. Then figure out how those three elements might go together, and what might happen in a story that has all three of them." Some of the items from Jean's "story stew" cards are shown in Figure 3.3. You can easily make up your own; our students love to suggest additions!

Because it can be impossible to work entirely random items into a story that makes sense, we almost always allow students to trade cards with each other, or to give some of their cards back for another try at selection. But because some will trade cards all day, we usually limit trades and tell students that after they've traded once (or twice at most), they have to go with what they have.

When students share their "stew stories," they tell what elements they got, and may read their writing aloud or tell how they combined them. As they hear each other's ideas, their own creative ideas are sparked. Creativity and ingenious ways of combining story elements are applauded. These short pieces can be kept in journals, notebooks, or writing folders, and sometimes are developed into fuller stories at a later time. Here are two examples written by sixth graders:

Character: bossy rich girl; Setting: pet store; Object: wad of bubble gum

Cindy was a little rich girl who was very bossy and always did just what she wanted. She lived two blocks from a pet store. Every day her limo would take her to the pet store. She would go in and pick a cage or tank and stick her used gum on it. One day she walked into the pet store and saw yesterday's gum on a rabbit cage. She smiled meanly. The storekeeper saw her and gave her a sly look. Just then, as Cindy was about to de-

Characters

circus clown	scientist who studies snakes	middle school principal
kindergarten teacher	school bus driver	rookie cop	taxi driver
100-year-old lady	K-9 police officer	nine-year-old twin boys	dentist
bossy little girl	mom with seven young children	a big mean dog	carpenter
lost kitten	lifeguard	hospital orderly	teenage babysitter

Settings

cemetery	kindergarten class	doctor's office	riding stable
animal shelter (SPCA)	used-car dealership	inside of an ambulance
dangerous neighborhood	Chinese restaurant	pet store	locker room
supermarket	public library	highway rest area	police station

Objects

a stolen CD	six pork chops	smelly gym shoes	talking parrot
bunch of bananas	a shovel	a silver dollar	a key
a dozen donuts	three pennies	sweater with a hole in one sleeve
one red carnation	a lost library book	a lottery ticket	an engagement ring

FIGURE 3.3. Examples of Jean's "story stew" cards.

posit her gum on the side of a fish tank, the storekeeper pressed a button with an alarm that made her jump. The door burst open blinding her with a white light! Two guys came in and grabbed her. She screamed and kicked but the men just held her tighter. They took her outside and threw her into a truck. Her head banged against the wall. They drove for a long time. Finally they came to a brick building with bars on the windows. It was Juvenile Hall! Cindy was led to a cell and chained to a bunk. They slammed the door shut. How could they just leave her in that wretched place?

"Wait 'til I tell my Daddy!" she screamed. "Bring me some water!" But no one answered. "You bring me some water this minute!" she kept yelling. But the guards just laughed.

"Cindy," she heard a soft voice say. "Cindy . . ." Cindy sat straight up in bed. She was in her own room. "It was just a dream," she said. But she changed her ways from that day on.

—by Shelley

Characters: a high school cheerleader and a zombie; Setting: a restaurant

Once there was a girl named Mary who went to the local high school. She was a cheerleader. Her best friend Cindy wanted to be a cheerleader too. Cindy and Mary always met at 11:00 at the cemetery. It was their one place to hang out. Every time they went to the cemetery, Mary would teach Cindy some cheerleader stunts. One time Mary was teaching Cindy to do a back flip. Mary got in her position and jumped. She went straight down and hit her head on a headstone, which split her head open. Cindy tried to stop Mary's head from hitting the stone but it was too late. She was dead. Cindy called

911 and the Rescue Squad came but they said it was no use. The next day they had Mary's funeral at the same cemetery where she died.

    A year later the cemetery was sold and they started to build a pizza restaurant on the very spot. They moved all of the graves to another place but for some reason they missed Mary's grave. One night just after the restaurant opened a man looked up from his pizza and saw someone looking in the window. It looked like a zombie and it had worms crawling through its arms and brains. The man thought it was wearing a ragged old cheerleader uniform. The man was terrified! He jumped up screaming and the manager came running over, but when the manager went outside he saw nothing. Then when he went to the window he saw worms on the ground. So the owner called the police. A detective looked all around and said that for sure a zombie had been lurking outside the restaurant. Of course, it was the ghost of Mary trying to get back to her grave.

—by Kevin

"Stew stories" are sometimes contrived, but students usually enjoy trying to figure out ways to combine the elements. Reluctant writers especially seem to enjoy being "given" a couple of story elements, even though it may be a challenge to combine them. This exercise often results in a lot of hilarity during both the writing and the sharing. It also gives writers practice in stretching their imaginations.

Great children's literature sometimes incorporates seemingly unrelated or unfamiliar elements in unforgettable ways. Patricia Polacco's *Pink and Say* is an example of the tremendous power that story elements can have. Most noticeable initially is the odd title, which the reader comes to discover are the names of the two main characters.

Characters' names alone can be the basis of an entire mini-lesson: What if the boys' names were Buford and Eugene, or Rambo and Max? What images do names conjure? Explore with students some memorable characters' names from high-quality literature. Story characters often have names that reflect personal qualities or abilities, such as Ian Fleming's Commander Caractacus Pott, inventor of the *Chitty Chitty Bang Bang* car, or the greedy John Midas from Patrick Skene Catling's *The Chocolate Touch*. So do Charles Dickens's characters, like the disgusting Uriah Heep and the skinflint Ebenezer Scrooge; and Natalie Babbitt's heroic Gaylen, contrasted with the traitorous prime minister Hemlock, in *The Search for Delicious*. Brian Jacques, author of the much-beloved *Redwall* sagas, often uses names to create characterization. For example, could any reader miss the point that a squirrel named Elmjak, a golden badger named Sunflash, or Dearie Lingle the baby mole are good animals, but Balefur the "dogfox," Lask Frildur the lizard, and Slashback the sea rat are bad creatures? Literature is full of memorable characters' names, which can be the basis for mini-lessons on the importance of choosing just the right name for story characters.

We often do mini-lessons in which students either invent names for characters we describe, or develop short character sketches based on a character's name. For example, we'll give them a few names we've made up, such as Lawrence Weldon Burkhead IV, Muffy Pinkney, or Rocky Flint. Using only what the names might suggest to them, they make up a few details (age, occupation, looks, etc.). For example, Zack, a sixth grader, wrote the following:

> *Lawrence Weldon Burkhead IV is a 40 year old lawyer who wears wire-rimmed glasses and suits with vests. He always wears a suit, even to mow the lawn or wash the dog. He drives a Volvo and sleeps with his briefcase next to the bed.*

> *Muffy Pinkney is 25 years old. She has curly brown hair and big lips and she always wears bright pink lipstick. She wears very short skirts. She works in a bakery where she decorates the birthday cakes, and she flirts with all the men who come into the bakery.*

> *Rocky Flint is a tough guy of about 19 who dropped out of high school. He lifts weights every day so he has huge muscles. All the girls like him. He drives a motorcycle and he goes to the gym every night. His dog is a Doberman.*

Alternatively, we'll give a brief description of a character, and students will brainstorm names for him or her. For example, what would be a good name for *a country preacher who gives loud sermons about sin, but secretly steals from the collection plate?* Our students suggested, among others, "Rev. Bob Lightfinger" and "Deacon Steele." How about *a plump, sweet-natured kindergarten teacher who greets each student with a hug each day?* "Mrs. Rosie Huggles" and "Irenia Love" were two suggestions.

Setting, too, is a story element students can explore. For example, Polacco's setting in *Pink and Say* is so vividly described that the reader actually experiences it along with the characters. How did the author achieve this? Many other stories have intriguing settings. A. A. Milne's timeless Hundred Acre Wood in *Winnie-the-Pooh* becomes an entire universe, its geography meticulously set forth in Ernest Shepard's maps; Alice McLerran's sun-baked, cactus-stubbled desert hill becomes the town of Roxaboxen in her book by that title; and E. B. White's barnyard in *Charlotte's Web* is so carefully described that readers can practically hear the slops sloshing into Wilbur's trough and smell the manure pile on which he sleeps. Setting helps writers create mood and credibility in their stories.

Webs

The purpose of any type of *web* is to organize information about a topic visually, so as to have various ideas from which to choose at one's fingertips. An effective way to help students generate ideas is to teach or review with the students how to make a web. In this lesson, the concept that *all* ideas are accepted and written down is the most important part. Students must turn off their Critic's voice and simply brainstorm. Judgments are not placed on suggestions; no answer is right or wrong. It's like a puzzle, where all the pieces are necessary to complete the idea.

Webs can be organized very strictly into several categories, or can be more loosely defined, more in the nature of a list. One student's web on animals may be divided by types, habitats, diet, and offspring, while another may just list all the animal things he or she can think of in a more random manner, as in Figure 3.4. Model the webbing process from start to finish, letting students choose the topic and add each item where they see fit. The end result is not the finished web, for that is really the beginning. The next step is to turn those webbed ideas into a story or nonfiction piece.

How can you write one story with a whole class? One way is to guide a dis-

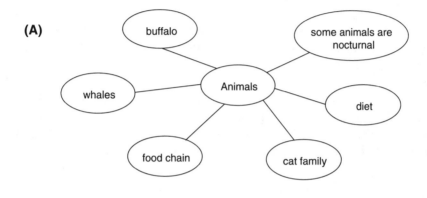

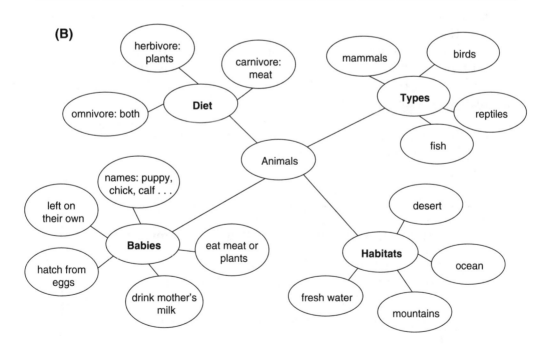

FIGURE 3.4. Sample webs. (a) Brainstorm web. (b) More organized web.

cussion of the story progression, letting the students direct the story events. Another way is to make a brief topical outline to remind students what they are discussing and in what order. This demonstrates the necessary connection and flow between parts. But at the beginning of the year, we most often write the story down on a chart or the board, as it is dictated by the students. In this way, it is not personally owned by just one student; many class members have contributed.

Because of its time-consuming nature, a group story may be started, but may not be seen through to its conclusion before the end of the writing period. However, save the story to complete during subsequent writing periods. In that way, students will have walked through the process with some guidance and a lot of modeling. They will enjoy these group stories if you keep in mind two things: They are in charge, and they have limited attention spans. If participation and enthusiasm begin to wane, *stop*. Save it for next time, or leave the story displayed as a good beginning that some may want to continue. Beware of letting a class story session turn into a marathon listening activity.

If you'd like the students to use the webbing technique independently, reinforce it. If you see a student making a web, announce it to the class. Have students share their webs before reading the stories created from them. Remind a struggling student that a web may be a helpful way to get "unstuck."

The Five W's

Do you remember the "Five W" questions you may have learned to write news reports? The Five W's—*who, what, where, when,* and *why*—are just as useful for writing fiction as for news accounts. Using these questions in a slightly modified form is also known as the *story grammar strategy* (Harris and Graham, 1996). The story grammar strategy uses the mnemonic device *W-W-W—What 2—How 2*, which stands for these questions:

- *Who* is the main character, and who else is in the story?
- *When* does the story take place?

BOX 3.1. Webs: Important Points to Remember

- Accept all responses without judgment.
- Model the process of transforming web ideas into stories.
- Move quickly through the content to keep students' interest.
- Encourage students to web on their own as part of the prewriting process.

- *Where* does the story take place?
- *What* does the main character do or want to do? *What* happens with other characters?
- *How* does the story end? *How* does the main character (and other characters) feel?

For example, Brittany knew she wanted to write about her grandmother; she had her topic, but she didn't know where to go from there. She shared her concern with the class, so we brainstormed questions to ask Brittany. Our first question dealt with *intention,* one of the most fundamental considerations of any writer: "What kind of piece do you want it to be?" Brittany said that she wanted it to be a fiction piece to give to her grandmother as a gift.

Knowing her intention clarified things, and we turned to the Five W's for help. We wrote each of the question words on the board, and the students then formed more W questions for Brittany: "*Who* else might be in this story?" "*What* do you want to happen?" "*When* and *where* does the story take place?" Brittany used these questions to discover the direction she would move the story from there.

Of course, sometimes the questions will not always help, and the student will respond "I don't know" to each one. This too can be helped. In such a situation, the class can offer suggestions. Most often the suggestions spark something in the student; this may occur because the writer likes one or more suggestions and wants to incorporate them into the story, because a suggestion reminds him or her of something else, or even because the writer rejects all the suggestions and comes up with his or her own alternative.

BOX 3.2. The W Questions (W-W-W—What 2—How 2)

- WHO is the main character? Who else is in the story?
- WHEN does the story take place?
- WHERE does the story take place?
- WHAT does the main character want to do?
- WHAT happens when the main character tries to do it? WHAT happens with the other characters?
- HOW does the story end?
- HOW does the main character feel? HOW do other characters feel?

From Harris and Graham (1996, p. 49). Copyright 1996 by Brookline Books. Reprinted by permission.

Read, Read, Read!

Of course, we all want our students to read. We read aloud to them and allow time for daily independent reading in our classroom. In doing so, we are already taking a big step in supporting their writing development. Reading benefits children in many ways with which we are all familiar: vocabulary development, growth in logical thinking, deepening of imagination, ability to see from another's viewpoint, and so forth. It's only a short step from reading to your students to develop their reading and thinking abilities, to using literature to enhance your writing instruction.

In *The Art of Teaching Writing*, Lucy McCormick Calkins (1994) called this "writing under the influence" of literature (p. 249). Calkins continued:

> When Cynthia Rylant was asked how to teach writing to children, she answered, "Read to them. Read them *Ox-Cart Man*, *The Animal Farm*, and *The Birds and the Beasts and the Third Thing*. Take their breath away. . . . Don't talk the experience to death. . . . Teach your children to be moved and you will be preparing them to move others." (pp. 251–252)

If children can determine what makes a story or book enjoyable, they can use this powerful knowledge to transform their own writing. When you read a book to the class, discuss with students what makes it so wonderful, hilarious, boring, scary, or whatever to them. How are the characters described? In what ways do problems occur? Do the illustrations add to or detract from the text?

When you analyze a story in this fashion, however, keep in mind Rylant's admonition. You're not picking it apart for theme and symbolism the way you did in English 201, or telling your students what makes it a good story. Instead, have a discussion involving the *whys* behind our opinions. *Why* is it funny? Sad? Intriguing? Model thinking deeply about what makes a story great, okay, or blah, and you'll find your students beginning to do the same as they think about and discuss stories.

⊡⊡⊡

TEACHER'S TIP: To help your students improve their writing, surround them with excellent literature; read *to* them and *with* them.

⊡⊡⊡

Nothing is as exciting as when students look at their own or someone else's writing and suggest a strategy developed from literature to enhance it. During peer conferencing one day, Lynn overheard this conversation between two second graders:

ERICA: This is a great story, but I think it would be even better if you tried that thing like in the book about Max and the wild things, and you had the girl's room turn into the place in her dream like Max's room turned into the forest.

JENNIFER: Oh, cool! Will you help me?

The two girls worked together to produce a piece far superior to the original draft, due in large part to their transference of Maurice Sendak's technique to their own story. Had they not experienced *Where the Wild Things Are*, they would not have been aware of this technique. It was exciting because Erica and Jennifer had achieved the level of confidence necessary to consider using the tools of a "real" author.

INDIVIDUAL AND GROUP TOPIC LISTS

Most teachers are already familiar with the lists of topics writers often keep to help remind themselves of good topics they might otherwise forget. So far, we have discussed numerous ways to generate topics. Most of them involve some cooperative group work, at least initially. *Group topic lists* may be recorded on charts, bulletin boards, or the like and displayed in the classroom for further use. Group topic lists are encouraged for a number of reasons.

First of all, a group format increases both the quantity and quality of ideas. For example, Sarah may not be able to think of anything on her own today, but she may be able to take Lee's idea, expand upon it, and improve it. Although she has not originated the thought, she has made it her own.

Second, group work allows time to think out loud. Those who easily come up with ideas daily can explain where their thoughts came from and how they developed them. This may help those who sit back and look at the "magical" process going on around them in awe. They become aware that this is actually achievable, once they've heard repeatedly how often the topics are conceived in a simple manner.

Third, group processing encourages risk taking. The atmosphere is designed

---

BOX 3.3. Summary of Activities to Generate Topics

- Create a free association word list.
- Make a timeline.
- Combine story elements such as characters, settings, and objects.
- Practice creating names for characters and creating characters from names.
- Use good literature as models.

to support many ideas, and most contributions are accepted. Most students find that it's safer to propose a new idea or try a new technique in a small group than to try it either alone, or in front of the whole class.

Fourth, a group approach may eliminate competition and enhance collaboration during writing. The group is encouraged to share ideas, and learns that sharing an idea only increases its value. The subsequent section on ownership deals more with this topic.

Individual topic lists, on the other hand, are also important. There are times when students will not want to, or be able to, collaborate in order to shape a story. Therefore, students must be able to complete this process by themselves. Individual topic lists are often kept in the writing folder or notebook, usually on the inside front cover; a form that can be used for such a list has already been shown in Figure 3.1. Students are encouraged to reflect on and add to this list regularly if it is to be maintained. In addition, as mentioned before, we encourage our students to add topics from group sessions to their individual lists as well.

SHARING TOPICS: "WHOSE IDEA IS THIS, ANYWAY?"

Sharing topics doesn't always go smoothly, even with adult writers. Children sometimes feel that it's unjust to appropriate an idea or topic. The way you handle this situation will do much to help establish a collaborative atmosphere, as well as a sense of personal justice, in your classroom, as the following scenario illustrates.

In Lynn's third-grade classroom, Patrice had a wonderful idea: to write a fantasy story in which the school is carried off to another planet. In fact, the idea was so attractive that Cecily decided to write a story about the very same thing! To Patrice's dismay, Cecily coolly insisted that she was *not* copying. The discussion was heating up as Lynn approached.

"You *stole* my idea!" accused Patrice angrily.

"It's not yours; we can share ideas in here," Cecily fired back.

This was the first dispute over topics so far this year, so Lynn knew she must handle it carefully. She began not by telling both girls to lower their voices, or by stating that they should not be arguing, but by empathizing with Patrice.

"It seems like you're upset because you came up with the idea for the story and you feel that Cecily is taking it from you," Lynn said. Patrice nodded emphatically: "It was my idea first, and she stole it!"

"But, Ms. Beverly," argued Cecily, "you always said we could get ideas from other people, and I *like* that idea! Besides, my story wouldn't be the same as Patrice's." A thoughtful expression crossed Patrice's face. "I know she can't take it from me because I can still write about it," Patrice admitted. For several minutes more, they discussed the idea that Patrice did *originate* the idea, but did not *own* it. Lynn reminded the girls of some familiar books—like *The Three Little Pigs* and *The True Story of the Three Little Pigs*, or *Little Red Riding Hood* and *Lon Po Po*—in which one author used another author's topic, yet the two versions were quite different. Patrice worried that Cecily would replicate her entire story, so Cecily shared her plans for her version. Since it was decidedly different, Patrice felt comfortable with the idea of sharing the topic with Cecily.

Patrice and Cecily's experience points up the importance of dealing directly with the concept of *ownership*. One way to deal with this concept is to demonstrate that no two writers will probably ever deal with the same topic in the same way, as Lynn did the very next day. She told her students that for that lesson, they would all write on the same topic, *school*. "I have a very good reason for doing this, and I will tell you what it is when we are finished," she told them. "For now, you may write what you choose, but it must be on the topic of *school*. We'll share in 20 minutes."

After 20 minutes, the students chose partners and took turns reading their stories. This operation was repeated with a second partner, and then the students were asked to come together in a group on the floor. They were told to listen to how their own stories were similar to or different from the ones being read, and four volunteers read their stories to the group.

Of course, no two stories were exactly alike. You wouldn't be surprised, but the students were. They couldn't believe that out of 23 people, all writing about the same thing, there were none of the same stories. Some students wrote about their present school, some about schools they had moved away from, some about fictional schools such as Louis Sachar's weird Wayside School, and so forth. Three students who wrote about the class had different ways of looking at their daily classroom experience, and they all shared the same classroom! A productive discussion followed about who owns ideas (*nobody!*) and when a topic gets "used up" (*never!*). This lesson took one entire day of the writing workshop, but the benefits lasted throughout the year.

TEACHER'S TIP: One good demonstration that no two writers ever write about the same topic in exactly the same way is worth a thousand reminders that "nobody owns topics."

WRITERS' NOTEBOOKS

Lucy McCormick Calkins (1994) first wrote about the use of writers' notebooks in *The Art of Teaching Writing*. As a writer and writing teacher, she had begun to move away from the notion that children should keep writing folders, filled with their drafts of pieces, and toward a technique used for many years by professional writers and poets: keeping a notebook of writing ideas and "stuff" through which one can sift whenever an idea is needed. In doing so, Calkins showed us yet another way that we can learn about writing by studying what professional writers do. This she referred to as "living the writerly life" (1994, p. 261), in which young writers see themselves as insiders in the writing process—full-fledged writers by themselves.

Many writers keep notebooks they fill with "treasures," like the shiny black stones in Marian's rusty tin box in *Roxaboxen*. Instead of shiny stones, they keep the images, scraps of overheard dialogue, descriptive phrases, characters' fanciful names, ideas for settings, story and poem titles, evocative photographs, pressed flowers, newspaper headlines, doodles, and everything else that a writer might find worth keeping. Their notebooks become "safe deposit boxes"—repositories of ideas and raw materials that might someday become a story, a poem, an article, or a letter.

Ralph Fletcher (1996), a poet and teacher, wrote:

> Keeping a notebook is the single best way I know to survive as a writer. It encourages you to pay attention to your world, inside and out. It serves as a container to keep together all the seeds you gather until you're ready to plant them. It gives you a quiet place to catch your breath and begin to write. . . . If I want to write movingly I must first pay attention to what moves me. I must be connected to it: I must be *fused*. That's what the notebook is for. It gives you a roomy place to record and explore what amazes, delights, disgusts, or appalls you. (pp. 1, 11; emphasis in original)

Notebooks may be preferred over writing folders because students can include more "stuff" in them than just the typical topic lists, successive drafts, and finished work usually found in a student's writing folder. Notebooks quickly become very personal for students, and they are used more to hold ideas, images, and bits of writing than to hold drafts or finished pieces. Students can use notebooks to record, to store, and to revisit as they search for topics and fresh ways to express themselves.

They can also use their notebooks to experiment, to fail, and to write badly. These are as necessary to good writing as anything else—as necessary as reading and listening to good literature and poetry, as people watching and eavesdropping on conversations, as close observation of everyday things and events. Fletcher (1996a) aptly quoted the philosopher Nietzche, who once wrote, "Much dung must be spread so that a single flower can grow" (p. 56) The notebook is a private place to write badly, to "spread dung," so that later great ideas, perfect turns of phrase, can bloom.

The best way for students to understand what a writer's notebook is, and how it differs from a writing folder, is to ask a writer who keeps a notebook to share it with your class. If you don't personally know anybody who practices such a strange ritual, start asking around. Local bookstores that feature local writers, the nearby community college or university, or even the English department chair at a local high school might help you connect with a real adult writer (published or not) who keeps a notebook; most writers do, in some form or other. (This might also be a good time for you to start your own; it will surely help your own writing, and it will give this part of your writing program an even more personal touch. Besides, chances are that once you start keeping a notebook, you'll want to continue.)

Again, writers' notebooks serve many purposes. They can hold pieces of writing ranging in length from a sentence or two to pages—experiments with different voices and styles; unsuccessful attempts to get a particular description, bit of dialogue, or character sketch just right; samples of poetry that work or don't work; bits of memoir; and on and on—just about anything a writer can produce, except perhaps perfect final drafts. In this way, a notebook *is* like a classroom writing folder. Notebooks also contain lots and lots of ideas for possible topics, although writers don't usually use a topic list in their notebooks, but instead may toss ideas in along with longer bits.

But the main way notebooks differ from folders is that writers usually include memorable "stuff" in their notebooks that remind them of something or help them preserve a memory. Letters, ticket stubs, notes, newspaper or magazine articles or headlines, photos, and many other kinds of realia can trigger memories and associations that can further one's writing. These can be some of the most powerful writing stimuli of all, for, as Fletcher (1996a) wrote, "Most of us find the past the steadiest, most reliable supplier of material for our work. . . . Your notebook is an invitation to . . . touch base with all the old selves you left along the way" (pp. 45–46).

Connecting with the past is one of the best ways to help young writers discover the wealth of topics, ideas, images, and emotions they have inside themselves. Although some may say that children have little "past" to write about, we think that children are only closer to their pasts than the rest of us; their childhood and adolescent memories are that much closer and more available to be relived. And a writer is never too young to learn the power of memory and the associations that ordinary objects can trigger. For these reasons, notebooks can be powerful writing tools in your classroom.

To begin using writing notebooks in your classroom, you will probably want to show your students one or more examples, and this is another good reason for beginning to keep your own personal notebook. Some teachers provide each student with a first notebook, while others invite students to supply their own and keep a few on hand for those who aren't able to. In the former case, sturdy spiral-bound notebooks or composition books with a sewn binding are good. In the latter case, students will probably experiment with different kinds of notebooks; standard three-ring binders (often with pockets, to hold scraps that can't be clipped into the binders) and bound blank books are often chosen. Size is also a matter of personal choice. The standard 8½" × 11" size accommodates lots of artifacts as well as writing and drawing, while the smaller 5" × 8" size may be more inviting to reluctant writers, or easier for students to carry and keep nearby.

In the beginning, you'll want to consistently encourage students to keep their notebooks with them and use them in every writing workshop. Every few days, a mini-lesson on notebooks is helpful; mini-lessons can focus on how you are adding to and using your own notebook, and can extend to having a few students at a time share something they've added or show how they've used a notebook item in a piece of writing recently.

⊡⊡

TEACHER'S TIP: Children learn the power of memory and reminiscence as they reflect on a treasured object and what it means in their lives.

⊡⊡

As their notebooks get fuller, you should systematically set aside time for all students to look back through their notebooks and share, orally or in writing, their reflections on what they've discovered. In small or large groups, or in personal reflective writing, students can share a favorite inclusion—something they forgot was there, something they aren't sure what to do with, something that strikes them as funny, and so forth. Sharing like this helps writers rediscover the richness of their notebooks; it also helps them get new ideas from each other, and experience celebrating their uniqueness.

WRITING FIRST DRAFTS

Whether you call the first version of a piece "sloppy copy," "rough draft," "first draft," or whatever, its purpose is to get ideas down on paper in a clear manner. Often ideas can get lost as young writers struggle to balance the creative force of their ideas with the criticizing force of their fears and uncertainties.

Encourage students to do the best they can with mechanics, grammar, and spelling while they get their ideas down. That does *not* mean you should tell them not to worry about these things. It's frustrating to see an advanced fourth grader write *GRIL* for *girl*, or a capable second grader write a sentence like "She *was talk* to her cousin." Once again, there is a fine line in determining what each student should already know and be putting in to practice automatically. But the emphasis in first, or early, drafts is on generating ideas, not on polishing the mechanics (yet).

Let the first draft be a time of experimentation for the students, and don't get in the way of the process. Suggestions are appropriate as long as they are given as such, and not as orders. "One way you could . . ." might seem like more of a suggestion than "You should . . ." or "Why don't you . . ." Encourage students not to get bogged down in any one detail or question by reminding them that there will be time to refine such issues later in the process.

As you observe and talk with students during the first-draft phase, make notes to yourself on individual progress and needs. Our favorite way to do this is to use self-adhesive notes that we can just transfer to their folders. An effective format for this is shown in Figure 3.5. For example, we may jot down, "Markesha: Punctuates sentences correctly" as a reminder that Markesha can be expected to be doing this in her first drafts without help. These notes will also come in handy at report card and conference times. But at this stage, these notes remind us what to ignore and what to point out as we look at first drafts.

Getting over the Spelling Hurdle

A major obstacle that you will encounter when teaching writing to young children is the dreaded whine, "I don't know how to spell it!" Teachers often wonder what the best response is to students' complaints that they don't know how to spell something, or requests for their teachers to spell it for them. We all want to be supportive, but giving too much help can be as bad as not giving enough.

Here are some strategies you can use when students expect more than occasional spelling help during the first-draft stage.

• *Don't give them all the words they want.* That is, don't tell them how to spell it, but make some encouraging comment like "Just give it your best try," or "Don't worry about spelling it correctly until you're ready to edit your paper."

Sometimes students just want to try you out to see whether they will get the word from you. Once they see that you will not give it to them, they will be more likely to try on their own. In general, the more you supply words for them the more often they will turn to you and the less often they will try to figure it out. We want to encourage independence, not dependence.

TEACHER'S TIP: The more you tell students how to spell words, the less likely they are to try to spell them on their own. Don't encourage dependence on you.

• *Encourage phonemic awareness by calling attention to the sounds in the word.* When asked to spell a word for a child, teachers and parents often say some version of "Sound it out." Kids often don't know what this means, or think it means they have to be able to spell *all* the sounds in the word. That, of course, is part of why they're asking for help in the first place! A better response is "What is the first sound you hear in that word? What do you hear next?" This takes longer than saying "Sound it out," but it helps the child to isolate the sounds and breaks the task down into manageable parts.

Mike A.	Billy E.	Desirée C.
3/12 Introduced quotation marks	3/10 Used cut-&-paste to revise	3/15 Shared her topic list w/group
Maria P.	Miles S.	Kaitlyn J.
3/16 Needs help with chronological order	3/18 Used a web spontaneously during prewriting	

FIGURE 3.5. Sample observation sheet with sticky notes.

Adapted from *Creating the Child-Centred Classroom* by Susan Schwartz and Mindy Pollishuke. Copyright 1990 by Irwin Publishing, Toronto, Ontario, Canada. Adapted by permission of Richard C. Owen Publishers, Katonah, NY.

• *Teach students how to stretch words like rubber bands.* Show the students a regular rubber band. Stretch it out between your fingers, and let it contract again. Compare this rubber band with the words they are trying to spell. For example, show the rubber band contracted and say, "Let's say I want to spell the word *flower.*" Then stretch out the rubber band as you say the word very slowly, extending each phoneme (as if you were speaking in slow motion):

"f f f f - l l l l - ow w w w- er r r r"

Repeat stretching the word out while students try to write the word using a letter or letters for each sound they hear. (Remember, they may not spell it right, but they'll probably be fairly close. The "closer" they can get, the better!) Most will need to practice this procedure before they can do it independently.

It is easier to spell a word if you stretch it out and say it slowly so you hear all the sounds. Remind students of this procedure by asking, "Have you stretched it out like a rubber band?"

• *Teach spelling directly and systematically.* Kids need systematic spelling instruction based on word patterns and frequency. It doesn't really matter whether you are using a basal spelling program, some locally developed spelling curriculum, or misspelled words from their own writing to teach them, as long as they are receiving systematic, direct spelling instruction regularly.

Remember to *continually make connections between what students are learning in spelling and the words they are trying to use in their writing.* If they have learned *can* and need to spell *can't*, remind them that they already know *can*, and that they only need to add the final sound. By making this association frequently, students begin to connect what they are learning in spelling with their everyday use of the words.

TEACHER'S TIP: When trying to spell a new word, remind writers of
similar words they've already learned.

• *Remind students of rhyming words and words from the same "word family."* Teach students to think of words that rhyme with the word that they're trying to spell. For example, Paxton, a fourth grader, had spelled *twice* as *TWISE.* She knew it was spelled wrong, but didn't recognize what was wrong with it. Prompted to think of a rhyming word that she could spell, she replied, "*Nice.* Oh, that's it! It should be a *C.*" Paxton's discovery was much more effective than someone's telling her how to fix it would have been.

Even very young students can use the word families they've learned. The rhyming idea will only help if it is a member of a pattern known to the child. A first grader who is trying to spell *computer* will obviously not be helped by a rhyme, but if he or she is trying to spell *that* and already knows *cat*, then this is an appropriate method.

   • *Remind students that corrections will occur during revision and editing.* The purpose of the first draft is to get ideas down on paper, and if students worry about spelling too much, they may lose their great ideas. The revision and editing stages are the specifically designated times in which students and teachers should be most concerned with spelling. These stages are discussed in detail in Chapters 4 and 5.

   • *Encourage students to try to use a dictionary.* This is not easy for many students, and not a response we give too often. It is difficult to use a dictionary for spelling help if you are not a very good speller and you can't readily identify all the possible combinations of letters that may make one sound. If Jack can't spell *suddenly* except for the *S*, it would be a waste of time, and very frustrating, for Jack to look through each page of the *S*'s. But we do want students to learn to use dictionaries. We often help students by having them find the section for the first letter, helping them locate the correct section or page, and then having them search for the word on that one page. At least they get practice in turning to the dictionary for help, and in recognizing the correct word. As they progress, we will teach them how to use the dictionary more effectively and independently.

   • *Correct spelling with a very light touch at the early draft stage.* Just as Goldilocks did not want her porridge too cold or too hot, teachers should avoid emphasizing spelling either too much or too little at this stage. Once again, the purpose of early drafts is to get ideas down, even if the form is incorrect. Overemphasizing correctness interferes with creating meaning. But if you notice frequent careless mistakes like *GRIL* for *girl*, gently point them out. Demonstrate that while you don't expect perfection, you have your expectations for correct spelling of words they do know and patterns they've learned. Opt for the "just right" amount of feedback.

Sharing First Drafts

An often overlooked step at this stage is *sharing the first draft*. This is an important prerequisite to the revision and editing stages. Sharing a piece with several peers or the whole class provides invaluable feedback to the writer. However, giving constructive feedback does not come naturally to children; it must be taught.

   Before we ever let a student get feedback from peers, we provide several short mini-lessons on how to give and receive praise and suggestions. We talk first about how important it is to be *constructive* and *specific*. We guide students

---

BOX 3.4. Ways to Respond When
Students Ask for Spelling Help

- Don't give them all the words they want.
- Encourage phonemic awareness by calling attention to sounds in words.
- Teach students how to "stretch" words like rubber bands.
- Teach spelling directly and systematically, using spelling patterns.
- Remind students of rhyming words and word families.
- Remind students that corrections will occur during revision and editing stages.
- Encourage dictionary use.
- Correct spelling judiciously, with a light touch.

---

in contrasting general and specific statements (e.g., "I like your story" vs. "The ending is exciting") and helpful and unhelpful statements (e.g., "You might shorten the beginning" vs. "It's too long"). We may even have students rehearse making specific statements, and have pairs role-play this for practice.

We emphasize that specific comments help writers see what could be changed, and we stress how important it is to put suggestions in positive terms. We may even list students' suggestions of statements that can hurt feelings, such as "I don't like it," "It's too . . . ," and "You shouldn't have . . ." With some groups, we may even share a story of our own and ask a particularly brave student to show the class a "don't" way to give feedback. This always draws a lot of laughter from the students as we appear crushed by the offending student's remarks. We discuss what writers feel in this situation, and what the writer might do differently next time, including never wanting to share writing again. Students always seem to get the message.

At the beginning of subsequent writing periods, we briefly role-play both the giving and receiving of appropriate feedback. Receiving feedback is easily overlooked, but students need to be reminded not to be either boastful or oversensitive. We also stress that suggestions are not mandates. Writers can choose whether or not to follow a suggestion given by another.

This sharing encourages continued collaboration. We have begun with collaborating on topics, and now we are working together to bring our first drafts to the revision stage. We have all benefited by learning how to cooperate and deal with peers in socially acceptable ways, while producing a piece superior to one completed alone. Furthermore, we have begun to develop a sense of who we are writing for, our audience.

> **BOX 3.5. How to Give and Receive Feedback on Writing**
>
> - All comments and suggestions should be constructive and positively worded.
> - Practice phrasing suggestions positively.
> - Role-play "do's" and "don't's" for conferring with other writers.
> - Discuss appropriate ways of receiving others' comments and suggestions.

Intention and Audience

Arthur Schopenhauer, a German philosopher of the early 19th century, once said of writing, "The first rule . . . is to have something to say" (quoted in Harris and Graham, 1996, p. 66). If you asked your students, "Why do you write?", what would they say? In many classrooms the teacher would hear some version of "Because you make us." A few students might be inspired enough to cite their love of it, but most write for their teachers. The collaboration described in this book is designed to change that. The audience a student is writing for is no longer just the teacher.

Writers have to consider their *intention* (why they are writing) and their *audience* (for whom they are writing) before they begin. These factors alone have more impact on a piece than you might think. How might a piece written for a graduate class assignment differ in style and form from an entry in your private journal after an exceedingly frustrating teaching day? Of course, these two pieces would be vastly different from each other in every way, because at the outset your intention and audience were different.

Students too have different styles, voices, and so forth. When collaboration comes regularly and naturally, students develop a sense of what might appeal to their target audience. They begin to think beyond "Will my teacher like this?" and move on to the more important questions of "Do *I* like this?" and "Does this fit my intended audience?" As adults, we always know who our audience is; it might be ourselves alone, the professor teaching us, the person we address in a letter, a parent, and so forth. In each case, we shape our writing to fit this audience.

Writers' sense of audience develops slowly, over many collaborations with others to improve a piece. The younger the writers, the closer they are to the cognitive state of *egocentrism*, in which children find it difficult to understand or take another's point of view. This means that young writers often assume their readers know what they know, so they may leave out or presume that readers already know parts of their stories. Consequently, their narratives often seem to jump about or jerk along without continuity. Only through the feedback of others can they grow to realize that they must explain and elaborate in order to communicate effectively.

A writer who overuses pronouns like *he* and *his* finds that his narrative confuses his audience, and they ask, "Who's talking here?" Another writer who tells about "my friend" without naming her finds her readers asking, "Who were you with?" And the one who places a story in a vague setting hears "Where is this happening? What is this place?" By coming up against the audience's confusion or misunderstanding, writers learn how to write so that a variety of audiences can understand and appreciate the writing. Likewise, by experiencing an audience's appreciation for a believable dialogue, a colorful description, or a character who can be mentally visualized, writers learn what works. They gradually learn to look at their writing not only through their own eyes, but also through the eyes of others who may read it, and make sure it communicates.

TEACHER'S TIP: Writers' sense of audience develops through repeated collaborations and opportunities to give and receive feedback.

The Importance of Teacher Modeling

The "Do as I say, not as I do" philosophy often infects adults who are around children, and teachers can sometimes fall into this trap. Lynn shares this anecdote in which she learned, to her chagrin, that sometimes her actions in the writing workshop belied her words.

"I confess I am a neat freak, but I try hard not to disclose this preference to my students. I thought I was so clever in my hiding, until the day I heard Desirée say to her friend, 'Ms. Beverly will like that; look at how *neat* it is.' I was horrified! Although I tried specifically *not* to impose my love of neatness in all forms into our writing workshop, somehow I had done just that!

"Thinking long and hard about this, I realized a few of my habits. When editing with my students individually, I would very often use the cut-and-paste technique [described in detail in Chapter 4], in which you show students how to actually cut apart a story to add or change something. I love this technique because you don't have to scrunch in any words that you want to add, and you don't have to scratch out the ones you want to get rid of. It's neat, neat, neat! Also, when we wrote group stories, I would actually 'white-out' any of my mistakes that were not part of the lesson! Even when brainstorming, I always used my best penmanship. Here I was, telling kids to just make it legible, while I was editing each mark on my paper. The moral: They will do as you *do*."

One particularly disastrous form of this has to do with expectations. We say we have high expectations for all our students, but do we really? Is there that one student who is so far behind that you're just happy when he or she produces anything at all? Realistically, you cannot have equal expectations for all students, for that would be a great injustice. But you can have a belief, way down deep, that *each student will progress.* Not all at the same rate, and not to the same extent, for their individual progress is shaped by so many factors, including prior experiences, motivation, personal and family attitudes toward success, and so forth. But in spite of these individual differences, you must be a firm believer that *each student in your room can and will do great things.* If you don't believe that, neither will they. They can hear you *say* you believe it, which is better than nothing, but if you don't act with that confidence and faith, they will see right through you.

Expecting great things from every student means both accepting where each one is today and pushing the limits just a little farther tomorrow. It means knowing where each one is, and where you want him or her to go next. It means devising tasks that each one can accomplish, but not too easily. It means being accepting of what students can do, but not allowing them to stay in one place too long. It means continually setting new goals, based on the fact that the more one learns, the more one can learn. And it means continually expressing your unshakeable belief that your students are capable of astonishing accomplishments.

TEACHER'S TIP: Believe that each student in your room
can and will do great things.

Modeling goes beyond the atmosphere of high expectations. It also constitutes the "nuts and bolts" of every successful classroom practice. Classroom organization, management, and all social and academic areas require teacher and peer modeling. As the teacher, you must do what you're expecting of your students. Don't tell them about it; *do it.* If you want students to write, you must write. If you want them to enjoy writing, you must show them how much you enjoy writing, and how much you enjoy what they write. If you want your students to use a dictionary or thesaurus, let them see you use these resources, and think aloud about what you're doing as you're doing it.

We all have to work at modeling what we want our students to do. It's tempting to check homework during sustained silent reading, but it's more important to be a reading model. We show our students letters we've received from friends or are about to mail. We make mistakes daily, some on purpose and some not, just to show that it's okay. If we don't know an answer, we'll tell them, "I don't know," and then we go find it out. You can't sit at a desk all day and just say things and hope they get absorbed; you have to live them.

This philosophy can be extended to include lessons. We act out, role-play, and demonstrate all day long. This is helpful to the students because they always know clearly what is expected of them; they've actually seen it *live*, not just in their imagination as it is described to them. We know that children are not very abstract in their thought processes, so modeling helps bring things to a concrete level. It's also important for students with attention disorders and short-term memory problems. The visual impact and the motor learning that takes place are helpful adaptations in the regular classroom.

Mini-lessons that include teacher modeling of what we want children to do are intrinsic parts of this approach to learning. The following section demonstrates a mini-lesson on topic selection.

Sample Mini-Lesson on Topic Selection: Top Ten Lists

This mini-lesson is written in the format one might use for a substitute's lesson plan, so it can be followed as a series of steps.

Day 1

1. Explain to the students, "Today we will be working on Top Ten lists." Have students brainstorm what Top Ten lists might be, and/or what kind of Top Ten lists they might have heard of before (hit songs, top money-making movies, etc.).

2. Offer an example of your own Top Ten list, either best or worst. For example, we might do our "Top Ten Favorite Foods." You can start with number 1 and work your way down, or the reverse.

3. Ask the students whether they can see any way that a list like this could be helpful in writing. Lead them in the direction of "It can give us ideas," if they seem to be on a different track.

4. Discuss what type of Top Ten best and worst lists would be most helpful for writing. Ask them to think about stories they've written and where they've gotten stuck before, to come up with some good ideas. If they seem to be floundering with this, walk them through the process of writing step by step. For example, you might say, "Think about when you start a story. What do you need to know?" (Character descriptions and names, setting locations, time period, etc.) Continue through the middle and end of the story, when topics like problems and solutions will arise. Make sure to keep track of all the suggestions on the board or a chart for use later. These can be made into lists of things writers need to know or think of.

5. Brainstorm a few of these lists together. For example, a class that chose "Top Ten Worst Problems for a Character" might have items such as the death of a friend or family member, moving away from home, being teased by

friends, and the like. This brainstorming serves as a model for the students to replicate independently later on.

6. Refer students back to the list of Top Ten list possibilities. Add any new ideas. Have students work in groups or independently to develop their own lists. (Some examples might be "Top Ten Scary Places," "Top Ten Best Names for Characters," or "Top Ten Time Periods for a Story Setting.") Remind students that these lists should be kept in a safe place, because they will be needed again.

Day 2

1. For the following day's mini-lesson, have children share some items from the lists they compiled previously. List several offerings to create categories: time period, setting, characters' names, problems, and solutions.

2. Have students agree on an item from each category and then write a group story. As students dictate, write down the story on a transparency or chart paper. This step is extremely important if you expect the students to learn to use these lists as tools to help them write. The list on its own will not benefit their writing if they have not experienced firsthand how it can be useful to them while composing.

3. Reread the completed group story together, and review with the students how the elements they selected were worked into the story. Encourage discussion of how the story would have been different if one element were changed— say, if a different problem from the list were chosen.

4. As students return to their own writing, remind them that writers are free to choose what goes into their writing at all points in its development.

In subsequent lessons, return to the idea of Top Ten lists occasionally. Review with students how such lists can help them have a range of ideas at their fingertips during writing. Encourage them to keep and add to their lists periodically, and to "borrow" freely from each other, so that all students begin to feel that they have a reserve of ideas available to them as they write.

OTHER MINI-LESSON TOPICS AT THIS STAGE

In choosing your mini-lesson topics, you should avoid following a preset schedule. This is because, ideally, you are developing lesson ideas based on what is actually occurring in your students' writing. Skills are taught as you observe that students are ready to receive them and have a need for them. Beginning first graders are unlikely to need or be ready for lessons on using setting to develop a mood, but are probably going to need lots of help with putting events in sequential order so readers/listeners can understand what's going on. One group of third graders may be ready to learn how to punctuate dialogue, while another group may need additional work with periods at the ends of sentences. Start with the basics and move toward more advanced skills and operations as stu-

> **BOX 3.6. Topic Selection Mini-Lesson Overview:**
> **Top Ten Lists**
>
> Day 1
>
> 1. Create your own Top Ten Best (or Worst) list as a model.
>
> 2. Brainstorm other lists with students that can help them in writing ("Top Ten Best Story Settings," "Top Ten Worst Problems for a Main Character," etc.). Record on a chart for future reference.
>
> Day 2
>
> 1. Use suggestions from lists to write a group story.
>
> 2. Encourage students to record interesting topics on individual topic lists.
>
> 3. Using group story as a model, have students begin individual stories.

dents show their readiness, rather than strictly following some established scope and sequence. Also, keep in mind what good writers need to be able to do. Plan lessons that share such practical information.

Other topics that *may* be appropriate at this beginning-to-write stage are described briefly below.

- *Management and organization of the writing workshop*—using time and materials, getting help, working with others. (This lesson is a must for writers of all ages and abilites, and needs to be repeated periodically.)
- *The writing process*—what happens in each of the various stages.
- *Using the five senses* to enhance writing.
- *Leads*—ways to start a story. Three main types of leads: (1) Action: Character(s) doing something. (2) Dialogue: Character(s) saying something (3) Reaction: Character(s) thinking about something. (For more about leads, see Chapter 4.)
- *Focus*—sticking to the point of the story.
- *Voice*—maintaining point of view.
- *Expansion*—using techniques to add detail to a story.
- *Mood*—setting and maintaining an appropriate mood for a story.
- *Repetition/patterns*—using repeating patterns, refrains, and the like effectively
- *Personification*—reasons and techniques for giving objects or animals human characteristics.

Most of these topics are taught best by using real literature as an introduction and a bridge into using the technique. A discussion about personification is not nearly as effective as one that is preceded by a read-aloud of say, a *Frog and Toad* book. Remember, it is not necessary to read the entire book. A few pages or paragraphs can introduce the concept just as well at times. After reading, you can discuss with the students what the author has done and how they might do something similar. Always bring the lesson back to the practical issue of its application in their writing, or it will not transfer.

Many of these mini-lesson topics overlap with the next step in the writing cycle, the *revision* stage. Because students will never all be at the same point in their overall writing development, or in developing an individual piece of writing, it is almost impossible to use only topics in mini-lessons that are relevant to the very beginning stage. Just as there is no clear dividing line between writing a first draft and beginning to revise it, there is no one set of mini-lesson topics that is useful only in the beginning stage. Again, your best guide to what to teach will not be a list like the one above, or any lists of composition skills sequences. It will be watching what your writers are doing—what's easy for them, what they're struggling with, and what they need to learn next.

In Chapter 4 we take up the issues of clarifying meaning in subsequent drafts, during the revision stage of the writing cycle. Some issues related to writing at this stage include overcoming children's reluctance to revise, developing positive attitudes about revising, teaching students how to confer with each other, conducting group and individual conferences, and a variety of methods for teaching revision. Some sample mini-lessons are offered, and the issue of spelling in revision is revisited.

REFERENCES

Bernays, Anne, and Pamela Painter. *What If?: Writing Exercises for Fiction Writers.* New York: HarperCollins, 1990.

Calkins, Lucy McCormick. *The Art of Teaching Writing* (new ed.). Portsmouth, NH: Heinemann, 1994.

Fletcher, Ralph. *Breathing In, Breathing Out: Keeping a Writer's Notebook.* Portsmouth, NH: Heinemann, 1996a.

Fletcher, Ralph. *A Writer's Notebook: Unlocking the Writer within You.* New York, Avon Books, 1996b.

Harris, Karen R., and Steve Graham. *Making the Writing Process Work: Strategies for Composition and Self-Regulation.* Cambridge, MA: Brookline Books, 1996.

Schwartz, Susan, and Mindy Pollishuke. *Creating the Child-Centred Classroom.* Toronto: Irwin, 1990.

CHAPTER 4

□■■

Revision:
Clarifying Meaning

Even a first draft is a revision of all the words I have yet to write.

—Barry Lane (1993, p. 5)

When writers revise, they consider and polish the content, or message, of the writing. They read and reread what they've written, and get help from others as they try to make the writing as clear, interesting, and memorable as they can. Because this is very hard to do alone, collaboration and sharing with other writers are required.

It's also very hard for young writers to distinguish between *revising*, in which the *content* of the piece is considered, and *editing*, in which the *correctness* of the writing is considered. (Editing is the topic of Chapter 5.) It takes a lot of effort, and much direct teaching, for students to learn to craft their meaning before they correct errors. But the more clearly we can define these two operations and separate them into distinct stages, the more likely it is that students will be able to make their writing more effective as well as more correct.

We can help students learn to consider content separately from correctness by explaining clearly and repeatedly the difference between writing that is effective and writing that is merely correct, by guiding them through a variety of revision activities that help them focus on the meaning of the writing, and by modeling how to consider meaning rather than correctness when we read or listen to a piece.

TEACHER'S TIP: Clearly distinguish between revising and editing, and separate them into distinct stages.

There is no getting around the fact that revising a piece of writing is hard work, and that it is usually not nearly as much fun as starting a whole new piece. Writers who generate topics and first drafts with enthusiasm may strongly resist efforts to get them to change and polish their writing. Their attitude seems to be "If I'd known how to do it better, I would have done it the first time." This is understandable, but is based on an incorrect premise—namely, that good writers "do it right" the first time, and that only poor writers have to tinker with their writing.

That's why it is important to have young writers begin revising as *soon* as possible, and as *often* as possible, right from the start. It is a mistake to put off beginning to teach revision until later in the year, when students have become more fluent at producing topics and first drafts. They will mistakenly begin to think that this is all there is to writing, and will resist changing their writing. Also, it's a mistake to put off teaching revision until later grades, or until students are a little older and have become more confident writers. The older the students are, the more often they have seen classmates who have "messed up" have to redo their work. Their belief becomes more entrenched that doing work over, or trying to change it, means that they did it wrong the first time.

As teachers, we may unwittingly engender and nourish their belief by the ways we treat students' work in subjects where there is one right answer—for example, in math. We hand out a page of subtraction problems, and mark their answers correct or incorrect; then we ask students to redo the incorrect problems, perhaps after explaining the process again. The problems done correctly aren't redone, only the wrong ones, and the students who got all their problems right often get to do something else (such as read or draw).

When students are subtracting, or outlining a chapter, or copying the "morning message" from the board, or diagramming sentences, or spelling plurals, or many of the other things they do in school, the correct answer isn't subject to discussion or dependent on their personal opinion. Seven minus five is two, and there is no range of possible correct answers or acceptable possibilities. After a couple of weeks in first grade, students figure out that having to do something over means they didn't do it correctly or acceptably the first time; most try hard to avoid getting into this situation. Then we teachers turn around and try to tell them that when they write, they should rework their writing when they finish their first drafts. We try to convince them that, all of a sudden, doing something over again is *not* a sign that it was badly done the first time. No wonder they begin to doubt us!

That's why it's important to stress to students over and over, from the first day of school on, that writing is not like subtracting or diagramming sentences or spelling. Good writing has to be both effective *and* correct, while the others only have to be correct. In math, there *is* a correct answer, although there may be more than one way to arrive at it. But in writing, there are many ways that a piece can be made more effective, and many ways to make it so. All writers, we must stress, rework and polish their writing to make it clearer, or more interesting, more effective. It may take students a long time to accept this.

This point can be clarified by having a writer visit your class or school to show students successive drafts of a piece or to demonstrate how he or she revises a piece. This is one of the best ways there are to convince students that even good writers, even professional writers, revise their work. (It's probably unlikely that you could get Jack Prelutsky or Betsy Byars to visit your class, but there may be local authors, poets, or songwriters who will.)

But it may not be possible for you to get a real writer to visit. You'll have to do the job yourself, showing students how to separate meaning from correctness and leading them through steps that help them clarify their messages before they edit. In the following sections, we'll describe ways to do so that worked for us.

INTRODUCING THE CONCEPT OF REVISION

You have to start by explaining just what *revising* means: *changing a piece of writing to make the message clearer.* The message is what a writer says, not how it was said.

There are four basic operations of revision. Writers can . . .

- *Add* more words, ideas, sentences, and so forth.
- *Delete* parts they deem unnecessary.
- *Substitute*, or *change*, parts of the writing.
- *Rearrange* parts of the piece by moving them around.

Adding and deleting are easier for most writers than changing and rearranging. We teach students to revise by teaching each process in order, and we have students work with each process separately before trying the next one.

▣▣

> *TEACHER'S TIP:* Students often mistakenly believe that good writers "do it right" the first time, and that only poor writers have to tinker with their writing.

▣▣

Since writers learn as much from our actions as from our words (if not more), it is important to model how to consider the message of a piece first, rather than reacting to its physical appearance or correctness. *Always respond to the content of a piece before you respond to correctness.* This is a cardinal rule of teaching writing. When a student shows you a piece, *don't* pick it up and look at it; instead, ask the writer to read it to you, or read the first part if it's a long piece. Listen to what the writer is saying; ignore, for the time being, mistakes in grammar, sentence fragments or run-ons, and so forth. Respond to what it was about, either with a supportive comment or a question.

Supportive comments are something like "It sounds like you know a lot about _____," or "It sounds like you really enjoyed _____," or "It sounds like you have strong feelings about _____." Questions that help writers focus on meaning include "How did you come to know so much about _____?" or "Where did you get the idea for this?", or even "I wonder what's going to happen next?" Responses like these help you model how readers react to the message of a piece rather than its correctness.

Another effective way to introduce the idea of revision is to present model pieces of writing and guide students in revising them to make them clearer, more vivid, or more organized. In a series of revision mini-lessons, we present

---

**BOX 4.1. Comments That Respond
to the Message of a Piece**

- "It sounds like you know a lot about _____."
- "It sounds like you really enjoyed [or disliked] _____."
- "I can tell you have strong feelings about _____."
- "How did you find out so much about/get to be so good at _____?"
- "Where did you get the idea for this?"
- "How did you go about choosing this topic?"
- "I wonder what's going to happen next?"
- "What do you think you'll do next with this piece?"

---

short pieces that we have written ourselves, or have adapted from student writings. We show the piece on a transparency, on the computer, on a large sheet of chart paper, or even on the board. Then we invite students to react to the piece, telling whether they find it interesting, easy to understand, or enjoyable to read. If we're focusing on making the writing interesting, we'll show them a piece that's deliberately made boring; if we're focusing on using vivid or precise vocabulary, we'll show them a piece that's studded with drab words and imprecise references; if we're focusing on organization, we'll show them a piece that gives information in the wrong order; and so forth. (The mini-lessons that follow demonstrate these points.)

As students make suggestions, we make the changes right on the story. We cross out words and write changes above them, draw arrows to show where sentences should be reordered, use a caret to insert more information, and so forth. Figure 4.1 shows a sample of a piece of writing that has been revised in a group mini-lesson.

In mini-lessons, we try to focus students' attention on just one revision operation at a time. If we're working on using vivid words rather than boring ones, we don't present disorganized examples or suggest that students reorder sentences. If we're demonstrating how to add dialogue to a piece, we don't show an example that's full of trite, overused words. And when they begin to revise their own pieces, we urge them to look for one particular way they can change the piece, rather than trying to make many kinds of revisions in the same piece. This helps limit confusion about the ways a piece can be revised, and it helps keep the operation in perspective. After all, one could keep revising a piece endlessly, since there are endless ways it could be changed. Because we want to

The   six   our family was   by a neighbor. I named
~~One~~ summer when I was ~~a little girl~~ ~~we were~~ given a tiny kitten. By   her Cindy.

December she was a beautiful grey cat with striped fur and a long thin tail.

She looked grown up but was still as playful as a kitten. She was always getting
into closets, boxes, and paper bags.
    A few days before Christmas my father brought home a huge

Christmas tree. We set it up in the living room, next to the stairs. My father
                              of the tree
thought he should tie the top to the stair rail to keep it from tipping over,

but by the time we got it set up he was too tired and forgot about it. After

we decorated it with ornaments and strings of lights, we went into the

kitchen to eat supper. We didn't know that Cindy was hiding in the living
    room, watching.
                                            dropped our forks and
    ~~While we were eating~~ we heard a tremendous CRASH! We ran to the
        Suddenly

living room ~~to see what had happened~~. The tree was lying on its side with
                scattered
broken ornaments everywhere. Cindy was tangled up in the lights and

branches, struggling to get out. She had tried to climb the tree and had

knocked the whole thing over. We were really mad at first, but we soon
    forgave her.

Readers' questions:

How old were you?
Who gave her to you?
What was her name?
What playful things did she do?
Top of the tree?
Was anyone there when it fell?
Does it matter that you were eating? Could you just say "Suddenly"?
Do you need "... to see what happened"?
What happened to Cindy?

FIGURE 4.1. Revised piece after group mini-lesson.

avoid this, we limit the ways students work on revision, until they are so accomplished at it that they can undertake it independently.

⊡⊡

TEACHER'S TIP: Always respond to the content of a piece before you respond to its correctness.

⊡⊡

GOALS AND CHECKLISTS FOR REVISION

It's also helpful to establish revision goals at the outset, and to display them prominently so that writers can keep in mind what they are trying to do when they revise. If they lose sight of what revision is, they'll soon be "revising" by correcting spelling errors and adding capital letters to proper nouns. That's necessary too, but it's editing, not revision, and it doesn't contribute to improving meaning. Editing should occur *after* a writer is satisfied that his or her meaning has been conveyed in the writing.

Goals can be established in a guided group discussion, in which students are asked to contribute suggestions on how to clarify meaning, either as statements or as questions. For example, students could compile a list of questions for writers to consider as they begin to revise, something along these lines:

Do I need to add information or details?
If so, where should they go?
Do I need to take out parts that aren't needed?
Are the parts in the right order?
Can I use more interesting words in some places?

Or students could come up with a series of statements that are guidelines for revision, such as the following:

Read the piece to someone else and have them ask you questions.
Find out from a partner if they can understand what you wrote.
Use strong, interesting words whenever you can.
Be sure the parts are in the right order.
Take out words or sentences that aren't about the subject.

These are not all the ways a piece can be revised, but they are steps along the path, and students will remember them better if they come from themselves rather than from you. And they are more likely to use the guidelines if they are prominently displayed and if students are reminded to refer to them when they revise. As the students become more proficient at revising, they may want to add to or change their guidelines. You can buy classroom posters or bulletin boards listing revision steps or rules, but the ones students produce are the ones they remember to use.

A simple revision checklist can be devised that students can staple to their first drafts and follow as they begin to revise. Figures 4.2a and 4.2b show two examples of such checklists; Figure 4.2a is a very simple one for primary graders, and Figure 4.2b is a more detailed one that children in middle grades and above can use. These can be adapted in many ways to fit the needs and abilities of your students.

TEACHING REVISING FROM LITERATURE

Literature provides a wealth of examples of good writing, and should be referred to often as we teach revision. One way to do this is to show students a paragraph or short piece that is dull or confusing, and then show them the same material as it appears in a piece of literature. An example from fiction might be to contrast passages 1 and 2 below:

> *Passage 1*: Stuart fell into a bunch of garbage. He got garbage all over himself.

> *Passage 2*: Stuart landed on his head, buried two feet deep in wet slippery garbage. Under him, over him, on all four sides of him—garbage. Just an enormous world of garbage and trash and smell. . . . He had egg on his trousers, butter on his cap, gravy on his shirt, orange pulp in his ear, and banana peel wrapped around his waist. (E. B. White, *Stuart Little*, 1945, pp. 58–59)

An example from nonfiction might be to contrast passages A and B:

> *Passage A*: All dogs are descended from wolves, no matter what breed or how big the dog is. All dogs act sort of like wolves.

> *Passage B*: The wolf is the ancestor of all domestic dogs, including the Irish wolfhound, which is much larger than the wolf, and the Pekingese, which is very much smaller. The outward appearance of these breeds may look completely different from the wolf . . . but every dog, inside its skin, feels and behaves like a wolf. (Juliet Clutton-Brock, *Eyewitness Books: Dog*, 1991, p. 34)

Another way to use examples from literature is to have students try to "reverse-revise." That is, present a well-written example, and then ask students to write the same ideas in less effective language. We don't ordinarily like exercises that require students to do something they are later supposed to avoid doing; used judiciously, however, this one can make a good point. Here, if students can

Name _____ Date _____

_____ I read my whole piece to myself.

_____ I read my whole piece to a partner. (My partner was _____.)

_____ I revised my piece to make it clearer.

_____ I stuck to the topic.

_____ I looked for places to add more ideas or information.

_____ I took out anything I didn't need.

_____ I wrote more than one lead and chose the one I liked best.

_____ I looked for places where I needed to move parts around.

_____ I used strong, colorful words.

FIGURE 4.2a. Revision checklist for primary grades.

From *Directing the Writing Workshop* by Jean Wallace Gillet and Lynn Beverly. Copyright 2001 by The Guilford Press. Permission to photocopy this figure is granted to purchasers of this book for personal use only (see copyright page for details).

Name _____ Date _____

_____ Did I plan my writing before I began?

_____ Did I follow the writing cycle (generate a topic, write a first draft, revise)?

_____ Did I share my draft with others and get suggestions from them?

_____ Did I add information or ideas where they were needed?

_____ Do I have a topic sentence?

_____ Do I need to add more details?

_____ Do I need to add a closing or concluding sentence?

_____ Did I delete any parts that were not related or needed?

_____ Did I include unnecessary details?

_____ Did I repeat myself?

_____ Did I say too much about any part?

_____ Do I need to reorder any parts of the piece?

_____ Do my ideas follow a logical order?

_____ Did I put my most important ideas first?

_____ Did I explain my ideas so readers could understand?

_____ Did I rewrite confusing or unclear sentences?

_____ Did I use strong, interesting words?

_____ Did I clarify any parts that readers didn't understand?

FIGURE 4.2b. Revision checklist for middle/upper grades.

From *Directing the Writing Workshop* by Jean Wallace Gillet and Lynn Beverly. Copyright 2001 by The Guilford Press. Permission to photocopy this figure is granted to purchasers of this book for personal use only (see copyright page for details).

identify what makes writing ineffective clearly enough to produce it from a high-quality example, they can (let's hope) identify examples of ineffective writing in their own work. Besides, they really enjoy vying with each other to produce the worst writing! We don't do a lot of this, but it does get the point across to students in an enjoyable, even humorous way.

Examples from literature help students see that effective writing is detailed, uses vivid and picturesque language, gives examples, helps the reader draw mental pictures, and *shows* readers rather than just *telling* them. We make it a habit to continually draw students' attention to examples of effective description, dialogue, and explanation as models for their own writing.

REVISION CONFERENCES

Writers are often dependent on others when they revise, because it is often difficult to see how one's own writing could be confusing or boring. After all, it's clear as can be to the writer! The younger the writer, the more difficult it is for him or her to perceive that others may not be able to "read between the lines," or to know what the writer knows but has not conveyed. In conferences with the teacher and with peers, young writers learn to see their writing through the eyes of others, and develop the critically important *sense of audience* that enables writers to communicate clearly with readers.

Sense of audience means the understanding that readers may not know or understand what the writer understands about the topic, and that writing must speak to the *reader*, not to the *writer*, in order to be effective. Primary graders typically have little or no sense of audience, partly because (as we have noted in earlier chapters) they are cognitively egocentric—that is, centered on or preoccupied with themselves rather than with others.

It is very hard for primary graders to take another's point of view, truly understand what another thinks or feels, or realize that a piece of writing does not

---

BOX 4.2. Ways to Teach Revising from Literature

1. Contrast examples of effective writing from literature with dull or poorly written versions of the same texts.

2. Have students "reverse-revise"—that is, deliberately try to rewrite good examples into bad. (Do this judiciously!)

3. Frequently draw students' attention to examples of effective writing in literature they read and listen to.

communicate to others. Their egocentrism shows in many ways: the way they start telling a story in the middle and jump around from event to event; the way they talk at the same time as others, or interrupt constantly; or the way they are sensitive to others' hurtful comments to them, but oblivious to the effect their comments have on others. These things are all normal aspects of early and middle childhood. But they stand in the way of developing a writer's sense of audience, and account for why young writers find it difficult to understand why someone else might be unmoved by their writing.

That's why we need to start right away—in the first days of school, and in the primary grades as well as beyond—to have students collaborate on their writing and give and receive feedback from peers as well as from the teacher. This can be facilitated by teaching them how to confer about a piece of writing in productive ways.

TEACHER'S TIP: Have young writers begin collaborating and revising as *soon* as possible, and as *often* as possible, right from the start.

Conferences with the Teacher

Teacher–student conferences will take many forms in your classroom. They range from a brief "base-touching" moment with a writer that lasts perhaps a minute or less, to a scheduled "sit-down" conference that takes 15–20 minutes or more, depending in part on the grade and the writer's needs. Regardless of their form, teacher–student conferences have only one goal: *to give the writer the support that is needed right now.* Keep your goal in mind by asking yourself, "What is most important to this writer now?"

Most important is a key idea, because there will probably be many ways in which a writer needs assistance and support, but you have to limit what you try to do in any one exchange. To try to do more is to risk overloading—and discouraging—the writer. If a writer has many very glaring needs at one time, resist the temptation to try to meet all his or her needs at once; instead, focus on one way to help the writer at a time, and meet with that writer more often, for short time periods.

As we have mentioned before, the first step in any student–teacher exchange is for the writer to read the work to the teacher. Young children love to do this, and may pester you nearly to distraction to listen to every last one of them! Older writers, however, become more and more hesitant to do so; they would much rather shove the paper at you and mentally leave the room while you read it. Don't let them do this; be gently insistent that they read it to you, explaining that you need to hear each writer's words in the writer's own voice in order to really understand it. (You can also explain that if they read it, you won't be distracted by any errors you might see. Older writers will readily understand and agree with this point.)

After you've listened to the writer read the piece, your first inclination will probably be to offer a compliment, a suggestion for improvement, or a judgment on the piece. *Don't!* Doing so comes naturally to us as teachers, but it fosters writers' dependence on us and our reactions to their work. Instead, ask questions about the piece, or about the process of writing it, that will get the writer talking about the work. Let the writer be the guide! As students talk about their writing, their concerns will begin to reveal themselves to you. That's where you pick up the ball, and offer support and guidance. Whether a writer is stuck with little more to say, bogged down by too much detail, lost in a wandering narrative, wondering whether what's been written makes sense to anyone else, or just needing somebody to listen to it, what the writer needs at that point will be revealed by what he or she tells you about the piece and its process.

□□

TEACHER'S TIP: Teacher–student conferences have one goal: to give the writer the support that is needed right now.

□□

Here are some examples, taken from our own daily writing experience with children.

Katie is stuck for a topic today, which is unusual for her and is making her uncomfortable. Sensing her discomfort, the teacher stops for a quick "base touch" and asks, "How's it going, Katie?" Katie unhappily explains that she can't think of what she'd like to write about today. Instead of telling Katie how to get herself unstuck, or even offering suggestions, the teacher asks, "What would you suggest to somebody else who was stuck?" Katie looks at the list of "Things to Do When You're Stuck" that is displayed in the writing area, and lists some of her favorites: "I'd tell them to read over some of their old pieces, or draw, or write about their favorite things." Before the teacher can ask her which one she could try, Katie says with relief, "I'll read some of my old stories for an idea." She begins to rummage in her folder as the teacher moves away.

Patrick is deep in the throes of writing a multipart epic on his usual topic, space heroes and their weaponry. Today he's writing Part 3, and he's progressed far enough into his story to begin feeling very successful. Patrick doesn't even wait for his teacher to approach him individually; as she roams nearby, glancing and noting what each writer is doing, Patrick pulls her over with an excited "Listen to this!" He leans into her side, his favorite "sharing" position, and reads his most recent part with mounting excitement. As soon as he finishes, he grabs his pencil and is off again. This morning, Patrick didn't need prodding, suggestions, or anything except that most precious commodity to a writer: a listener's willing, interested ear. This "conference" has simply offered Patrick validation that he is a writer. At various times, a listening ear and a validating comment may be all a writer needs to keep moving.

Paula and Courtney are writing a story together, but have fallen into squabbling over whose idea will come first. When the teacher asks, "Girls, where are you in writing this piece?", their frustrations pour out. They expect her to decide for them what they should do next, but she resists. Instead, she asks them to come up with at least three ways they could solve their problem, and tells them she'll return in a few minutes. On her return, they have decided to try to take turns deciding what will happen next in their story. She congratulates them for solving their problem creatively, and moves away as they settle down to work.

The teacher continues on her wandering way, seeming to have little in mind as she stops and kneels by first one, then another writer. She gets down close to the writers rather than towering over them, and sometimes closes her eyes as they read to her, the better to concentrate on their words. To each, she offers a question: "What do you think is the best part of this piece?" "How did you learn so much about _____?" "What do you think you'll do next with this piece?" "Who could help you with that?" She listens to their replies, and nudges them all to maintain ownership of their writing.

There are as many questions to ask writers as there are topics to write about. What you ask will depend on many factors, including the age and grade of the class, the writer's ability and enthusiasm, the topic of the piece, and so forth. But some questions are useful in many situations, and some of these are shown in Figure 4.3.

Another kind of teacher–student revision conference occurs when you talk with a student about his or her writing in general over a period of time, rather than discussing a particular piece of writing. In this case you are not working with the writer to revise a piece, but rather helping the writer become aware of his or her own growth and set goals for continued progress.

We periodically confer with writers about their progress over time—say, a quarter or a semester. Our purposes here are twofold: to help writers see how their writing has changed over time, and to guide them in setting personal goals for improving their writing further. We ask two general questions in this conference: *"How has your writing changed from the beginning of this time period to now?"* and *"What do you think you could do to continue to improve your writing?"* In this way, we begin positively by having writers survey their work to see all the many ways it has improved, and then we help them set a goal that they will concentrate on for the next period (usually a few weeks).

In a first-grade class, we set aside time for these individual conferences after students have been writing freely on self-selected topics for several months. After this fairly long period, most first graders' writing has changed dramatically, and their growth is very apparent. Every writer is able to see many ways in

- What's the most important thing you are saying in this piece?
- Where is the most important part of this piece?
- What part do you think readers will like the most? Why?
- Is there a part or parts that don't seem to belong with the rest?
- Is there a part or parts that you think belong somewhere else in the piece?
- Is there a part or parts you're not comfortable with? What could you do?
- What could you do to get help from another writer?
- Is there a place where you know a lot more information, but didn't put it in? Why not?
- Are there places you think you need more details?
- How is this piece different from your very first draft? What revisions have you made already?
- What was the hardest part of writing this piece? What was easiest?
- What do you think you'll do now?
- What help do you need now to move ahead with this piece? How can you get that help for yourself?

FIGURE 4.3. Questions for revision conferences.

which he or she has grown as a writer. Typically, they notice that their writing is more readable, their pieces are longer, they can now spell many common words correctly, their temporary spellings are usually longer and more complex, and they are beginning to use periods and capital letters reliably.

When asked, "What is one thing you could concentrate on doing that would improve your writing even more?" many first graders say, "Put periods at the ends of sentences," "Check the Word Wall to spell little words," "Write more neatly," and "Read over my writing to see if I left any words out." Although these are largely editing concerns, we are satisfied when these young writers set a personal goal (whatever it may be) and try to apply it when they write. In subsequent conferences, we'll guide them toward goals more closely related to revision per se, such as using descriptive words, using precise verbs, and sticking to the topic. For beginners, the process of self-evaluation and goal setting is more important than what goal they set or how well they accomplish it.

In second grade and beyond, we follow the same general procedure for these goal-setting conferences, but with a few differences. First, we try to hold these conferences more often, perhaps every month or so. Second, we encourage writers to review their work with a partner prior to the conference, to get a peer's view of their writing progress. Third, we encourage writers to set specific writing goals. And fourth, at subsequent conferences we ask them to review their work specifically to see how well they have accomplished the goals they set for themselves. We continue to emphasize the importance of regular self-evaluation, as well as the value of self-determined writing goals rather than those a teacher develops.

Conferences with Other Writers

As important as it is for writers to confer regularly with their teachers, it is even more important for them to confer with fellow writers on a regular basis. Developing writers can only develop that critically important sense of audience if readers other than their teachers have to make sense of their work. After all, teachers will automatically "fill in the gaps," so to speak, when they read children's writing. Peers generally need—and demand—greater clarity, accuracy, and precision in the writing in order to understand and appreciate it. Peers, then, can be a writer's most demanding audience, but ultimately the most helpful.

◰◰

TEACHER'S TIP: Writers need to confer with fellow writers
on a regular basis.

◰◰

We have mentioned previously how important it is to begin the revision process early, with the youngest writers and as soon as possible in the year. The same is true of peer conferences. If your students confer only with you for the first several months, they will be less likely to turn to or listen to each other,

---

BOX 4.3. Hints for Teacher–Student Writing Conferences

- Ask yourself, "What is most important to this writer now?"
- Resist the temptation to try to meet all the writer's needs at once.
- When a writer needs several kinds of help at once, focus on one area at a time and meet with that writer more frequently.
- Have the writer read the piece to you; don't read the piece yourself.
- Ask questions that help the writer talk about the piece.
- Respond to what the writer has to say about the piece, rather than to the piece itself.
- Periodically ask writers to reflect on how their writing has changed over time and to set personal writing goals.
- Use conferences to emphasize the importance of writers' self-evaluation and goal setting.

preferring your adult counsel. But if they begin early to share with each other, ask each other questions, ask each other for help, and offer their opinions as writers, they will learn to value each other's help as much as yours. This is important, for it helps them become independent writers, not dependent on a teacher's help or opinion.

The first peer conferences are informal and take place right while writers are working. To begin, tell your students that you want them to help each other and share with each other. Explain that you want them to read parts of their writing to each other, to ask each other for help, and to offer *helpful* suggestions as they work. (This will come as a great shock to those who have come from classrooms where "No talking during writing!" was the rule!)

Then remind the students every day when they begin that they can get help from (and give it to) each other, as well as getting help from you. Whenever opportunities arise, encourage them to get help from each other, rather than waiting for you or turning exclusively to you. Remarks like "Who could you ask to help you with that word?", "So-and-so knows more than I do about that topic, and I bet he [or she] would love to tell you about it," or "I know you're good at [whatever it is]; could you give So-and-so some help with that?" remind students that help is all around.

After students have begun to turn to each other informally, and the "workshop climate" we have referred to in Chapter 1 has begun to develop, it is appropriate to begin more formal peer conferences. Pairs, threes, and small groups can confer; however, you must teach them how to do so productively. Most students need guidance and modeling in order to be appreciative, supportive, and tactful when responding to each other. Nowhere is that more evident than when they respond to each other's writing.

It is easiest for us to begin peer conferences with pairs. Periodically we pair students and ask them to complete a very specific task, such as one of the following:

- "Listen to your partner read his or her piece, and ask him or her one or two questions about the topic."
- "Listen to your partner's piece, and tell him or her two things you especially liked in the piece."
- "Help your partner find two [or more] hard words and help him or her spell them."
- "Help your partner find a place to add one more sentence to the piece."

We keep the task specific and the time allowed short; we "patrol" to make sure each pair is on task; we compliment pairs that are working effectively; and we immediately "debrief" with the whole group when the time is up, having each pair summarize in one sentence what they did. We look for and point out positive behaviors, so that others will know just how to conduct themselves.

We have our students work in pairs a number of times, varying the task each time, before we have them confer in threes or fours. We usually do the pairing or grouping, so we can control who works with whom; we keep changing the pairs and groups, so that students have to work with many partners; and we rarely establish conference groups of more than four, because the larger the group, the less involved some group members will be.

It is important to continue to teach and demonstrate how to confer with another writer, even after small groups have begun to conduct conferences fairly successfully. We continue to include periodic mini-lessons on peer conferences, and we often ask writers to talk about conferences they recently participated in, telling what went particularly well and what was not so successful.

Frequently, writers will say that the best peer conferences occurred when the partner or group showed genuine interest in the piece, expressed appreciation for particular parts or ideas, and gave suggestions rather than issuing edicts. Likewise, we frequently hear writers complain that partners or group members were inattentive to the piece, made seemingly offhand remarks about the writing, appeared to be demanding instead of suggesting changes, or "took over" the piece and suggested changes that made it their story rather than the writer's.

A student-generated list of helpful reminders, like that shown in Figure 4.4, can be displayed to help students remember how to be helpful in peer conferences.

Peer conferences may be less helpful to writers and more time-consuming than teacher–student conferences, and so we are sometimes tempted to do away with them altogether and just confer with writers ourselves. It's important to stifle this impulse, though, and remind ourselves that the *process* of conferring and assisting another writer is what's important here, not the *product* of such assistance. Students will not be able to work collaboratively with each other as well as adult writers can, but that's because they're just learning how to do this. The more they help each other and receive each other's help, the better they'll get at this process. It's better to let them struggle with it than to intervene and do it ourselves.

TOOLS FOR REVISION

Revising a piece to make it clearer and more effective requires that students know what to do when they want to add, delete, change, or rearrange a part of their writing. As we mentioned previously, we teach revision step by step. That is, we show writers how to add to a piece, and have them practice adding to their drafts, before we show them how to delete; when they are comfortable with adding and deleting, we focus for a bit on changing; and we teach rearranging after that. For each revision operation, students need to learn specific procedures.

- Tell where you are in the writing process (this is a first draft, revised once, final draft, etc.).
- Read the whole piece out loud; read in a strong voice and not too fast.
- Everyone should listen to the piece without saying anything. Be an active listener.
- Tell what kind of help you need; don't just say, "I need help with this whole thing," or "I don't like this piece."
- Give the help the writer asks for; don't make other suggestions that the writer didn't ask for. Especially, don't say, "Write it over."
- Make suggestions; don't give orders. Say, "Maybe you could . . ." or "Why don't you . . ." rather than "Do this."
- Be nice. Don't say things like, "I don't like this story," or "Is this the best you could do?" Be respectful of other people's feelings.
- Be specific. Tell what parts you liked, or what parts you didn't understand. Don't say things like, "I don't like the beginning," or "The whole thing is okay."
- Don't use words that hurt people's feelings, like *stupid*, *dumb*, or *boring*. If you think something is boring, help the writer make it more interesting.
- Don't say how *you* would write it. Remember, it's not your story!

FIGURE 4.4. Students' suggestions for peer conferences.

Revision Symbols

Simple marks can help students note what they want to do to a piece as they read through it or work with a partner. The first symbol we teach is the *caret*, a small arrow that shows where something is to be added. The caret can point up or down, depending on where there is space to write the addition; because we ask our students always to skip lines as they write, they usually have space above in which to write additional words. On a transparency or on chart paper or in some other manner, we show students how to do this, as shown below.

next door   big brown
Myₐneighbor has aₐdog.

We tell younger students, "A caret says to the reader, 'Look up or look down, to see what I added here!' " After several lessons on the use of carets, our first graders' reading of each other's work was often punctuated with cries of "Look up!" as they encountered carets.

Adding is the easiest revision operation and the first one we teach. Students like using the caret because they don't have to squeeze additional words into lines or erase to make room. With young writers, we start by having them add a word or two here and there, then a single sentence, and finally longer pieces of text. By the time they're ready to add several sentences in one place, they're ready to learn about cutting and pasting, described in the following section.

Deleting is most easily done by crossing out, and we emphasize to students that if they cross out with one line, rather than erasing or blacking out parts, they can easily put them back in again if they change their minds. Many writers, especially young ones, enjoy adding to their work but dislike deleting. They hate to part with any of their words, even when the deleted part doesn't work anyway. We continually reassure them that if they cross out with just one line through, they can easily restore the deletion later. This seems to make it easier for them to learn to delete.

We teach students to use the inversion symbol ($\frown$ $\smile$) to show that a word or phrase has been moved to another spot in the sentence, as shown below:

We're going to get ice cream and go to the mall.

We use parentheses and arrows to show where longer pieces of text are to be moved. These operations work best when the parts to be moved are on the same page. Moving sections of text from one page to another requires cutting and pasting, or other operations discussed in the section to follow.

Cutting and Pasting

Sometimes writers want to make changes that require adding, deleting, or moving large sections of text. Marking up a piece to show where to make big changes can make the work very confusing. It's often easier to cut the work apart and tape it back together in its new form. We demonstrate this process in mini-lessons in which we physically cut apart pieces and move the parts around (see the sample mini-lesson that follows). In separate mini-lessons, we also show students how to add text on sticky notes or on adding machine tape, which can be stuck or taped on where desired. These are all part of what we think of as *cut-and-paste* revision.

When we teach the cut-and-paste operation, we encourage students to make just one change at a time and to work systematically, so they don't end up with numerous cut-up parts that they don't know what to do with. For young writers, as well as "organizationally challenged" writers of any age, this takes supervision and is best practiced either with a partner or in a small revision group that can be supervised closely. With practice, they'll be able to cut and paste their work independently.

Although many students enjoy the activity of cutting their work up and reassembling it, some are disturbed by it. Those of our students who are very concerned with neatness and the attractive appearance of a piece (not many of them, but there are a few!) are uncomfortable about cutting and pasting; they don't like to make it "ugly" or "messy," as they put it. But writers who resist making their work "messy" may be much more comfortable with revision on the computer, described below.

The other side of the cut-and-paste coin is that many writers, especially young ones, take to the process with joyous abandon—but the end result is messiness that doesn't contribute to the clarification of meaning. In other words, for many young writers, revision becomes an end in itself; they revise to revise, not to improve.

Calkins (1994) recounted the experience of watching a young writer carefully compose a first draft, then crumple the page and smooth it out again. When Calkins asked what she was doing, the youngster replied, "Revising. See? It's all loved up" (p. 208). Likewise, we've seen young writers cut apart their paragraphs, then painstakingly tape them back together—in the same order. It seems there's one writer in every class who latches onto the notion of cutting the piece apart, but nothing else; he or she usually ends up cutting each sentence or line apart, and ends up with a litter of strips on the desk. We've seen students vie among themselves to make the most changes to a single piece, as if the sheer number of changes constituted effective revision.

All this is pretty predictable, and it doesn't mean that revision isn't being taught effectively. Rather, it means that young students, who tend to be fairly literal in their interpretation of our instructions, are focusing more on the "how" than on the "why" of revising. We try not to overemphasize the physical aspects of revision, and we keep reminding students that revision means *improving* a piece, making it more effective or meaningful—not just making it messy or "loved up." Finally, we keep reminding ourselves that revising requires an objectivity about one's own writing that most writers struggle to achieve, and that most efforts at revision are at least steps in the right direction.

▨▨

> **TEACHER'S TIP:** Don't overemphasize the physical aspects of revision;
> keep reminding students that revision means making a piece
> more effective or meaningful.

▨▨

Sample Mini-Lesson: Revision on a Transparency— Cut-and-Paste Lesson

Materials needed:

   Overhead projector and screen
   Sample text on a transparency (student-written or your own)

A blank transparency
Transparency marker
Scissors
Tape

Procedure:

1. Show the sample text on the overhead projector, and read it aloud or have a student read it.
2. Invite students to suggest places where more information is needed.
3. Mark suggested revisions on the transparency with the marker, using carets for small additions and other revision symbols as needed.
4. Have students identify a place in the text where a major addition should occur.
5. Mark the place with the marker; then cut the transparency apart and spread the sections apart on top of the blank transparency.
6. Use the marker to write the addition on the blank transparency, using space as needed.
7. Tape the cut-apart sections to the blank transparency above and below the added section.
8. Review the steps you followed to add a new section to the draft.
9. Distribute scissors, tape, and additional paper.
10. Tell students to find a place to add a new section in a current piece of their own writing, working alone or with a partner. Then have them use the cut-and-paste technique to create a space for the new section.
11. Debrief by summarizing steps, and allow time for sharing, comments, and questions.

Revision at the Computer

Teaching students to use word processing as they write is no longer a frill, but a basic life skill. Even if they don't have a computer at home, most students will be expected to produce typed, edited, and proofread papers by high school or before. Many colleges now require that every student have a personal computer, and some include the cost of a computer in their fees. Using word processing effectively is a basic writing skill.

Revising at the computer is so much easier than revising by hand that many students take to it immediately. Writers don't have to physically cut their work apart to reorder parts; they can store successive drafts on a disk to reexamine if needed; and they can move even large blocks of text in just seconds. Once they've mastered the basic operations, most writers enjoy revision at the computer and become quite effective at it.

You need to familiarize yourself with the word-processing functions of inserting, deleting, copying, and pasting, and to be comfortable with them before you teach them to your students. Each process can be the topic of a demonstration lesson, which can then be practiced by students working on their own text on disks.

If you have access to equipment that shows what is on one computer screen on a large TV monitor, you can demonstrate these operations to a whole group or class at the same time. If students are then able to practice the operation at an individual computer station, you can circulate and supervise. But if you have only your classroom computer to use, then you'll probably need to divide your class into several smaller groups and repeat the lesson so that each student can see what you're doing on your monitor. Students should then practice the operations on text stored on their own disks. Figure 4.5 lists a number of different word-processing operations that can be taught in computer mini-lessons.

A sample mini-lesson on computer revision follows.

Sample Mini-Lesson: Revision at the Computer— Adding, Deleting, and Moving Text

Materials needed:

   Student-written piece or your own writing on a disk
   Computer and monitor

Procedure:

1. Put your text sample on the screen and read it aloud or have a student read it. (Be sure students can see the keyboard and monitor.)
2. Invite students to make suggestions for revisions, including identifying a place for text to be added.

Saving text

Changing font style and size

Changing spacing (single, 1.5, double)

Keyboarding drills (important keys, where and how much to space, etc.)

Capitalizing (the Shift and Caps Lock keys)

Moving the cursor with the mouse

Using spell-check

Using the computer's dictionary

Using the editing functions of copying, cutting, and pasting

Using the Enter and Tab keys to begin new paragraphs

Using the "scroll," Page Up, Page Down, Home, and End keys to find parts of text

Printing final drafts

FIGURE 4.5. Word-processing techniques for mini-lessons.

3. Demonstrate how to use the mouse and/or keys to place the cursor at the spot where text is to be added.
4. Type in the text to be added.
5. If desired, repeat steps 2 through 4 to demonstrate how to highlight and delete text; how to delete and substitute words or sentences; and how to highlight and use the editing functions of copying, pasting. and cutting to move text portions to other locations. (Or these operations may be taught in separate lessons.)
6. Demonstrate how to save changes on the disk.
7. Have students bring up a current piece from their disks and practice the operations just demonstrated.
8. Debrief by summarizing the steps, allowing time for sharing, comments, and questions.

REVISING LEADS

Leads are beginnings of pieces. Because a good lead can immediately draw a reader into a piece, whereas a poor lead can turn the reader off entirely, we spend a good deal of time helping students learn to revise their leads. This makes for more interesting beginnings, but it is more valuable than that: *Revising leads is a microcosm of the whole process of revision.*

If students can approach their leads with objectivity, compose several different versions, get peer feedback on their alternative leads, and select the one they think works best, they can use the same processes to revise an entire piece. By teaching how to revise leads, we can actually teach writers how to approach all revision.

Writing the first sentence or two of a composition is often the scariest part for many writers. Many writers believe that if they can just find the right lead, the piece will write itself. For those who still labor under the misconception that it has to be "right from the start," the lead is a difficult hurdle to get over. These writers can be observed writing a first sentence, considering it, crossing it out and writing another, and repeating these steps over and over, never getting beyond the first sentence. The worst scenario is the "blocked" writer who sits and stares numbly at the blank paper (or screen), unable even to begin. What is commonly referred to as "writer's block" is nothing more than an advanced case of "lead-o-phobia," or fear of starting a piece.

□□

TEACHER'S TIP: Revising leads is a microcosm of the whole
process of revision.

□□

These writers conceive of writing as somehow permanent. As we have noted in Chapter 1, they feel that writing is like sculpting in marble or cutting a diamond. One slip of the chisel, and the piece is ruined; one poor sentence, and the composition is spoiled. This notion prevents writing from occurring. Writers who think of themselves as working with clay rather than marble understand that writing is dynamic: Slips can be easily fixed; parts can be changed in innumerable ways; and, if desired, the whole piece can be entirely reshaped before the piece is declared finished.

This is, of course, exactly the way we want our students to see themselves—as artists working with a very fluid, dynamic, adaptable medium, which can be shaped, molded, elaborated, and streamlined in any number of ways without damage to the medium or the final product. So we teach them to work with their leads as though they were wet clay, and then to apply those strategies to the rest of their writing.

One way to teach leads is to *use models from literature*. Donald Graves often asks teachers participating in his workshops to bring several favorite books with them, and to share how each favorite story begins. Comparing them, teachers quickly discover that good leads place the reader immediately into the setting and action of the story, convey a sense of immediacy, and often cause the reader to wonder or be puzzled. Anne Bernays and Pamela Painter (1990) have also described a number of activities in which students compare the first one or two sentences of stories in magazines and story collections in their very helpful book, *What If?: Writing Exercises for Fiction Writers*.

Strong leads often make the reader ask questions that make the reader want to read on. We look for examples of these; then we write these leads on the board and invite students to list the questions that arise in their minds. Sometimes we contrast these with weak leads, often found in strictly expository material like biographies, that leave no questions in readers' minds. "Which piece would you rather read?" we ask. "Why? How can you write a lead that will cause your readers to wonder and be curious about what's to come?"

Contrasting weak and strong leads can be used by writers of many ages; it works particularly well in middle grades and above. Comparing the beginnings of different novels and stories helps students make an immediate connection

---

BOX 4.5. Strong Leads . . .

- Place the reader immediately into the setting and action of the story.
- Convey a sense of immediacy.
- Often cause readers to wonder or be puzzled.
- Often ask questions that make the reader want to read on.

between the literature they read and what they write. Drawing conclusions about what makes a lead effective helps students appreciate a writer's technique, as well as encouraging them to use such techniques in their own writing. As with other lesson topics, one lesson will not suffice; we reteach this skill systematically by periodically comparing leads in literature and inviting students to work on their own leads.

☐☐

TEACHER'S TIP: Connect reading and writing by sharing the beginnings of good literature with writers.

☐☐

A second way to teach lead writing is to have students *compose several alternative leads* for the same piece and determine which they think "works best." They can do this either alone or with partners or small groups, as is demonstrated in the sample mini-lesson that follows. Peer conferences can focus on helping writers select the most effective leads from several alternatives.

A third way to help writers revise leads is to have them *ask each other questions* to help their partner find the strongest or most interesting idea to begin with. Young and reluctant writers especially like discussing their leads orally and questioning each other about their topics before they write. More practiced or fluent writers may use questioning occasionally, but they prefer to compose several alternatives before sharing them with a partner.

An intriguing twist on using questions to develop leads has been described by Barry Lane (1993), who called this exercise "The Navajo story circle meets Ted Koppel." When a Navajo speaker holds the "talking stick," it gives the speaker the power to generate total, undivided attention. Students in this exercise use a ballpoint pen instead of a talking stick, but each writer in turn holds the magic pen while reading a piece being revised. Listeners then *write*, not ask, their questions about the piece as though they were Ted Koppel, the investiga-

---

BOX 4.5. Ways to Teach Lead Writing

- Share good examples from literature.
- Compare examples of strong and weak leads.
- Have writers try alternative leads and choose which work best.
- Have writers ask each other questions to help find the best way to begin a piece.

tive journalist. This allows writers to consider the questions privately and thoughtfully, and to select the questions that intrigue them and make them want to write more.

By critically studying how professional writers craft their leads, and by constructing alternative leads for their own pieces, writers develop the objectivity and sense of audience they need to revise entire pieces. They learn to approach topics from a variety of directions, to hone their word choices to convey their meaning precisely, and to give and receive constructive help—all of which are necessary to becoming effective writers.

Sample Mini-Lesson: Writing Alternative Leads

Materials needed:

A short sample piece on transparency or chart paper
Blank transparency or chart paper for writing new leads
Transparency markers or felt pens

Procedure:

1. Display the sample piece and read it aloud or have a student do so. The piece should have a fairly colorless lead.
2. Underline or highlight the sentence or sentences that constitute the lead, and invite students to suggest more interesting or colorful ways to begin the piece.
3. Compose three or four different leads for the same piece, or let students suggest alternatives. Write them on the blank transparency or chart paper so all can see them. (With student suggestions, downplay who offered the suggestion, and avoid comments like "Ronnie's suggested lead . . .")
4. Read the piece again, each time substituting an alternative lead. After each reading, invite students to comment about what makes that lead effective and how it improves the piece overall.
5. Choose, or invite student input on, the one lead that works best for this piece. Use the "think-aloud" technique to explain your reasoning and reactions to students. If desired, cut off the original lead and substitute the new version, taping it onto the paper or transparency.
6. Direct students to select a piece from their writing folders that could be improved by a better lead. Next, have each student try composing three different lead sentences, and then choose the lead he or she thinks works best.
7. Debrief by summarizing the steps in this procedure, and allow time for sharing, comments and questions.

ADDING DIALOGUE

Another useful revision technique is to learn how to add dialogue to a piece. As much as anything else, dialogue makes characters come alive. Often the way they speak, more than any action or description, reveals characters fully to readers.

Think about some of your favorite stories. How do different authors use dialogue to create scenes and develop characters? Looking at some of your own favorite books can help you explain the importance of dialogue to your students.

Using Literature Models

We often start introducing dialogue by sharing examples from literature with students. We look for portions of stories (often the beginnings) that use dialogue skillfully, and discuss with students how dialogue is used to help build a scene. If we can find some, we also share examples of ineffective dialogue—that is, dialogue that sounds phony, or goes on much too long, or feels like it was put in just to break up the narrative. We ask students to watch out for examples of good and bad dialogue as they read, and we make copies of them for sharing as students share them with us. Good and bad examples can be arrayed on posters or a bulletin board as students are working on dialogue.

We also use literature examples in two other ways. First, we find examples of straight narrative containing no dialogue, and invite students to work in pairs or threes to write dialogue for the characters; second, we find examples of extended dialogue with little narrative, and have students condense the dialogue and intersperse sections of narrative into it. Working with dialogue in the context of an already written piece is easier than creating the entire piece from scratch, and gives students practice in manipulating this challenging part of writing.

Listening to People Talk

Writing good dialogue is much harder than it looks. Most writers struggle with it, because it's hard to get just the right sound, to put in enough without making it go on too long, and to make the dialogue add to the scene. One pitfall that young writers often stumble into is creating overly long, repetitious exchanges that don't reveal anything about the characters or move the action forward—for instance, the mindless back-and-forth of a sibling argument ("Yes, you did!" "No, I didn't!" "Yes, you did!"), or the banal exchange of small talk between two uninteresting people ("Hi!" "Hi!" "How are you?" "Good, thanks. How about you?" "Can't complain.").

One way to help young writers become attuned to dialogue is to invite them to "eavesdrop" on conversations around them—to deliberately listen in at home, on the bus, in the halls and lunchroom, and in stores and restaurants to people talking to each other. They can even keep pocket notebooks to jot down scraps of interesting conversation to share. When they study dialogue closely, they often discover that much of what passes back and forth as conversation is either unnecessary or unclear. Much conversation is just small talk, intended to "grease the wheels" of social interaction. And much of it is also intelligible only to the participants, since facial expression, gesture, pitch, and volume lend as much meaning to speech as the words themselves do. By paying attention to how real people speak to each other, students can develop insights into what makes written dialogue effective.

Using Dialogue, "Snapshots," and "Thoughtshots"

Barry Lane (1993) developed a way of helping writers integrate dialogue with narrative by using what he called "snapshots," or narrative that relates action, and "thoughtshots," or narrative that tells what a character is thinking or feeling. Skilled writers balance their use of all three in their storytelling, so that readers can see what characters are doing and know what they are thinking or feeling as well as hearing what they are saying. Usually dialogue is interspersed with "snapshots" and "thoughtshots" to reveal a character fully. Here is an example, from *The Hobbit* (Tolkien, 1966, pp. 47–48):

> Bert and Tom went off to the barrel. William was having another drink. Then Bilbo plucked up courage and put his little hand in William's enormous pocket. There was a purse in it, as big as a bag to Bilbo. [snapshot] "Ha!" thought he, warming to his new work as he lifted it out carefully, "this is a beginning!" [thoughtshot]
>
> It was! Trolls' purses are the mischief, and this was no exception. [snapshot] " 'Ere, 'oo are you?" it squeaked, as it left the pocket; [dialogue] and William turned round at once and grabbed Bilbo by the neck, before he could duck behind the tree. [snapshot]
>
> "Blimey, Bert, look what I've copped!" [dialogue]
>
> "What is it?" said the others coming up. [dialogue and snapshot]
>
> "Lumme if I knows! What are yer?" [dialogue]
>
> "Bilbo Baggins, a bur—a hobbit," said poor Bilbo, [dialogue] shaking all over, and wondering how to make owl-noises before they throttled him. [thoughtshot]
>
> "A burrahobbit?" they said, [dialogue] a bit startled. [thoughtshot] Trolls are slow on the uptake, and mighty suspicious about anything new to them. [snapshot]
>
> "Can yer cook 'em?" said Tom. . . . [dialogue]
>
> "P'raps there are more like him round about, and we might make a pie," said Bert. "Here you, are there any more of your sort a-sneakin' in these here woods, yer nasty little rabbit?" said he [dialogue] looking at the hobbit's furry feet; and he picked him up by the toes and shook him. [snapshot]
>
> "Yes, lots," said Bilbo [dialogue] before he remembered not to give his friends away. [thoughtshot] "No, none at all," he said immediately afterwards. [dialogue]

Examples like this from stories students are reading can help them understand Lane's concept—that skilled writers integrate bits of dialogue with characters' thoughts and actions to create scenes.

Students can practice creating scenes in this way by brainstorming and choosing situations to write as scenes, not as whole stories. For example, different scenes can be created from situations such as these:

- *A teenage girl who is babysitting talks on the phone to her boyfriend while the children start a soccer game in the house.*
- *A store security guard catches someone who just shoplifted an expensive watch.*
- *Two kids walking in the woods discover a small door at the foot of a tree.*
- *The family dog, chasing a squirrel, jumps over the fence and disappears down the street.*
- *A shopper returns to the parking lot to find his or her car missing.*

Lane suggested that writers practice creating scenes, rather than entire stories, to practice integrating meaningful dialogue with narrative description of thoughts and actions.

We also encourage young writers to confer with partners and peer groups as they construct dialogues, and to have readers read the speakers' words aloud. One of the best ways to critique dialogue is to read it aloud; if it doesn't sound right, it won't "read" right, either. Peers can help writers identify ineffective dialogue and suggest changes that can strengthen the writing. In the process, writers relearn the important lesson that good writing is often collaborative.

OTHER WAYS TO REVISE A PIECE

There are as many ways to revise a piece as there are individual writers and approaches to writing. Depending on the age, grade, and writing skill of the students, revision lessons can run the gamut from the simplest (e.g., adding descriptive words) to the most complex (e.g., effective character development or conveying mood). Each revision lesson should focus on one skill students can observe being demonstrated and then practice applying in their own writing, either immediately or at another time. Key concepts should be reviewed frequently and retaught periodically to ensure that students internalize them. The following is a partial list of some useful revision topics.

Adding details that help explain or clarify
Naming characters
Describing characters
Creating a character's personality with furnishings, clothing, and so forth
Creating authentic settings
Using dialect, figurative language, and colloquialism to make dialogue sound real
Using a narrator to tell a story

Writing in the first person versus the third person (point of view)
Using personal memoir in stories
Developing plot; creating characters' problems and challenges
Using strong adverbs and adjectives; avoiding trite expressions
Creating sound effects with words
Varying sentence structure
Creating mysteries; giving clues that don't reveal too much
Writing good titles
Taking out anything that doesn't contribute to the story

TEMPORARY SPELLING IN EARLY DRAFTS

The issue of spelling always comes up during revision, as students often have difficulty keeping the stages of revision and editing separate. Revision, we remind them, is the process of clarifying what they mean, whereas editing is the process of correcting and polishing the work. Concern about correct spelling is appropriate, but it is best considered during the editing stage of writing.

That being said, we continue to encourage students to use *temporary spellings* while they are revising. We never tell them, "Spelling isn't important" (or anything like this), because of course we don't believe that ourselves; spelling *is* important, so that readers can make sense of what's been written. But we don't want students to agonize over correctness yet, or to let it distract them from the immediate task of writing exactly what they mean in as effective a way as they can.

We encourage students to use the words they want to use in their writing, not just the words they know how to spell. We want them to spell correctly those words that they have already learned, but we don't want them to limit their vocabulary selection to words they can already spell. When they don't know how to spell a word, we encourage them to spell it as best they can *for now*; we remind them that spelling and other mechanical features will be checked and corrected in the editing stage. Often we refer to the writing cycle chart we have displayed and ask writers to point out where they are in the cycle at this moment. When they see that they are in the second (revision) stage, and that the next stage is the editing stage, they often feel less unsure about temporary spelling.

If students are sharing revised work at home, be sure you have explained to parents that correction of spelling and other errors (capitalization, punctuation, sentence formation, etc.) are going to be corrected in the *next* stage. Otherwise they will begin to worry that you are not being rigorous about spelling, and some may attempt to take over and "proofread" their child's work, or force the child to correct the errors right now. When revised work is shared at home, it is important for parents to celebrate the work and notice how much clearer, more descriptive, and so forth it is becoming, rather than expecting a correct final copy yet.

▣▣▣

TEACHER'S TIP: Share your expectations and procedures with parents so that they can reinforce and support at home.

▣▣▣

RESPONDING TO STUDENTS' REQUESTS FOR SPELLING HELP

When students ask for spelling help in the revision stage, we are careful to encourage their best effort while not requiring correctness yet. We do not tell students how to spell a word very often, for this seems to encourage dependence; once we've given words to students, they are often less likely to try words on their own and more likely to ask us again. We remind ourselves that help doesn't mean giving the word; it means giving support to a student's effort, or helping a student over a rough spot in a word. (We have discussed this issue in Chapter 3 as well; you may want to look again at Box 3.4.)

With students in primary grades and older students who are primarily *phonemic* or sound-based spellers, we most often encourage them to say the word slowly and clearly, "stretching it out like a rubber band," and writing letters that represent the sounds they hear as they stretch it out. We'll encourage their developing phonemic segmentation ability by saying, "What do you hear at the beginning? What do you hear next? In the middle? At the end?" and so forth. When they make mistakes (as they frequently do), we congratulate them on what they have been able to do with comments like, "That's a very close spelling for that word," or "You've got almost all of that word right," or "I hear a _____ sound in the middle too." And when they ask, "Did I get it right?", we'll usually say something like "Almost! We'll take another look at it when you edit this story. For now go on with getting your ideas down."

What we're trying to do here is not to dodge the issue, to mislead students into thinking that they've spelled words right that are incorrect, or to downplay the importance of correctness. Rather, we're trying to empower students to make their best try and then go on, with the promise that we'll come back later and consider these hard words again. And we're trying to keep each writer's attention focused on the meaning of the piece, where it appropriately belongs in the revision stage, and keep meaning at the forefront of the writer's purpose for the time being. After writers have worked at honing their meaning—clarifying their ideas so that readers understand and connect with the writing—then and only then are they ready to tackle the issues of correctness that are the proper subjects of the editing stage. This stage is the topic of Chapter 5.

REFERENCES

Bernays, Anne, and Pamela Painter. *What If?: Writing Exercises for Fiction Writers*. New York: HarperCollins, 1990.

Calkins, Lucy McCormick. *Lessons from a Child: On the Teaching and Learning of Writing*. Portsmouth, NH: Heinemann, 1983.

Calkins, Lucy McCormick. *The Art of Teaching Writing* (new ed.). Portsmouth, NH: Heinemann, 1994.

Clutton-Brock, Juliet. *Eyewitness Books: Dog*. New York: Knopf, 1991.

Lane, Barry. *After the End: Teaching and Learning Creative Revision*. Portsmouth, NH: Heinemann, 1993.

Tolkien, J. R. R. *The Hobbit* (rev. ed.). New York: Ballantine, 1966.

White, E. B. *Stuart Little*. New York: Scholastic, 1987. (Originally published 1945)

CHAPTER 5

■□

Editing:
The Final Shaping

After a draft has been revised, and the writer is satisfied with the meaning and message of the writing, the next step is to edit the piece. *Editing* means *giving the final shaping to the work*—finding and correcting errors in mechanics (spelling, punctuation, grammar, etc.), and creating a finished version.

As we have discussed in Chapter 4, many writers confuse editing with revision. When they revise, they often try to do too much at once—changing the wording of sentences, adding and deleting sentences or paragraphs, and correcting mechanical errors at the same time. Often they get sidetracked by looking up spellings or breaking up overlong paragraphs, and they shortchange the process of revision. And they often become overwhelmed by changing so many things that they get discouraged and quit working on a piece, or simply copy it over neatly and forget about it.

That's why it is important to help young writers remember that revision and editing are two separate stages in the writing process, and that writers do very different things in each stage. They should not concentrate too much on mechanics or surface features of the piece until *after* they have crafted the message and have made their writing as interesting, understandable, and memorable as they can. When they are satisfied with the message, then they can turn their attention to correcting errors and creating a well-shaped final draft.

WHY IS EDITING SO PAINFUL?

Many students resist editing as much as, or more than, they resist revising. As with the revision process, many writers seem to believe that if they could have done it better, they would already have done so. Especially after working on revising a draft, they are now faced with yet another task: improving it even more, and in ways they couldn't think of while they were writing it. How in the world can they fix it up if they can't figure out what needs to be fixed? Left to their own devices, many writers will quickly scan a piece for any mistakes they can locate, and then call it a day.

A second reason why many students resist editing involves the time and effort required by revision, which often leave writers feeling vulnerable to any sort of criticism of the work. They're ready to bask in the satisfaction of having produced a meaningful piece, but we're ready to have them correct their errors! The more personal or meaningful a piece is to the writer, the more difficult it may be to continue to approach it objectively. For many writers, having to edit a piece is a signal that they have been "unsuccessful" again.

A third reason editing may be resisted is that many students tire of working on a piece before we think they are done with it. They've brainstormed topics, perhaps webbed or outlined what they know, produced a tentative first draft, conferred with teacher and peers, experimented with leads, added and deleted parts, and shared their efforts. By this time, they may be sick of their stories; isn't the fat lady singing yet? We need to be very careful about this, because it's one of the reasons reluctant writers tell us they hate writing. We need to make sure that writers move on to the next stage in the process *before* they reach the "I can't stand working on this another minute" point. We'll return to this point in Chapter 6 (see "Publishing as a Student-Directed Process").

For these reasons, we need to approach the process of editing in as positive a way as possible, deemphasizing the "correcting mistakes" aspects (while admitting that correcting mistakes is just what we're doing). We maintain to students that their good ideas *deserve* to be expressed clearly, correctly, and neatly, so that others can understand and appreciate them.

Depending on the age of our students, we also try to convey the notion that readers may make assumptions about a writer based on the correctness of the piece as well as on its content. These assumptions may be wrong, but they exist regardless. As teachers, we would cringe at the idea of sending home a note or classroom newsletter containing mechanical or grammatical errors; parents rightly expect us to do such things correctly! Students beyond the primary grades can think of many real-life situations in which mistakes would create a negative impression: a job application, a letter requesting information or services, and so forth. In this light, editing becomes the process of making sure the writer's good ideas are packaged in a way that creates a positive impression.

TEACHER'S TIP: Approach editing from the positive side:
Students' good ideas deserve to be presented correctly
and neatly, so that others can appreciate them!

Hand in hand with teaching editing is the teaching of necessary skills in composing, grammatical usage, and mechanics, which make up much of our language arts curriculum. Students can't correct errors if they don't know they made them, or if they don't know how to do things right in the first place. In the following sections, we'll discuss the skills students need to produce correct writing.

DEVELOPING SKILLS IN SENTENCE
AND PARAGRAPH CONSTRUCTION

One fundamental way that most writers must edit their work is in the construction of complete sentences and organized paragraphs. This takes longer than many people think. Developing writers typically master sentence construction by about second grade, and paragraph construction by about fourth; by sixth grade they should be able to write organized papers and essays with multiple paragraphs, each organized correctly and following a logical order. (They *should* be able to, but many can't; it's necessary to keep hammering away at sentence and paragraph formation at every grade.) Figure 5.1 shows a suggested sequence of writing benchmarks in sentence and paragraph construction for each grade, first through sixth.

Teaching young writers how to construct complete sentences is very difficult. Young children's writing is very much like their speech; that is, they write as they talk. But much of our informal speech is not organized into separate, complete sentences. In speech we use many sentence fragments, and many

First Grade

- Write to express ideas and experiences.
- Write two or more related sentences that the writer can read to another.
- Compose complete thoughts in simple sentences.
- Use mostly complete sentences.
- Begin sentences with capital letters, and use end punctuation.
- Use appropriate vocabulary for self-expression.

Second Grade

- Write stories, letters, and simple explanations.
- Produce writing that contains a beginning, middle, and end.
- Write an organized paragraph with a topic sentence and two or more supporting sentences.
- Write simple declarative, interrogative, and exclamatory sentences.
- Begin each sentence with a capital, and use appropriate end punctuation.
- Use some descriptive words and strong verbs.

Third Grade

- Write stories, letters, simple explanations, descriptions, and short factual reports.
- Write two paragraphs related to a central idea, each with its own topic sentence and two or more supporting sentences.

(cont.)

FIGURE 5.1. Sequence of skills in sentence and paragraph construction.

- Include descriptive details that elaborate the central idea.
- Use vivid vocabulary (adjectives, adverbs, strong verbs, precise nouns).
- Maintain focus or feeling throughout the piece.
- Use complete sentences with correct capitalization and punctuation.
- Use mostly simple sentences with occasional complex sentence forms.
- Use some internal punctuation, such as commas and quotation marks.

Fourth Grade

- Write extended narratives, explanations, and factual reports.
- Write organized pieces comprising three or more paragraphs on the same topic, each with its own topic sentence and supporting sentences.
- Include specific relevant details to support the main idea.
- Maintain central idea and feeling throughout the piece.
- Utilize elements of style including vivid word choices, personal voice, and consistent style.
- Use a variety of simple and complex sentence forms, with correct capitalization and correct internal and end punctuation.
- Utilize subject-verb agreement, use *I* correctly in compound subjects, and avoid double negatives.

Fifth Grade

- Write for a variety of purposes—to inform, entertain, describe, and express oneself.
- Write extended narratives, explanations, and reports with multiple paragraphs.
- Use organizational strategies appropriate to the form and purpose of the writing.
- Use correct standard grammar, capitalization, punctuation, and spelling.
- Punctuate dialogue and possessives correctly.
- Use elaborate, precise vocabulary.
- Use compound and complex sentence forms.
- Vary sentence structure.

Sixth Grade and Above

- Write for a variety of purposes, including narrative, expository, persuasive, and poetic writing.
- Write extended pieces, using a variety of appropriate organizational schemes.
- Maintain focus, point of view, and voice within and among paragraphs.
- Select vocabulary and information specific to the purpose and tone of the writing.
- Use correct forms of homonyms, pronoun–antecedent agreement, subject–verb agreement, and verb tense consistency.
- Use correct pronoun case, verb tense inflection, and adjective and adverb comparisons.

FIGURE 5.1. *(cont.)*

spoken sentences sound like what our teachers called "run-on" sentences, without discernible breaks between them. When children write their thoughts as they might say them, they naturally produce many incomplete and poorly constructed sentences.

That's why it is so necessary for young writers not only to practice speaking correctly, using grammatically correct sentences and precise words, but also to be surrounded by the *language of print read aloud*. When children are read to a great deal, they internalize the patterns of written language, and these patterns show up in both their speech and their writing. In other words, the more young children are read to, the more their language (both oral and written) benefits. The less they are read to, the more they must rely on their own and others' speech to create written language.

Today most young children are surrounded more by the sound of TV and videos than by the sound of books being read aloud. TV and other electronic media are speech-based rather than print-based; therefore, their language sounds more like talking than like reading. This does not help children develop the language of writing they will need to write themselves. Many programs and videos for children have very little elaborated language, relying instead on short utterances, body language, and sound effects. The more of this they are accustomed to by school entry, the more their writing will sound like talk, not like writing.

Teachers have been saying, "Turn off the TV and read!" for many years, and they will keep on saying it, even though very few seem to be listening. But it remains true that in order for children to learn to recognize, use, and produce the elaborate, precise, fully formed sentences that make up effective writing, they must be surrounded by the language of print—first by listening to someone read aloud, and then by reading a great deal themselves. The more time they spend watching TV, the less time they have for reading and books.

□□

TEACHER'S TIP: Read to your students every day, even
in middle school! The more they are read to, the more
their oral and written language benefits.

□□

Learning to Construct Sentences

It doesn't do much good to tell young children that a sentence is made up of a subject and a predicate, or a subject and its action, or even a complete thought; they just don't know what these terms mean. Until they get into the late primary or middle elementary grades and can distinguish between nouns and verbs, it doesn't help to tell them that each sentence has to have a subject and a verb.

We've had some success, however, with teaching young children to read their writing aloud and put periods where their voices naturally pause. This often results in their using too many periods for a while, but it's easier to take these out than to put them in, so we don't worry too much when we see periods beginning to proliferate in writing.

We teach writers to read their writing aloud, not hurrying too fast, and to listen for the places where their voices drop or pause; those places, we tell them, are probably where periods belong. (They can do this with a partner until they get the hang of it.) We have them practice putting periods in sample pieces (as in the mini-lesson that follows) and in their own writing, as well as having them assist each other, until they begin to put periods in spontaneously as they write.

When they can write fairly fluently and use periods, even if these aren't all correctly placed, we progress to mastering sentence construction. We start using this "voice-dropping" lesson in first grade, but older students can do this as well. We've used the technique even with sixth and seventh graders who are still grappling with fragments and run-ons.

What follows is a sample mini-lesson on sentence construction using the technique of "listening for the voice dropping," which can be adapted for a variety of grades as needed.

Sample Mini-Lesson: Putting Periods at the Ends of Sentences

Materials needed:

On the board or chart stand:

A series of related sentences written in paragraph form, but lacking any periods or capital letters, written on the board or on chart paper
Small sticky notes with periods and other end punctuation marks on them
Felt pen or crayon

On the overhead projector:

Unpunctuated sentences as above, printed on a transparency with adequate space between words
Transparency pen or marker

Procedure:

1. Read the writing sample aloud in a natural way. If students have not commented that there are no periods, elicit this discovery by asking what's missing.

2. Tell them that they are going to decide where to place the periods, by reading the piece out loud and listening for the places where their voices seem to drop or pause.

3. Ask a volunteer to begin reading aloud, stopping where he or she thinks

the first sentence ends. If this is being done at the board or chart, hand the reader a sticky note with a period written on it and have him or her place it where the period should go. If it is being done at the overhead projector, hand the reader a transparency marker and have him or her write the period on the transparency in the correct position.

4. Ask the other members of the group to determine whether they agree, by reading the preceding words aloud and listening for the place where their voices drop. If they do not agree, have someone move the period until it is in the correct position.

5. Continue having volunteers read aloud, dropping their voices at appropriate spots and placing the periods in the text as required. Have students check for accuracy by reading aloud and listening for the "voice drops."

6. After the lesson, have students work together to review a current piece of their own writing, adding periods as needed.

Young children may enjoy "acting out" where the periods go by lifting and dropping their arms as they read the sentences, or by standing up to read and sitting down when they come to the periods.

This mini-lesson can easily be adapted to the skills of combining sentence fragments to make complete sentences (in this case, sentence strips are made and cut into parts) and of breaking up run-on sentences. It can also be used as a "center" or independent activity, with the necessary pieces stored in large zip-locking bags; working alone or together, students can arrange the sentences and punctuation on a pocket chart or on a table or the floor.

Other punctuation skills that are appropriate for mini-lessons are listed in Figure 5.2. Several lists of children's books that are useful in teaching various types of punctuation are provided in Appendix A.

Learning to Construct Paragraphs

Once students have gotten the general idea about complete sentences, the same procedures can be used to teach and practice the process of building paragraphs by combining sentences into organized paragraphs. We teach the idea that a paragraph is made up of sentences related to the same idea, and we familiarize our students with many examples from literature and nonfiction of well-organized paragraphs. Then we proceed to mini-lessons in which students must group together related sentences, putting them in logical order, while deleting sentences that are not related to the topic.

Many grammar books provide sentence and paragraph construction exercises, but most of them are not "hands-on" enough. That is, they require students to do too much rewriting, without doing much of anything active. We've had better success with mini-lessons and practice activities where students actually move the sentences and punctuation marks around physically. This can be

- End punctuation for statements (*Today is Monday.*), questions (*How are you?*), and exclamations (*Stop!*)
- Commas to separate items in series (*She bought milk, bread, rice, and apples. He took a nap, ate dinner, and then finished his homework.*)
- Commas in direct address (*Mark, did you raise your hand?*)
- Commas to separate clauses connected by conjunctions (*He raised his hand, but she didn't call on him. Was she sick, or did her car break down?*)
- Commas to set off introductory phrases (*In the end, she was glad she had gone. First, you should read the directions.*)
- Commas to set off appositives (*Ms. Beverly, my third-grade teacher, is absent today.*)
- Periods in abbreviations (*Mr., Dr., Tues., Oct.*)
- Colons when making a list (*The steps in the procedure are as follows:*)
- Apostrophes to show possession (*the dog's paw, Ms. Gillet's car, six cats' footprints*)
- Apostrophes in contractions (*I'll, you've, we're, can't*)
- Parentheses within sentences (*here, for example*) or lists
- Quotation marks in dialogue (*"Help, help!"*)
- Commas and end punctuation in dialogue (*"Hold on tight," Piglet called. "I'll be back as soon as I can!" "Please hurry," Pooh replied, "for I can't hold on much longer."*)

FIGURE 5.2. Punctuation skills for mini-lessons.

done in several ways: by using sentence strips and a pocket chart, by using sentences written on chart paper and scissors, or by using a transparency and scissors (see the mini-lesson at the end of this section). To create "living paragraphs," we write related sentences on sentence strips without end punctuation, and we hand them out to members of a group, along with periods, question marks, and exclamation marks on file cards. Each group member will have either a sentence or a punctuation mark. They then arrange themselves in a line across the front of the room, with each sentence in the correct order followed by the appropriate punctuation mark.

Young writers rarely use paragraphs spontaneously. Their writing is usually arranged in a single long paragraph, which is not indented unless they have been told to indent the first sentence. Each sentence appears as it occurred to the writer, not necessarily in sequential order. Sentences that are unrelated (or only loosely related) to the topic often intrude, also included as they occurred to the writer. So for young writers, the idea of paragraphs as groups of related sentences, with the first or topic sentence of each one indented to show the beginning of a new paragraph, is usually a novel one.

Somewhat older writers (say, in third grade and above) usually have some idea of what a paragraph is, but their understanding is usually limited; many think a paragraph is simply a number of sentences written together, with the first one indented. We have seen writers trying to apply the notion of paragraphs by writing two, three, or four sentences and then indenting the next sentence, over and over. Never mind that the sentences in each group are not necessarily related to each other; on paper, the groups look like paragraphs!

These writers already know that a paragraph is made up of several sentences with the first one indented. What they don't yet understand is that *all the sentences in a paragraph must be related to a single topic*, and that a new paragraph begins when the topic shifts. So their paragraph practice must involve finding the related sentences and grouping them together.

It is useful to teach students to use the proofreader's mark for a paragraph (¶) at the beginning of a sentence that appears to start a new paragraph. For some time they will tend to overuse this sign in their editing, and some may make separate paragraphs out of nearly every sentence. Don't worry too much about this; overgeneralizing is a predictable part of learning to apply a new strategy. As we have noted above, young writers often do the same thing when putting in periods; first graders just getting the idea of periods often sprinkle them across a story like salt on a hamburger! After they've overused a strategy for a while, they'll begin to firm up the notion of when to use it correctly.

⬚⬚

TEACHER'S TIP: It's natural for students to overuse a strategy when they first learn it. Practice will help them learn when to use it appropriately.

⬚⬚

BOX 5.1. Some Ways to Teach Sentence and Paragraph Construction

- Have students read run-on sentences aloud and listen for the places where their voices "drop."
- Have students create "living paragraphs" by holding up sentence strips and punctuation cards in the correct order.
- Have students physically arrange sentence fragments and punctuation marks, using cut-up sentence strips.
- Have students find and group together related sentences to form cohesive paragraphs.

It is often easier for writers to help each other figure out where the paragraphs break than it is to do it in their own writing. Somehow, such things often seem clearer in someone else's piece. Again, it is important to stress that getting editing help from another writer is just another form of collaboration, and that it is a good thing to do. Often young writers will be able to help each other understand a concept or operation more simply and easily than you can; we're always surprised when one student is able to explain to another a concept that we've been banging our heads on for days! So we encourage writers to assist each other in figuring out where their paragraph breaks belong.

Sample Mini-Lesson: Creating Paragraphs by Using Sentence Strips

Materials needed:

A pocket chart for holding sentence strips
Sentence strips
Markers

Procedure:

1. Create or find a paragraph made up of four or five sentences. You may write one yourself, use a literature model, or use a student-written paragraph.

2. Copy each sentence onto a sentence strip. Include one or two sentences that are unrelated to the others. Display the sentences in the pocket chart.

3. Read each sentence aloud or have volunteers read them. Invite volunteers to identify and remove the sentence strips that are unrelated to the others. Explain that these sentences may be used in other paragraphs or may be deleted from the writing, but that in either case they do not belong in this paragraph.

4. Invite volunteers to physically arrange the sentence strips in a logical sequence to create a meaningful paragraph. Have someone move the first sentence over so that it appears to be indented, and (if necessary) explain that the space before the indented sentence is a signal that a new paragraph has begun. (If you have previously introduced the idea of a *topic sentence*, have students locate the topic sentence and make sure it is placed at the beginning of the paragraph.)

5. Invite students to rearrange the sentences so that the paragraph makes sense. If they can be arranged in more than one way, point this out to students.

6. Have students read a piece they are currently editing and follow the same procedure, deleting unrelated sentences and arranging the others in order to create logical paragraphs. Students may need to cut and paste their drafts to do so.

This mini-lesson can be adapted to use with sentences on chart paper or a transparency; you can give volunteers the scissors, and allow them to cut apart the draft and tape the sentences together as a paragraph. Students can also practice this procedure at their seats with individual scissors and the necessary sentences on a sheet of paper.

DEVELOPING SKILLS IN STANDARD ENGLISH USAGE

Standard English usage—what many of us think of as "correct grammar"—is most often taught in English lessons, separately from writing instruction. When this is the case, we have to reinforce what students are learning in these lessons when they are editing their writing. Whatever is being taught in grammar should be reinforced during editing lessons. If there is no prescribed curriculum for teaching standard English usage in your particular grade, then you can teach the various skills as students need them in their writing.

For example, many first-grade teachers do not teach English as such, so they teach sentence and paragraph formation, plurals, verb tenses, and so forth as students begin to use them in their writing. But in second grade and beyond, there typically exists a grammar curriculum that may dictate the skills to be taught and their order. If so, then by all means use the writing period as an opportunity to reteach and reinforce these skills, for they are most useful in speaking and writing.

It is beyond the scope of this discussion to describe what English grammar skills students should learn at each grade; most schools have such curriculum goals already in place. However, it is important to note that the linguistic and cultural diversity that now characterizes most American classrooms makes teaching and learning standard English grammar more challenging than ever. In the typical elementary classroom, not all children will be standard English speakers. Regional and dialectical differences in speech and grammar, as well as the presence of learners whose first language may be other than English, may interfere with students' using standard English in their writing. Young writers write as they speak; if they are accustomed to using expressions like "I ain't got none," "Is we going now?", and "It cost ten cent," these usages will occur in their writing as well as in their speech.

Many teachers have no problem with correcting children's grammar in their speech as well as in their writing. Others, however, fear that doing so will embarrass children, infer that their home speech is inferior, or otherwise stigmatize them. This is indeed a sensitive issue. Certainly, though, we have a responsibility to teach children how to speak and write standard English usage. All states with statewide curriculum and performance standards require students to demonstrate mastery of standard English grammar and usage, at least in their writing. So the issue is not *whether* to correct and model usage, but *how* to do so in ways that show respect for the language of their home and culture.

Some teachers explain that home and school speech are sometimes different, and that in school we are expected to speak and write in certain ways that we might not use in our informal talk. You may wish to avoid using value-laden terms like *wrong* or *bad grammar* in favor of a more connotatively neutral term like *standard English.*

Older children can certainly understand the idea that there are different ways of talking to different audiences, and that skilled speakers and writers suit their language to the situation. Most already understand that they would probably not use the same slangy, informal speech to talk to a grandparent or a teacher that they would use on the street or to their friends, or that they would use very different styles of writing to compose a note to a close friend or a letter requesting a job application.

TEACHER'S TIP: Correct nonstandard grammar or usage respectfully. Avoid value-laden terms like *wrong* or *bad grammar.*

An area of English usage that may be problematic for many writers is the confusion of similar-sounding words that are often confused. Some of these usage errors involve *homophones,* or words that sound the same but have different spellings and meanings, such as *to, too,* and *two.* Others are common in some regional and/or cultural dialects, like *a apple, We laid down to sleep, He don't feel too good,* or *She learned him to dance.* Figure 5.3 shows a list of common homophones and similar-sounding words that are often confused. They can be taught directly and displayed for quick reference.

EDITING IN PRIMARY GRADES

In primary grades, we are more interested in familiarizing children with the process of checking over their work than we are in having them correct many of their errors. After all, beginning writers probably do more things incorrectly than correctly, and it is unreasonable to expect them to be able to fix more than a few errors in any piece. But we want to help them develop the editing habit early, so that from the start they see editing as a natural, predictable part of the writing cycle. Also, we encourage them to collaborate as they edit, so that they feel supported rather than overwhelmed as they enter this stage of the writing process. Eventually, we want primary graders to be able to proofread their own work and locate at least a few errors to correct in each piece.

What can we expect primary-grade writers to be able to do? By the end of first grade, most writers should be able to . . .

an, and	ant, aunt	ate, eight	already, all ready	
by, buy, bye	bear, bare	beat, beet	birth, berth	bred, bread
break, brake	bail, bale	boy, buoy	blue, blew	been, bin
bald, balled	bored, board	bow, bough	boar, bore	be, bee
clothes, close	cent, scent	choose, chews	cheap, cheep	cell, sell
colonel, kernel	capital, capitol	course, coarse	creek, creak	
dear, deer	die, dye	doe, dough	do, due, dew	desert, dessert
days, daze				
four, for, fore	forth, fourth	find, fined	fir, fur	flower, flour
feet, feat	fair, fare	foul, fowl		
gate, gait	guessed, guest	groan, grown		
hair, hare	heard, herd	hear, here	heal, heel	hole, whole
him, hymn	horse, hoarse	hey, hay		
I'll, isle, aisle	its, it's	I, eye	in, inn	
led, lead	loan, lone	lose, loose		
made, maid	meet, meat	medal, metal	main, mane, Maine	minor, miner
mall, maul	morning, mourning	mail, male		
need, knead	no, know	not, knot	night, knight	new, knew, gnu
or, oar, ore	oh, owe	one, won	our, hour	
pain, pane	peel, peal	piece, peace	poor, pore, pour	peer, pier
plain, plane	pair, pear, pare	principle, principal	past, passed	pole, poll
pause, paws	pray, prey	petal, pedal, peddle		
quite, quiet				
rode, road, rowed	role, roll	rain, rein, reign	raise, rays, raze	read, reed
red, read	right, write	real, reel	ring, wring	rap, wrap
rung, wrung	rose, rows			
see, sea	seen, scene	sail, sale	steak, stake	seem, seam
so, sew, sow	some, sum	son, sun	steal, steel	soar, sore
sight, site, cite	sweet, suite	soul, sole	side, sighed	sense, cents, scents
sheer, shear	sleigh, slay			
tail, tale	to, too, two	throne, thrown	through, threw	there, their, they're
tide, tied	time, thyme	told, tolled	tear, terror	than, then
violet, violent				
waist, waste	wear, ware, where	witch, which	well, will, we'll	would, wood
who's, whose	we, wee	wait, weight	way, weigh	we'd, weed
we've, weave	week, weak	weather, whether	wade, weighed	
your, you're	you, ewe			

FIGURE 5.3. Easily confused homophones and similar-sounding words.

- Find and mark at least a few words they're not sure are spelled right, and check the spellings by using a Word Wall, primary dictionary, spelling list, or the like.
- Spell a body of high-utility sight words (e.g., *they, that, my, his, how, like, have, to,* and *with*) correctly.
- Use developmentally appropriate spelling attempts for new or unfamiliar words.

- Read the work aloud, listening for the voice dropping at the ends of sentences, and use at least some end punctuation correctly.
- Use capital letters at the beginning of each sentence, for names, and for the pronoun *I*.
- Use plural and verb tense endings in most cases, although they may be spelled phonetically (i.e., *WASHT/washed*, *GLASSIZ/glasses*, etc.)
- Use at least some complete sentences, although sentence fragments and run-ons will still be common.

And by the end of second grade, most writers should be able to . . .

- Write a piece with at least two separate paragraphs.
- Indent the first sentence of each paragraph, and make sure all sentences in a paragraph are related to the same topic.
- Use end punctuation correctly in nearly every case.
- Capitalize the first word in each sentence, proper nouns, and *I*.
- Use plural and verb tense endings appropriately and correctly in most cases.
- Use mostly complete sentences, with fragments and run-ons becoming increasingly rare.
- Use end punctuation consistently and correctly, including question marks and exclamation marks.
- Correctly spell an increasingly large body of high-utility words, while using developmentally appropriate spelling attempts for unfamiliar, complex words.
- Find and mark a number of words that may be misspelled, and check their spelling by using a dictionary or other aid.

In addition, by the end of second grade most writers should be familiar enough with the writing cycle that they can revise and edit selected pieces of their work fairly automatically, without constant reminders of what they need to do next. They should be able to collaborate with other writers, both giving and receiving assistance as they complete a piece, and should consistently show respect for others' work. They should be developing increasing independence, so that their requests for teacher assistance and support are less frequent and/or less urgent than they were in first grade, and they should be able to work on a piece for longer periods of time with moderate support and encouragement.

EDITING IN MIDDLE GRADES AND ABOVE

Beginning in third grade, we want students to become increasingly independent in their ability to edit their own work. Each year their independence should increase, so that by the end of the elementary years students should be able to read over their own revised work and correct most of their errors in spelling, usage, and mechanics. Many will probably not be able to do this entirely on their own, but will need to refer to dictionaries and other references, spelling lists, checklists, and so forth, and may need to get help from other writers. But they should no longer be dependent on the teacher (or a parent) to proofread their work and mark their errors for them, and they should know how to correct many of their mistakes.

Daily Group Editing

Barry Lane (1993, p. 189) wrote, "Editing is as much a habit as a skill," and this habit must be developed in (or by) the middle grades if it is to develop at all. Lane described *daily group editing* as a way to "affirm a class's editing skills and make it fun." He suggested writing a passage on the board before students arrive; each passage should have as many editing errors, related to what students are learning at the time, as there are students in the class. Students go to the board in pairs, each correcting one error and explaining the correction.

We adapted this procedure because we found it cumbersome to write a passage containing 20-plus errors every day! But we use a passage with a number of errors, somewhere between 6 and 12, often taken from the day's reading. Students sometimes work in pairs, threes, or fours to find and correct as many mistakes as they can. We often do this activity as a "Do Now"—an activity students are to complete as soon as they come in. It doesn't take long, and we think the daily practice is helpful.

Editing Goals for Middle Grades

It is important to remember that in middle grades we are actually working toward two main goals: One is that they will possess the skills to find and correct many of their own errors, and the other is that they will do this on their own as a natural part of the writing process. So we need to keep reminding ourselves that we must gradually draw away the support we provided these writers when they were younger, and do everything we can to foster independence rather than dependence on us.

We can only foster independence by *refusing to do anything for students that they can do for themselves*. We don't mean *refuse* in the sense of saying, "No, I won't help you," but we do have to make students rely on themselves instead of on us. For example, it's fairly common to find middle- and upper-grade teachers who routinely mark all the errors in their students' written work, returning it to the students for correction. That's a job students should increasingly be taking on themselves. Ask yourself, "Who needs the practice in editing—the writers or I?" Of course, the writers do.

We knew a parent who told us her college student son brought her all of his papers for her to edit. Her rationale for doing it was that at least his written work would be correct. We lacked the courage to tell her that she ought to let him learn to correct his own mistakes, but we were sure she wasn't doing him any favor.

We have found ourselves at times doing too much for this student or that one, or for the whole class, because it was easier just to do it ourselves or because we wanted the end result to be correct. But these are *not* sufficient reasons for doing too much for students. Remember, our job is not to make ourselves indispensable to writers, but to make ourselves obsolete!

> **TEACHER'S TIP:** Refuse (gently) to do anything for students they can do
> for themselves. This includes editing their writing!

If you are teaching editing by pointing out your students' errors to them, you will find it hard to stop all at once. It may be best to begin weaning them away from your support. There are several ways to do this.

One way is to *limit the kinds of errors you will point out*, making clear to writers that they are responsible for finding other types of errors. For example, you might continue for a while to point out errors in sentence and/or paragraph construction, but refrain from marking spelling or grammatical errors, reminding students that they must locate and correct these themselves. When you do this, frequent reteaching of the skills they will need to do these editing tasks independently is helpful.

Another way is to refrain from pointing out specific errors, but instead *tell writers where to look* for certain problems. Instead of marking the errors themselves, you can write notes like this: "There are two run-on sentences in the first paragraph; see if you can make them into four complete sentences," or "I see three spelling mistakes in the first two sentences. Can you find all three?"

A third method is to *make a list at the end of the piece* indicating what kinds of errors you want the writer to concentrate on. For example, you might list spelling of *there* and *their*, capitalizing names of cities and states, and dividing long paragraphs into shorter ones as things a writer needs to focus on in a particular piece. In this way you have reminded the student of particular skills he or she needs to practice, but haven't told the student where the errors are.

It's also important to remember to *point out what writers have done well*. Teacher editing can become very negative, and this becomes unpleasant for both teacher and writer. Whether you are conferring with a writer directly or writing comments on a piece turned in to you, try to make it a habit to remark on what was done well before you point out any weaknesses. Lucy Calkins (1994) has reminded us that beginning an editing conference by celebrating what the writer *did* do and the risks the writer took, even if these resulted in errors, helps to make editing a positive experience rather than a negative one.

Even if a piece is simply studded with mistakes, there will be something the writer has done well; find it and point it out to the writer. This puts you in a more positive frame of mind when approaching the rest of the paper, and helps the writer know what to do again next time. A simple comment like "Good for you! You remembered to give Charlottesville a capital C!" or "I see that every sentence begins with a capital and ends with a period! Way to go!" can be more reinforcing than all the reminders in the world. Calkins (1994) wrote, "Children, like adults, learn best in a supportive context. Like all of us, children are more apt to remember kind words about their successes than harsh words about their failures. They will take risks if we support risk-taking. The tendency instead is to reinforce correctness" (p. 303).

It's also important to ensure that the collaborative atmosphere you fostered during the first-draft and revision stages is still operational during editing. Make sure that you are not the only resource available to writers when they edit. Continually encourage them to seek help from each other when they are editing their work. Make sure that editing aids—dictionaries, a thesaurus, spelling lists, editing checklists, and so forth—are readily available for students to turn to as they edit. (You'll read more about these in the "Editing Aids" section later in this chapter.)

What can we expect middle and upper graders to be able to do for themselves in editing? With increasing skill and independence in each successive grade, they should be able to . . .

- Write a piece on a single topic that is made up of multiple paragraphs, each well organized and logically sequenced.
- Create a clearly organized piece with a discernible beginning, middle, and conclusion.
- Use complete sentences; avoid or correct sentence fragments and run-ons.

BOX 5.2. Ways to Foster Self-Reliance in Editing

- Choose judiciously what types of errors you will point out to students.
- Tell students where to look for errors.
- Make a list of types of errors for students to focus on.
- Point out what students have done well.
- Encourage peer collaboration.
- Provide dictionaries and other editing aids.

- Be consistent in voice, verb tense, and so forth; avoid switching back and forth from "He says" to "He said," from first to third person, and the like.
- Use end punctuation systematically and correctly.
- Use internal punctuation such as commas, apostrophes, and quotation marks with increasing correctness.
- Capitalize correctly.
- Use apostrophes correctly in contractions (*isn't, they're*, etc.) and possessives (*Dan's, teachers'*, etc.)
- Spell and use plurals and verb tenses correctly.
- Spell most words correctly, using developmentally appropriate spelling strategies for incorrectly spelled words. Spell high-utility words correctly.
- Spell and use homophones or easily confused words (e.g., *you're/your, there/their, an/and, to/too/two, we'll/will, no/know*, and *ever/every*) with increasing correctness.
- Use subject–verb agreement and pronoun–antecedent agreement; avoid common errors like "*Each student* will correct *their* work" and "The *books* we use in history class *is* outdated."
- Vary sentence length and style.
- Use vivid, precise vocabulary.
- Write for a variety of purposes: to persuade, to report or explain, to express opinions or feelings, to describe, to provide a sequence of steps or events, and to narrate a story.

▫▫

TEACHER'S TIP: Students in third grade and beyond should be able to find and correct their errors on their own, as a natural part of writing.

▫▫

TEACHING STUDENTS TO "PLAY COPS"

COPS is a method we use to encourage independence in editing. It stands for four editing operations we expect writers to perform before they seek help from us or consider a piece finished. COPS is an acronym for Capitalization, Organization, Punctuation, and Spelling.

When we are ready to begin teaching editing skills—that is, when students are fairly fluent with selecting topics, writing first drafts, and revising their ideas—we begin to mention that soon we'll be showing them how to "play COPS" with their writing. We don't tell them right away what that means; after a couple of days, some brave soul will finally ask us, thinking that maybe everyone else already knows.

If we want to build a little more anticipation, we don't even tell them then, but mysteriously reply, "Not yet!" or "You'll find out soon!" We might even drop a sly hint in the ear of an individual student or two here and there. When one says, "I finished my story. What do I do now?" we might murmur, "Well, you don't know how to play COPS yet, do you?" "What? What?" the student wonders. "Never mind," we reply. "Just read it over and see if there's anything you're not sure is right. I can't wait 'til you learn to play COPS. That's when you'll *really* get good at this." We'll then say no more, but let a little curiosity build. (We have to be careful not to overplay our hands here, though. Too much anticipation, and they'll be disappointed when they find out that it has nothing at all to do with handcuffs or police cars!)

When we *do* introduce the COPS game, we create a poster (see Figure 5.4) with the four letters arranged vertically, and explain that each letter stands for something we'll do to fix up our writing. We invite predictions of what each letter might stand for, and often someone guesses "capital letters" and "spelling," but O and P are somewhat more obscure. So we list each of the operations, and then in successive mini-lessons we deal with each operation in turn. After we have done one mini-lesson on each operation, explaining what it means and a little about how to do it, we reteach these skills again and again. In particular, organization (making sure that each sentence and idea is in the right place, and that everything makes sense to others) and punctuation (in all its various forms) will be the focus of many mini-lessons throughout the year. A sample mini-lesson on capitalization, adaptable to a range of grade levels, follows.

After we've introduced the concept of "playing COPS" with a piece, we make sure that we remind students to go through this process with a revised

Capitalization

Organization

Punctuation

Spelling

FIGURE 5.4. COPS poster.

piece *before* they bring it to us as finished or start making plans for their final copy. An editing checklist that includes places to check off as students edit for capitalization, organization, punctuation, and spelling can be paper-clipped to each edited piece; we run these off and keep them in the editing center (see the section on "Editing Aids" that follows).

Sample Mini-Lesson: Capitalization

Materials needed:

Text, either entirely lacking in capital letters, or with some capitals used incorrectly; this can be written on chart paper, on the board, or on a transparency. (We like to take a passage from a good book and copy it on a transparency, changing it so that there are lots of capitalization errors. After the lesson, we show students the correct text as it appears in the story.)

Tools for correcting errors (damp tissue and transparency marker for transparency; eraser and chalk for chalkboard; brush-on correction fluid or sticky notes for chart paper)

Procedure:

1. Refer to the COPS chart and remind students that the first step in playing COPS is to check for correct use of capital letters. Ask volunteers to recall what they already know about where capital letters should be used.

2. Invite volunteers to locate places in the text where capitals should be used, and have each correct one of the errors in the text by removing or covering up the lowercase letter and substituting the correct capital. Ask each one to explain why he or she made that particular change. (Learning is enhanced when students verbalize what they did.)

3. If capitals have been inappropriately included in the text, ask volunteers to locate places where capital letters *don't* belong, and correct as in step 2 above.

4. Summarize, or ask students to summarize, where capitals are required (and optionally, where they don't belong, as noted above).

5. Have students apply the skill just practiced with a piece of their own writing, either alone or with an editing partner.

EDITING AIDS

Another way to make editing a more positive process is to provide special materials and procedures exclusively for editing purposes. Besides making editing a

---

BOX 5.3. Capitalization Mini-Lesson Summary

1. Copy text with capitalization errors on chart, transparency, or the like.
2. Have students make corrections and explain their rationale. (Refer back to literature if appropriate.)
3. Summarize where capitals are and are not required.
4. Have students apply procedure to a piece of their writing.

---

little more fun, this also helps students remember that editing is a separate stage in the writing process, complete with its own tools and procedures.

Editing Tools

Having available particular tools that are reserved for the editing process makes it a little special. Some materials students will find useful are the following:

- Dictionaries, including picture dictionaries, and related reference works (e.g., a thesaurus and desk encyclopedia).
- Spelling aids, such as a Word Wall of high-utility words, lists of "spelling demons" or frequently misspelled words, and spelling books.
- Grammar books or easy-to-use handbooks like *Writers Express* (Kemper, Nathan, & Sebranek, 1994) for checking on grammar rules.
- Colored pens, pencils and/or markers, brush-on correction fluid, correction tape, erasers, sticky notes in various sizes, scissors, and tape.
- Editing checklists.

Editing Center

Organizing and storing editing materials in a special place will also help keep materials accessible and make editing a special part of the writing process. You only need a small table with a couple of chairs and storage for editing materials to create an editing center, where students can go when they are ready to edit a piece. A set of stacking office trays or plastic storage boxes can provide organization for materials.

A sign labeling the editing center and posters displaying important things to remember in editing, including the COPS procedure, help students use this area independently. If you have a roster or system for assigning classroom chores, the task of straightening the editing center and keeping materials neatly organized can be added to it.

Editing Checklists

Editing checklists are a great way of helping students apply spelling, grammar, and usage skills they are learning and develop independence in editing their work. Checklists should be developed cooperatively with students, and should be appropriate to the age and grade of the class. As the year progresses and more skills are taught, they can be added to the checklist so that students are reminded to apply these new skills to their writing.

Figures 5.5a, 5.5b, and 5.5c are examples of editing checklists appropriate for different grade levels. If peer editors or editing partners are used, this can be indicated on the checklists.

Editing Partners and Peer Editors

You can encourage students to collaborate on editing tasks by inviting them to choose an editing partner to review their work or by assigning students to serve as peer editors on a rotating basis. Young writers may prefer to choose their own editing partners, whereas older ones may enjoy the responsibility of a more formal job.

In either case, it is important to *train peer editors* so that their efforts are helpful, not hurtful, to writers and supportive of the collaborative workshop atmosphere you've worked so hard to establish. Before assigning anyone to be a peer editor, conduct at least one formal lesson on the "Do's and Don'ts of Peer Editing."

Peer editors do . . .
- Check a writer's work *after* the writer has edited it individually.
- Point out errors kindly and helpfully.
- Help writers find the correct way of doing something.
- Suggest changes to make the writing more correct.

Peer editors don't . . .
- Do the editing for the writer.
- Point out errors rudely, embarrass a writer, or make fun of a writer's errors.
- Make put-down remarks about the writing.
- Tell others about the writer's mistakes.
- Mark up the writing or make changes on the paper.
- Revise for meaning, delete parts, change the title, or tell the writer it's too long (or short).
- Give orders or act bossy.

Name _____ Date _____

1. I read my whole piece to myself. _____

2. My piece makes sense to me and to someone else. _____

   (I read my piece to _____.)

3. It has . . .   My name. _____

                    A title. _____

                    Periods. _____

                    Capital letters. _____

                    Spaces between words and sentences. _____

                    Pictures (optional) _____

4. I checked my spelling and made some changes. _____

5. I wrote neatly. _____

FIGURE 5.5a. Sample editing checklist for primary grades.

From *Directing the Writing Workshop* by Jean Wallace Gillet and Lynn Beverly. Copyright 2001 by The Guilford Press. Permission to photocopy this figure is granted to purchasers of this book for personal use only (see copyright page for details).

Name _____ Date _____

Sentences

_____ Sentences are clear and complete. I corrected fragments and run-ons.

_____ Sentences are of different lengths.

_____ Sentences begin in different ways.

Punctuation

_____ Each sentence ends with a punctuation mark.

_____ I used commas in series and in dialogue.

_____ I used quotation marks around each speaker's words.

Capitalization

_____ Each sentence starts with a capital letter.

_____ Proper nouns (names of specific people, places and things) start with capitals.

Usage

_____ I used strong, colorful verbs, nouns and describing words.

_____ I used the right form of words like *to/too*, *your/you're*, *for/four*, and so forth.

_____ I used correct standard grammar.

Spelling

_____ I marked words that didn't look right to me.

_____ I checked my spelling with a dictionary or other aid.

_____ checked my spelling.

FIGURE 5.5b. Sample editing checklist for middle grades.

Author _____   Title _____

Start date _____   Editing date _____

Peer editor(s) _____

_____ Final revision check for sense, order, meaning

_____ Sentences complete

_____ Sentences varied in length and style

_____ Paragraphs complete, all sentences related to topic, indented

_____ Vocabulary checked: strong, colorful, precise

_____ Punctuation checked and corrected (end punctuation, commas, quotation marks)

_____ Capitalization checked and corrected (sentence beginnings, *I*, proper nouns)

_____ Grammar checked and corrected (subject–verb agreement, pronoun– antecedent agreement, plurals, possessives, verb tenses)

_____ Usage checked and corrected (homophones, *a/an*, *good/well*, *alot*, *alright*, etc.)

_____ Spelling checked and corrected

FIGURE 5.5c. Sample editing checklist for upper grades.

From *Directing the Writing Workshop* by Jean Wallace Gillet and Lynn Beverly. Copyright 2001 by The Guilford Press. Permission to photocopy this figure is granted to purchasers of this book for personal use only (see copyright page for details).

Students should be reminded periodically that peer editing is a helpful collaborative process, not an opportunity for showing off, acting superior, or making another writer feel inadequate. A peer editor's job is to suggest and help, not give orders or do the editing for a writer. The writer retains the right to make changes and take or ignore suggestions.

⊡⊡⊡

TEACHER'S TIP: Peer editors must be taught how to suggest and help, while refraining from doing the editing for a writer.

⊡⊡⊡

To ensure accountability, it may be helpful to have peer editors sign or initial the work, or the editing checklist, when they are done. It is also useful to review the peer editing process periodically in an informal class discussion, with students telling what is most helpful in peer editing and what practices are annoying or not helpful. It may also help things run smoothly if there are several students serving as peer editors at a time. (Young writers enjoy wearing special pin-on "Student Editor" badges that can be stored in the editing center.)

USING DICTIONARIES

One of the most useful editing skills we can teach students is how to use dictionaries to check spelling, word meanings, derivations of words, and all the other information these volumes offer. Using a dictionary is a functional life skill. However, dictionary use cannot be taught effectively in one lesson. Many lessons and much practice will be needed before students can use dictionaries effectively and independently. We want our students to feel that dictionaries are useful and accessible, and not to be intimidated by the task of finding something in them.

We begin teaching dictionary use in first grade, as soon as students begin to check their spelling, and continue to use dictionaries systematically throughout the year and across all grades. We urge students to work with a partner to find needed words, to help each other when they are having trouble finding a word, and simply to browse in dictionaries whenever they choose.

We were surprised to find that even with primary graders, a few minutes of browsing through a well-illustrated dictionary often helped writers think of a topic when they were stuck for one. With an attractive dictionary, it's hard to scan very many pages without finding something interesting or new. (The same is true of encyclopedias, atlases, and related reference works. That's why we display such books in our classrooms and invite browsing at any time.)

Finding the Right Dictionary

The biggest problem we've found with elementary dictionaries is that they are usually too hard for the students' grade level. Too often, the only sets of dictionaries available are most appropriate for the oldest students in the school, and many schools appear reluctant to invest in the simplest primary dictionaries or picture dictionaries that young children need. But without this investment, we'll continue to turn kids off year after year to this most useful resource.

For primary grades, you won't need a whole class set of dictionaries, but you will need at least five or six. We like to collect several copies of different dictionaries—some easier than others, so we can tell a student, "Look in the big green dictionary for that word," or "You'll probably find that word in the red picture dictionary." For elementary grades, the most important features to look for are *lavish use of illustrations, short entries, easy readability level*, and *durability of construction*. Overall, it's better for kids to use a dictionary that's too easy than one that's too hard.

A collection of dictionaries belongs in every classroom. We're always amazed to visit an elementary classroom that has no student dictionaries, or maybe only one adult version. Any teachers' supply catalog or library catalog will list a variety of children's dictionaries, and the principal or media specialist is the first person to ask to purchase them for your class. But if purchasing isn't possible, you may be able to supplement what's in your room by looking in the book storage room for single copies that were sent on approval, combining and sharing with another teacher, or finding usable copies at book fairs and library sales. With your principal's approval, you might also let parents or the PTA/PTO know that your students need more dictionaries, and that donations will be appreciated.

Teaching Dictionary Use

Teaching students to use a dictionary isn't hard, but you'll have to go over the same ground many times, keep dictionaries readily accessible to students, and keep reminding them that they can find the word they're puzzling over in a dictionary. To use one, students need to know the alphabet, so dictionary practice

---

BOX 5.4. Features to Look for in Primary Dictionaries

- Lavish illustrations, especially photographs.
- Short, concise entries.
- Easy readability level.
- Durability of paper, covers, and binding.

is a particularly useful activity for primary graders (who will probably need to refer to an alphabet strip as they go along). The key to using a dictionary efficiently is to know what section to go to, so that's where we begin.

Finding the Right Section

We show students that words appear in a dictionary in alphabetical order, and start by having them figure out which part of the book they'll be looking in. We *don't* want them to have to start looking on the first page! An effective way to do this is to divide the alphabet into either two or three sections. We create spaces in the alphabet displayed on the wall, and then divide the available dictionaries into corresponding sections.

We assign each section of the alphabet a color, and use colored paper strips to mark off the sections—say, *A–H* with red paper, *I–O* with blue, and *P–Z* with yellow. Kids can use colored markers to mark off the sections on their desktop alphabet strips. Then we use colored highlighter markers to mark off the corresponding sections of each dictionary, making a broad line down the right-hand edges of the pages with the book closed. In this way we don't mark on the pages themselves but on the very edges of each one, and it's easy to open the dictionary to the correct section. (If you're not allowed to mark on the volumes, you can use colored sticky notes to mark off the sections like bookmarks—but these notes come off!)

We spend a few practice sessions just having students figure out which third to look in and turn to it quickly. For example, we may say, "Where would I look to find the word *horse?*" Students check the alphabet strip, see that *H* is at the end of the first section, and turn to the first section. Some may actually be able to locate the *H* words, but mostly we work at first on just going to the right section. When everyone can do that fairly easily, we move to finding the specific part of the section—for example, turning to the *P* words for *pancakes,* and so forth. As yet we don't emphasize finding the exact word, but rather developing facility with getting close.

TEACHER'S TIP: Divide each classroom dictionary into thirds. Color-code each section with colored markers on the right-hand side of the closed pages. Have students mark the sections on their desktop alphabet strips.

Using the Guide Words

The next key skill we teach is the use of the *guide words*—the pairs of words at the top of each page that show the first and last entry on that page. Once students can find the right section of the alphabet, we show them how the guide words can help them find the right page quickly. This requires teaching them that after the first letter in a word, they have to look at the alphabetical order of the second letter, then the third, and so forth.

We do lots of alphabetizing practice even in upper grades, with students putting lists of words in correct order by first letters, second letters, third letters, and so forth. For first graders, we might have them practice with lists of five or six words at first, only two or three of which have the same first letter, and gradually make the task more challenging. With fourth graders, we might have them order lists of 15 or so words, all of which begin with the same letter and a few with the same *two* letters, and increase the difficulty gradually. (This is a good way to have them work with their spelling words and other content-area vocabulary.) Most students need more practice with this than you might think, and they must be able to do it in order to use a dictionary. If they can't alphabetize to at least the third or fourth letter, finding a word in the dictionary is more a matter of luck than of skill.

We then start selecting misspelled words from students' writing, or asking them to volunteer words they need to look up, and having them find the page with the correct pair of guide words. A useful dictionary practice activity is to give students a list of words, and have them find and write down the dictionary page number on which the word appears, using the guide words to help them find the page. Again, this is a good way to have them manipulating their spelling or vocabulary words, as well as other content-area words we want them to study.

Once they've learned how to use the guide words to find the page, it's a matter of scanning the entry words in each column to find the right word. We remind them to look only at the bold-print entry words until they find the correct entry; otherwise, finding the right word can take forever.

Once in a while, they'll find the right page, scan it carefully . . . and the word they're looking for just isn't there. Instant discouragement! That's one reason we like to have a variety of dictionaries available. An unusual word may not appear in a primary dictionary, whereas a common one may not be included in a harder volume. They may not *like* having to look in another dictionary for their word, but life is full of instances of having to seek somewhere else for an answer. This, too, is a useful skill to learn.

The following sample mini-lesson emphasizes using guide words to locate the correct page. It presumes that students already know how to turn to the right section and letter in the dictionary when they begin.

Sample Mini-Lesson: Using Dictionary Guide Words

Materials needed:

At least one dictionary for every two students in the group

Procedure:

1. Ask for volunteers to suggest words to look up that they've struggled with in their writing recently—for example, *fourteen*.

2. Select one of the words and ask the student to write or spell aloud the word as best he or she can—for example, *FORTEEN*.

3. Ask students to predict the word's first letter *(F)*, and to turn to the appropriate section in their dictionaries.

4. Ask students to predict the word's second letter *(FO)*, and to use the guide words to find the first page on which words beginning with *fo* appear.

5. Ask students to predict the word's third letter. In this case some will predict *R*, but some may suggest *U*. Ask for suggestions of alternative ways to spell the word, and suggest its relation to the word *four* if necessary. Ask students to find the page with the guide words having the same first three letters. (Continue until they have found the page with the word being sought.)

6. If they are now on the page that contains *fourteen*, direct them to scan the entry words until they find the word. Have the student who suggested the word read its correct spelling.

7. Briefly review the procedure for predicting and looking at each successive letter in the guide words. Then have pairs apply what they have learned by selecting misspelled words from their own recent writing to locate. Have each pair write the predicted spelling, the correct spelling, and the pair of guide words at the top of the page on which they found it.

EDITING AT THE COMPUTER

Students who have been composing and revising at the computer will find that editing is also simplified. You may need to review procedures for moving the cursor, placing the cursor just after an error, backspacing to remove text, and highlighting and deleting text for replacement.

Many word-processing programs contain a variety of editing aids that alert the writer to mechanical errors that have occurred. You'll need to review the editing aids available to your students, and be sure they know what they mean. For example, some programs will highlight or underline portions of text in which grammatical errors occur; others signal misspellings, or words that aren't in the computer's internal dictionary, by underlining, making the words appear in color, or producing an audible signal.

These programs can be very helpful to writers, but they also encourage students to revise and edit as they go along, rather than composing first and then revising and editing. Some students will have no difficulty with this, but others may need to keep the operations separate until they get all their ideas down. For those who want to edit in a separate step, tell them to ignore the signals and save their work as it is for later revision and editing.

BOX 5.5. Dictionary Guide Words Mini-Lesson Summary

1. Choose a word to look up.

2. Have students predict what the first letter is, and turn to that section in their dictionaries.

3. Repeat for second and third letters if necessary.

4. Ask students to find the page with the guide words having the same first three letters.

5. Teach students to scan entry words until they find the desired word.

6. Have students work in pairs to apply this skill by looking up selected words from recent writing.

Using the SCAN Strategy

The SCAN strategy (Harris and Graham, 1996) was first developed as a systematic way to help struggling writers revise and edit essays when using the computer. SCAN is an acronym for the four operations the writer is to perform as each sentence is reread (see Figure 5.6). Harris and Graham (1996) write:

> Each sentence is "scanned" to see if it is (1) *clear*—will the reader understand it; (2) *useful*—does it directly support the development [of the argument]; (3) *complete*—do more details need to be added to make the sentence better; and (4) *error free*—are there any mechanical errors that need to be corrected? . . . To help [students] remember these four evaluation criteria, the mnemonic SCAN is used to remind students of the key words: **Sense, Connected, Add, and Note errors.** (p. 103; emphasis in original)

SCAN each sentence:
- Does it make Sense?
- Is it Connected?
- Can I Add more?
- Note errors.

Make my changes on the computer.

FIGURE 5.6. SCAN strategy.

Adapted from Harris and Graham (1996, p. 107). Copyright 1996 by Brookline Books. Adapted by permission.

Using Spell-Check

Word-processing programs also contain *spell-check*, which is a feature that checks the spelling of every word in the text when commanded to do so. Each word is checked by the computer against its internal dictionary, and if a word is found that does not appear in the computer's dictionary, the program indicates that it is misspelled and usually suggests several alternatives that do occur in the dictionary.

This can be an aid to proofreading, but it also has shortcomings, as we have noted in Chapter 1. A computer cannot think; all it can do is look in its internal dictionary. If a word isn't there, it must be wrong. When we can't find a word in a dictionary, we may think that we've made a mistake, or we may think we have to look for it somewhere else.

What Spell-Check Can't Do

Almost all proper names will be highlighted as misspellings. Students have to learn to check the spellings of proper names themselves, and when they are written correctly, the computer must be commanded to ignore the apparent misspelling. The adequacy of the program's computer is also a factor; many words we use in various kinds of writing do not appear in any computer dictionary. In our own professional writing, for example, our software frequently queries our use of educational terms such as *freewriting* and *cloze procedure*. Again, students will have to learn to check terms with special usages by another means.

▣▣

TEACHER'S TIP: Teach students not to overdepend on spell-checking
as an editing tool.

▣▣

Perhaps the most important limitation of a spell-check program is this: It does not catch errors that really are words, but are errors in that particular context. For example, such a program would not catch errors in sentences like "We went to the mall *for* times," "*There* dog ran away," or "Don't *peak* at the birthday presents." In fact, you could type, *"Wee want too the maul fore teams,"* and a spell-check program would pass it right by. Remember, computers can't think; they can't read, in the sense of creating meaning from print; and they can't make decisions about the correctness of words that are not truly misspelled.

Teach your students *not* to overdepend on spell-checking as an editing tool. It's fine for catching typos that result in nonwords, but text has be to read for meaning in order to edit it correctly.

REFERENCES

Calkins, Lucy McCormick. *The Art of Teaching Writing* (new ed.). Portsmouth, NH: Heinemann, 1994.

Harris, Karen R., and Steve Graham. *Making the Writing Process Work: Strategies for Composition and Self-Regulation.* Cambridge, MA: Brookline Books, 1996.

Kemper, Dave, Ruth Nathan, and Patrick Sebranek. *Writers Express: A Handbook for Young Writers, Thinkers, and Learners.* Burlington, WI: Write Source, 1994.

Lane, Barry. *After the End: Teaching and Learning Creative Revision.* Portsmouth, NH: Heinemann, 1993.

CHAPTER 6

■■

Publishing, Sharing, and Celebrating

For writers, one of life's milestones comes the first time they see their work in print. Whether the product is a textbook or novel that took years to write, a poem or short story in a magazine, an article in an educational journal, or a carefully crafted letter to the local newspaper, publication is a thrilling event.

As a writer's familiar work is transformed into a new, strangely unfamiliar form by the process of publication, so too is the writer transformed by it. A momentous transformation has taken place: The person has gone from being a *writer* to being an *author*. Publication brings the writer to a new self-awareness. The writer now joins the world of authorship and becomes part of an inner circle of authors.

Authorship is no less thrilling and transforming for students, though their publication is on a smaller scale. Our students never tire of simply watching their pages emerge from the printer, transformed from handwriting or pieced-together typed pages into their final form. When groups of individuals publish books with typed pages, illustrations, and bound covers, the works become some of the favorite items in the classroom library. Day after day, these writers rhapsodize over their work.

"I never thought I could do it," they muse.

"Isn't my book beautiful? Do you want to hear it?" they ask any classroom visitor.

"For my next book, I think I'll . . ."

Teachers know that young children who handle books with enjoyment, are read to, and feel themselves capable of authorship progress as readers more quickly, successfully, and enjoyably than those whose book experience is limited. They also recognize that children who regularly take part in book projects, creating books of their own, reap the following benefits, to paraphrase Johnson (1997, pp. 10–11):

- Greater self-esteem and pride in their work.
- New awareness of themselves as storytellers, authors and artists.
- Growth in language fluency and vocabulary.
- Improved cooperation and interpersonal skills.
- Familiarity with book language and story structures.
- Growth in ability to plan ahead, develop strategies, and solve problems.
- Improved fine motor skills through practice folding, cutting, sewing, and manipulating art media.

Authorship changes students as readers, too. For example, after struggling to create believable action scenes, Patrick became more critical of such scenes in books; Lauren, who patiently revised her dialogues over and over, became a critical reader who read dialogue passages aloud to herself to savor the words. Once students have labored over their own writing, they become more aware of what commercial authors have achieved. Even young writers begin to wonder, "Why did this author begin the story in this way? What is it about this author's descriptions that makes readers able to see, hear, and feel these places? How did this writer create characters that seem so real?" Authorship enables students to make connections with the books they read. After they have become published authors, reading another's writing is never quite the same again.

That's why the final stage in the writing process—bringing the work to a wider audience—is such an important one. Whether the writing is published in a national magazine, a school literary journal, or a classroom book, publication brings writing to a wider audience. It gives the writing wings and, by association, gives the writer wings as well. Publication is not the end of the writing, but a new and different beginning: the beginning of the writing's own life, independent of the author.

We want to ensure that every writer who wants to publish does so "early and often." *Publication* need not necessarily mean producing a bound volume, although it often does; it can also mean learning and reciting each other's poetry, acting out another's play, mailing a letter to the newspaper, or following the steps in someone's recipe to prepare a class treat. In each way, we celebrate the completion of a project and give it its rightful, wider audience.

PUBLISHING AS A STUDENT-DIRECTED PROCESS

We have friends who regularly carry home tote bags of students' written work to be corrected, graded, and edited. They spend evenings and weekends choosing which piece of a student's work deserves to be published, and typing the pages for publication. Naturally, they tire of it and wonder why their students don't enjoy publishing more.

Their students don't enjoy it because they are not *doing* the publishing. These hard-working, well-meaning teachers have taken publication out of the students' hands, where it belongs, and have fallen into the trap we have described in Chapter 5: that of doing for students what they can and should be doing for themselves.

▣▣

TEACHER'S TIP: Let students take control of publishing their work.

▣▣

First of all, *writers should choose for themselves which works they will publish.* Doing so requires that writers develop objectivity about their work, sensitivity to their potential audience, and the ability to reflect on their own efforts. These are important skills that will be increasingly called on as children progress through the grades.

Second, *writers should choose what form their published work will take*. Not all writing is best showcased between covers as a book. Plays, for example, may best be shared by printing scripts and producing them. Poetry deserves to be recorded and recited, whereas expository writing might make a better accompaniment to a display or mural than a bound book.

Once they become published authors, writers will often begin to shape their work from the beginning toward a particular end. They begin to ask themselves, "What can I make of this? Could this be better as a poem than a story? Could this story be a play instead of a book? Where is it going?"

Third, *writers should decide for themselves when the revision and editing phases are completed* and a work is ready for publication. This often causes teachers problems, because most students think they're finished before their teachers do. We can urge students to continue to revise and edit their work until it is as good as they can make it, but we must let them retain the right to tell us when that is. We may have to bite the bullet on this issue, but if we want our students to experience authorship, we have to give them the right to decide the fate of a piece.

Students who rush a work into publication, leaving issues and errors uncorrected that they could have resolved with a little more work, may find their peers critical of just these aspects of the finished product. The power of audience is such that, having once published a poorly written or edited piece just to get it done, most writers will take more care the next time. The natural and logical consequence of not doing the best job possible is that readers are likely to be critical of the work. Many students learn this difficult but valuable lesson more quickly from peers than they ever would from us.

We once watched a very experienced teacher handle this issue in a way that was illuminating for us. Each time a writer brought her a revised, edited piece to be published, she would ask gravely, "Is this your very best work?" On this occasion the youngster bringing her the work had, we knew, given his first draft only a cursory read-through before showing it to her. "Evan, is this your very best work?" she asked. "Yep!," Evan replied breezily. "Can you tell me what you've done to make your story the best it can be?" she asked. "Well . . . ," Evan mumbled, "I . . . I didn't really . . . I guess I better read it over again." Taking his paper, he hurried back to his desk.

Later we asked what she thought made Evan decide to give his story a bit more work. "They know I expect their best work," she explained, "but they also know I think *they're* the best judges of that. I didn't have to tell him it wasn't his best. He knew it, because he hadn't done anything to improve it. He knew what he needed to do; he just didn't want to do it. If I'd told him, 'No, it's not done yet,' he would have gone back to his desk and wasted the rest of the time, resentful that I'd made him work on it more. This way, the effort came from him. Even if he only changes a couple of words, and the final product is far from perfect, he will have learned something of the responsibility that goes with owning the piece."

> **BOX 6.1. Guidelines for Student-Directed Publishing**
>
> **Writers should . . .**
> - Choose for themselves which works they want to publish.
> - Choose the form their published work will take.
> - Decide for themselves when a piece is ready for publication.

SIMPLE SHARING

Work need not be published and bound to be shared with a wider audience. It can be very rewarding for authors to read and show their work to their class-mates in a special, formal way. Reading their work to any attentive, interested audience, and displaying work in the classroom, a hallway, the library, an office, or a showcase, are other ways of sharing and celebrating work.

The Author's Chair

Many teachers use the Author's Chair to have students read their work to oth-ers, but often this technique is misused and its power diluted. Ideally the Au-thor's Chair is a special chair used only for this purpose, placed in such a way that listeners can group themselves around it comfortably, free of other distrac-tions. All attention should be focused on the reader; no one should be fiddling with papers, whispering to a friend, or finishing seatwork. However, we often see just these things happening during the so-called "sharing time."

Too often we've seen young writers sitting up at the front of the room, yards away from their audience, while listeners sit at their desks working on other work or playing with materials. We've listened to readers read their work haltingly and inaudibly, without rehearsal or preparation for reading aloud to the class. We've even seen teachers correcting homework or preparing lessons while a child reads, unwittingly presenting a negative model.

Such conditions devalue the process of sharing and celebrating writing. Children realize that they need not pay attention while someone else reads, and that it's not important to be able to read your own work fluently in a clear voice. We cringe when we see young authors trying to read to an uninterested, distracted audience. What will they do when someone else reads? What do they think of their own work?

Effective sharing doesn't just happen. You have to set up the environment so that it is conducive, not destructive, to sharing. These guidelines will help:

- ***Locate the reader close to the audience,*** so that everyone can see and hear.

• *Have listeners sit up,* with eyes on the speaker, ears open, and hands empty and still.

• *Be a model listener* **yourself.** Don't correct papers, read, or talk.

• *Limit the size of the audience.* it may be better to share with fewer listeners at a time.

• *Make being part of a listening audience an earned privilege.*

• *Require that authors rehearse* so that they can read their pieces smoothly, clearly, and expressively; give writers at least a day's preparation time. Also, allow reading only of finished work.

• *Never force a student to share* who doesn't want to. A few students may prefer to share in other ways (see the following section), or with only a small group of peers.

• *Require active listening* by expecting listeners to do something with what they've heard. For example, they can ask the writer a thoughtful question about the topic, identify a part they liked best, or draw a picture of something from the piece (a character, place, etc.). Thoughtful questions help the writer talk about the piece; they include such questions as "How did you learn about this topic?", "What part is your favorite?", "How long have you been working on this piece?", and "What was the hardest part of writing this?" Emphasize that questions and comments should be positive and encouraging in tone, and that it is not the job of listeners to share *their* experiences with the same topic.

TEACHER'S TIP: Teach and model active listening to create an
environment conducive to sharing.

BOX 6.2. Facilitating Good Listening

• Place the speaker close to the listeners.
• Have listeners sit up, with empty hands and eyes on the speaker.
• Model good listening.
• Limit audience size.
• Make it a privilege to be part of an audience.
• Require that speakers rehearse.
• Never force someone to share.
• Require listeners to ask questions, identify an interesting part, draw a picture, or the like.

Displaying Writing

Writing should be displayed around the room and in special displays in the hall, the library, and on the outside of your classroom door. Displaying work is another way of sharing it, so writers should revise and edit before their work is displayed.

Traditionally teachers have displayed children's work as a reward. However, this has drawbacks: The teacher, not the writer, selects which work will be displayed; and some students may have work displayed more frequently than others. These are good reasons to think of displaying writing not as a reward or a room decoration, but as another means of publishing it.

TEACHER'S TIP: Let students help choose work to be displayed.

Displayed writing can be used to teach and reinforce writing skills. If students are working on a particular skill, displayed work can demonstrate and celebrate their progress. Such displays might include examples of how writers have experimented with different leads, written vivid descriptions, created effective titles, or organized paragraphs. Displays help writers remember what they are learning, and are informative to parents and other visitors. Students themselves can decide what skills to showcase and which examples should be included.

A continuing display of "work in progress" is useful for demonstrating how writers use the stages of writing to progress from initial ideas to final products. Students save and date their successive drafts and revisions to display in consecutive order. A "work in progress" bulletin board can stay up all year, with displayed materials changed periodically to show different aspects of drafting, revision, and editing, and to give all writers opportunities for inclusion.

Displays can be used to showcase students' self-selected "best work," but it is important to make sure that all students are included. "Student of the Week" or "Writer of the Week" displays can include writing as well as other work the selected student chooses. Every student should be featured in turn. Also, students can mark their favorite part of displayed work, freeing them from the expectation that the entire piece has to be "best."

Student writing doesn't have to be elaborately displayed. Some teachers insert the writing into inexpensive plastic photo frames or art-store picture mats, which can be used over and over and are easy to hang or stand for display. Others "frame" final drafts with borders of colorful plastic mending tape, or old bulletin-board borders, around all four edges of the paper to hang on a bulletin board or wall. Laminating some pieces may also be a possibility.

However work is displayed, some important things to remember are the following:

BOX 6.3. Types of Displays and Ways to Display Writing

Some types of displays:

- To show off a new skill (lead writing, effective titles, paragraph organization, etc.).
- "Work in progress."
- "Student of the Week."
- Writing on a common theme.
- Writing in a common genre.

Some ways to display writing:

- Mount it on a banner.
- Create a bulletin board.
- Write it on sentence strips.
- Frame it.
- Border it with colorful tape or bulletin-board border strips.
- Laminate it.

- Displays should teach, reinforce, and inform, not just decorate the room or reward writers.
- Students should view displaying as a form of publishing, and should be active in selecting the means and the work to be displayed.
- All students should have equal opportunities to publish their work by displaying it if they so choose.
- Having work displayed outside the classroom can be highly motivating to many writers.

MAKING BOOKS

Transforming a student's writing into book form makes it permanent, and may be a fulfilling culmination to the writing process. We are often surprised at how many times students from past years have told us how much pleasure and pride they experienced when their writing was published in book form.

Group Books

The simplest books are collections of individual papers with simple covers of tagboard, construction paper, wallpaper, or similar sturdy materials stapled together along one side; such books are referred to as *side-bound*. Side-bound books are fine for group efforts, especially in primary grades, where all the children contribute a page by writing or dictating and illustrating. These books have instant appeal because everyone helps write them, and they quickly become classroom library favorites. The writing done is often highly structured and predictable, which makes it easy for everyone to read.

For example, primary group books often feature letter recognition, counting, and concepts like colors and shapes (e.g., *What Is Round?* or *A Big Book of Big Things.*). Each student is given a page or two with a sentence to copy, such as "A _____ is round," or "A _____ is big." They draw or cut out magazine pictures of objects illustrating the concept for each page, and write or dictate the object word to fill the space. Illustrated pages are collected and stapled or bound together. This creates a simple, predictable book in which each page has almost the same words, with the new words on each page illustrated. Books like these are quick and easy to make and to read, reinforce familiar concepts, and give participants an authorship experience. Some sample book topics, with examples of titles we've used, are as follows:

- Colors and patterns (*Things That Are Red*; *What Has Stripes?*)
- Alphabet letters (*Our Alphabet Picture Book*; *What Starts with B?*)
- Shapes (*What Is Round?*; *Rectangles Are Everywhere*)
- Textures (*Fuzzy Things*; *Soft and Hard*; *The Big Book of Squishy Stuff*)
- Numbers (*One to Ten*; *How Many?*)
- Familiar objects (*What's in the Kitchen?*; *Favorite Animals*; *Foods We Love*)

Group books are not just for primary graders, and need not have a highly structured format like those above. Group books or anthologies can be created from collected works on a shared theme, such as jokes, Halloween stories, pet stories, or autobiographies. Students can begin to collaborate by agreeing on a topic. They can then contribute individual episodes to a fictional saga, or can do research and expository writing on such topics as *Caring for Dogs and Puppies* or *The History of Our Town*.

Such group projects are excellent for integrating writing into subject areas like science, social studies, and health. Each contributor's part may be revised and edited, with final productions typed on the computer or handwritten for inclusion. Some group members may specialize in creating illustrations or visual aids like charts and maps, as well as writing.

For example, our sixth graders one year wrote and illustrated biographies of famous men and women of the Revolutionary War period, in conjunction with their study of that time period in social studies. Each student received a copy of the whole collection. Likewise, students created several volumes of poetry to which each student contributed an original poem; the finished poems were typed, duplicated, and distributed to all students and other interested teachers.

Individual Books

From contributing to group books, students can move to producing their own individual books. Many writers view producing their own bound books as the pinnacle of authorship. It provides an impetus for putting in the necessary effort at revising and editing to create a polished final version.

The subjects and types of books produced are limited only by students' imaginations and interests. Books don't have to be rectangular; covers and pages can be cut after tracing around a large simple shape corresponding to the topic, like a snowman, truck, house, apple, basketball, or fish. (Collections of templates for making dozens of such "shape books" are widely available at teachers' stores and in school supply catalogs.)

The most durable and permanent books are made with sewn bindings and will last from year to year, with moderate care in handling. They are perfect for work students really want to preserve, such as pieces for a Young Authors' Conference or books to be presented to parents, classroom volunteers, teachers, the school library, or other classes.

When final drafts are ready to be bound into a sewn binding, students use sheets of unlined paper folded down the middle to create double pages (usually three to six sheets per set). They copy or type their finished text onto the pages (some word-processing software has templates that produce double pages), and include illustrations. Then they sew the double pages together along the fold with a needle and thread. The sets of sewn pages, called *folios*, are glued securely into separate covers made of cardboard covered with decorative paper, wallpaper, fabric, or other materials. Finished writing and illustrations can also be cut and pasted onto already sewn pages. Younger writers may prefer this method, since the blank pages are already attached to the book. The steps in making sewn books are shown in Figure 6.1.

Older students can sew their own folios; younger ones will need adult help. Responsible older students can sometimes be drafted to help younger ones sew their pages. (This is a great project for an older class teamed with another class of younger students as "buddies.") Some teachers ask volunteers to sew together folios of three to six folded pages each and keep them on hand to give out as needed. (This is a project that can be done at home by adults who want to help but can't volunteer during the school day, or by a school Scout troop or service club.)

Some teachers have writers compose a few sentences about themselves or complete an "About the Author" form (see Figure 6.2) to be glued inside the covers of these books. A student can also complete a biographical statement and glue a school picture to it; a photocopy is then placed in each book the student produces. Students' own books should be prominently displayed and readily available for pleasure reading. Your school media specialist can probably provide you with checkout cards and pockets to glue into the books, if you want them to circulate.

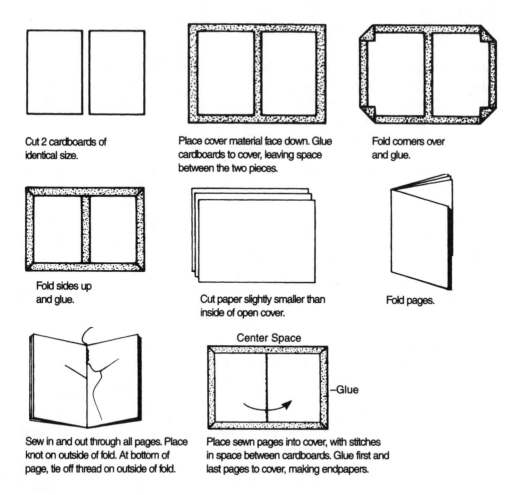

Cut 2 cardboards of identical size.

Place cover material face down. Glue cardboards to cover, leaving space between the two pieces.

Fold corners over and glue.

Fold sides up and glue.

Cut paper slightly smaller than inside of open cover.

Fold pages.

Sew in and out through all pages. Place knot on outside of fold. At bottom of page, tie off thread on outside of fold.

Place sewn pages into cover, with stitches in space between cardboards. Glue first and last pages to cover, making endpapers.

FIGURE 6.1. Steps in making a sewn book.
From Temple and Gillet (1996, p. 231). Copyright 1996. Reprinted by permission of Allyn & Bacon.

ILLUSTRATING BOOKS

Illustrations in children's books used to be thought of as merely decorative. Now we know that illustrations are very nearly as important as the text. Most often it is the illustrations, not the text, that first attract children to a book. We recognize that children "read" illustrations as another way of getting information from books, and that illustrations paralleling the written text provide a rich context for creating meaning.

When children illustrate their own writing, particularly their original stories, they must create images that support and enhance the meaning of their words. They learn to interrelate the language of words and the language of images. Doing so enhances their communication skills, understanding of stories, and creativity.

My name is _____ .

I am _____ years old. I am in grade _____ .

My teacher is _____ . Some things I really like

are _____ , _____ , and _____ .

Some of my favorite things to do are _____ , _____ , and

_____ .

I wrote this book because _____

_____ .

Here's my picture:

FIGURE 6.2. "About the Author" form.

But many teachers think teaching children illustration is the art teacher's responsibility, and many admit that they "couldn't draw a stick," as one colleague confessed to us. That's unfortunate, because children can quickly pick up on the negative notion that only what they call "good drawers" should try to illustrate their books. This notion is just about as nonsensical and destructive as thinking that only good writers should write stories, or only good readers should read books! Teaching about illustration isn't about art at all; it's really about understanding and planning stories, and how to support the text with pictures.

It's good for all writers to think about and experiment with ways to support and extend the meaning of their words with illustrations, regardless of their artistic skill. Whether or not the teacher is "artistic" is also unimportant. Teaching children a little about illustration helps deepen their understanding of how stories are conveyed, extends their appreciation of the effort involved in creating commercial books, and gives them a challenging, satisfying authorship experience.

□□

TEACHER'S TIP: Teach students that story illustrations support the text by sharing and discussing illustrations in books and magazines.

□□

Using Literature Models

Before we taught our students anything about illustration, we noticed several things about their spontaneous illustrations. One was that they often drew pictures that were quite unrelated to the story. For example, Cherrelle frequently illustrated her writing with heart-shaped balloons, although they had nothing at all to do with the text; Tavon often drew large tree-like plants, no matter what the topic. Many decorated their pages with colorful designs and borders that added nothing to the story, or drew buildings, weapons, and vehicles that were similarly unrelated. It seemed clear that illustration meant decoration rather than extending the story line.

By systematically studying the pictures in well-illustrated books, however, students discovered that illustrators didn't just draw what they liked, or what they were good at drawing; instead, the artists thoughtfully considered what the story was about when they illustrated. Even young students were able to come up with important generalizations about what illustrators did and didn't do. By looking at a wide variety of trade books, they discovered that *they had to think carefully about the story* in order to illustrate their books. This is an obvious conclusion to adults, but not so obvious to children, and it was an important step for them. When they realized that they weren't really free to draw whatever they liked, their illustrations changed in fundamental ways, and we realized that they were beginning to make a deeper connection with their stories.

We periodically planned short lessons in which we would present one or more examples of good illustration, inviting children to talk about what they saw. Sometimes we looked at two or three examples of large, double-page illustrations, and pointed out that these illustrations often occur in the middle of a story, where a lot of action is taking place. Other times we looked at how authors often alternate a page of text with a page of illustration; how some authors use a series of small pictures to show action instead of one large one; or how borders can be used to show details about a story, as well as to decorate pages.

Invariably, whatever we had recently discovered together would show up in some form in someone's pictures, immediately or a few days later. We were always glad to see our students take some piece of information and try to incorporate it into their own work.

▣▣▣

TEACHER'S TIP: Use high-quality literature to examine effective illustrating styles. Point out particular features, and invite children's observations.

▣▣▣

Once we began studying illustrations with students, as well as reading the stories to them, we found that students spent more time reading and looking at trade books, and that they began to discuss and analyze illustrations as well as the stories, thus deepening their interest in and appreciation of trade books. (See Appendix A for a list of children's books that can be used to teach mini-lessons on illustrating styles.)

Dividing a Story into Parts

An effective way we found to help students illustrate their stories was to introduce, or reteach, the idea that a story has a beginning, a middle, and an end. We used three-panel *story maps* like the one shown in Figure 6.3 to help them organize summaries of stories they'd read and heard into three major parts. This helped them learn to extract the most important idea from each part and ignore details and side issues. As they became more skilled at stating the most important beginning, middle, and final events in a story, they began to incorporate these features into their own stories; they began to plan and discuss the beginnings, middles, and ends of their stories before they wrote them, instead of letting them ramble all over. This resulted in better-organized, more coherent stories that readers could more easily understand and enjoy.

We continued to draw upon literature models, pointing out how authors used the beginning of a story to introduce the characters, setting, and problem or goal; the middle to create action and propel the story forward; and the end to resolve the problem and tie up loose ends. This helped our students better understand and appreciate the stories they read, and tighten up their own stories.

Once your students understand this organizational concept, can write and illustrate these parts from familiar stories (as Leslie, then a second grader, did in Figure 6.3), and begin to organize their original stories in this way, it is only a short step to have students create illustrations for the beginnings, middles, and ends of their stories. Because they have thought carefully about the parts of their stories, their illustrations tend to be much better integrated into the stories, and much more meaningful. We were pleased to see fewer heart-shaped

FIGURE 6.3. Leslie's story map of *Curious George and the Pizza*.
From Temple and Gillet (1996, p. 193). Copyright 1996. Reprinted by permission of Allyn & Bacon.

balloons and tree-like plants, and more use of the stories, in our students' illustrations! We knew this meant that the students were making much deeper connections with their stories, and thinking harder about communicating their ideas to their readers.

Using Storyboards

A *storyboard* is a visual organizer for a story. It is a more complex organizer than the three-part story map, because it has as many elements as the book will have pages. Storyboards allow writers to plan what will happen on each page of the story, and what will be most important in each illustration. Figure 6.4 shows a blank storyboard for a six-page story.

Using a storyboard is a highly structured approach to planning a story and its illustrations. It helps writers develop greater skill in crafting a narrative, extracting the main developments, and sequencing events. Students' story sense is enhanced by using a storyboard to plan their writing.

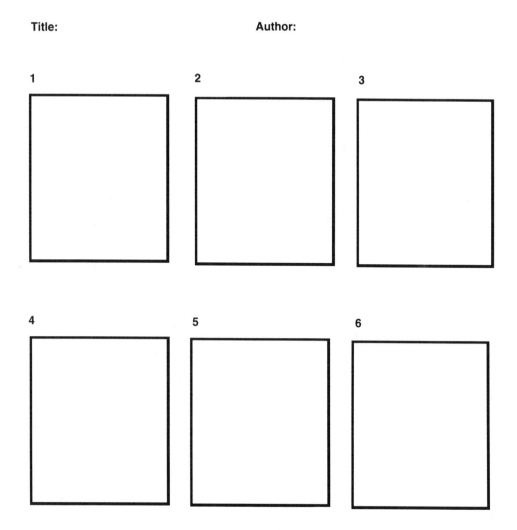

FIGURE 6.4. Blank storyboard.

This figure is adapted from *Pictures and Words Together: Children Illustrating and Writing Their Own Books* by Paul Johnson. Copyright 1997 by Paul Johnson. Used by permission of the publisher, Heinemann, a division of Reed Elsevier Inc., Portsmouth, NH.

TEACHER'S TIP: Use a storyboard to help students plan
and illustrate a story.

Since illustrations must follow the story, writers' first task is to condense their stories into as many parts as their books will have pages. As with the simpler story maps, they must develop the main ideas, but their stories can be more elaborate with more main parts. Writers must mentally pull out those main ideas, then decide how they will break up their stories so that something important happens on each page. These main ideas are written in condensed form in each box on the storyboard, as David, a first grader, did in his story about dinosaurs (see Figure 6.5).

Writers then use their storyboards to actually write each page of their story. Here they can add details and "flesh out" their narratives, as long as they stick to

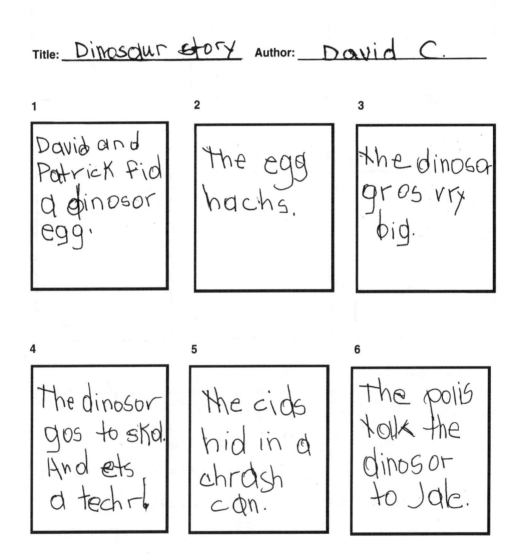

Title: Dinosaur story   Author: David C.

1

David and Patrick fid a dinosor egg.

2

The egg hachs.

3

the dinosa gros vry big.

4

The dinosor gos to skol. And ets a techr.

5

the cids hid in a chrash can.

6

the polis tolk the dinosor to Jale.

FIGURE 6.5. David's completed storyboard.

This figure is adapted from *Pictures and Words Together: Children Illustrating and Writing Their Own Books* by Paul Johnson. Copyright 1997 by Paul Johnson. Used by permission of the publisher, Heinemann, a division of Reed Elsevier Inc., Portsmouth, NH.

the original story line they have created. We encouraged our students to write their drafts of each page on a separate, numbered page so there would be plenty of room for revisions; they were not given the actual folios to write on, or to glue their typed final copies on, until after they had completed revision and editing.

When the text for each page had been planned, written, revised, and edited, they turned their attention to planning their illustrations for each page. After the careful planning they had done for their stories, it was much easier for the students to create illustrations that supported and extended the stories, rather than just decorating the pages.

Finally, we showed our students how to plan the layout of their books, using a book layout template like that shown in Figure 6.6. Again we referred to literature models to show how book planners place the text and illustrations in different places on pages, and sometimes incorporate the print as part of the illustration, for visual variety. Students can use a layout template to plan where their text and illustrations will be placed on each page, and to plan the appearance of their covers.

Taking the time to teach your students these fundamental aspects of story illustration will add enormously to their understanding of stories, their ability to plan and create organized narratives, and their appreciation of high-quality literature. It will also give students' pride and self-esteem a great boost, as they produce books they are proud to publish and share.

YOUNG AUTHORS' CONFERENCES

A *Young Authors' Conference* (or *Young Writers' Conference*) is a writing project in which individuals, classrooms, and even entire schools participate. Weeks of sustained effort may be spent writing, revising, editing, illustrating, and publishing fiction, nonfiction, and poetry. If a competitive component is planned, work can be evaluated by panels of judges, and honors can be awarded.

The effort may culminate in a variety of ways, such as a Book Fair, opportunities for children to share their work with a wide audience, or a visit from an author or illustrator of children's books. Young Authors' Conferences are held annually at many schools and colleges. They can be highly motivating experiences for young writers, and great culminations of extended units of study in writing and publishing.

These events are often held in the spring or late in a school year. Children in participating classrooms begin producing compositions several months beforehand, and eventually choose work that will be revised and edited for final production. Categories such as fiction, nonfiction, poetry, and drama may be specified in advance.

Young Authors' Conferences are often organized into phases or units corresponding to the stages in the writing process, so that each participating class works in unison toward the final production. Phase 1, usually several weeks

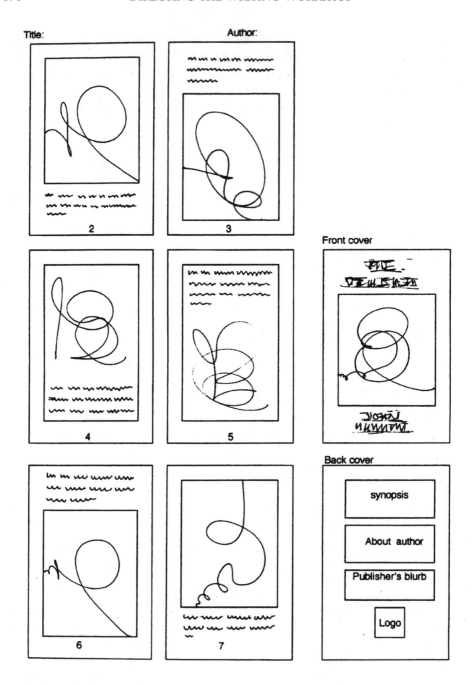

FIGURE 6.6. Book layout template.

This figure is reprinted from *Pictures and Words Together: Children Illustrating and Writing Their Own Books* by Paul Johnson. Copyright 1997 by Paul Johnson. Used by permission of the publisher, Heinemann, a division of Reed Elsevier Inc., Portsmouth, NH.

BOX 6.4. Some Ways for Students to Publish Their Writing

- Read it from the Author's Chair.
- Create a display for the classroom, hallway, office, or showcase.
- Make group books (multiple authors).
- Make individual books (a single author).
- Make a single book copy for display or circulation; or type it, print it, and duplicate multiple copies for distribution.
- Have a Young Authors' Conference.
- Record the author reading the work aloud and put it in a listening center.
- Create a puppet who "tells" the story in a puppet theater.
- Give it to a special person as a gift.
- Create a collection of student-written books for the classroom or school library.
- Read it to another class, the principal, or other staff members.
- Read it over the intercom.

---

long, is devoted to direct instruction and each writer's production of a variety of early drafts from which to choose. Phase 2 is devoted to the actual production of final manuscripts and can be subdivided into units on editing, illustrating, and binding books. During this phase, each student selects a composition for final work, revises and edits it, and produces it as an illustrated bound book. Phase 3, the culmination of the project, is devoted to evaluating and sharing the published works.

Typically criteria for evaluating work are determined and agreed upon at the beginning of Phase 1, often by students and teachers working together. Both content and form are important. Aspects of content that are considered include story originality, creativity, characterization, and dialogues, as well as organization and clarity of nonfiction writing. Aspects of form that are important include correctness of mechanics, neat writing and binding, and illustrations.

Some Young Authors' Conferences are essentially writing contests. In these, each classroom selects its best work in each category to be evaluated with similar works from other classes of the same grade, and a panel of evaluators is created that may include teachers, students, administrators, parents, and special guests (e.g., local authors, book editors, or college writing professors).

Other Young Authors' Conferences focus less on competing than on sharing. Any evaluation occurs within the individual classroom, and awards other than those for participation are deemphasized. Sharing activities—such as Book

Fairs; "read-ins"; visits by children's authors, illustrators, and/or editors; or field trips to a publishing company or book bindery—are the highlights of this type of conference.

⬚⬚

TEACHER'S TIP: Young Authors' Conferences can be competitive
or not, by design.

⬚⬚

Whether competition and awards are emphasized or deemphasized, it is important for every participant to be recognized as successful. Attractive certificates of participation, signed by the teacher and principal, are appropriate for every writer. Works that are judged to be exemplary can be given a fancy gold seal for the cover or a special bookplate inside. Every writer should participate in whatever culminating activities are planned. In any Young Authors' Conference, there may be special awards or recognitions, but every writer should feel like a winner.

REFERENCES

Johnson, Paul. *Pictures and Words Together: Children Illustrating and Writing Their Own Books.* Portsmouth, NH: Heinemann, 1997.
Temple, Charles, and Jean Wallace Gillet. *Language and Literacy.* New York: HarperCollins, 1996.

CHAPTER 7

□□

The Special Demands of Nonfiction Writing

In previous chapters, we have discussed how writers negotiate the journey from ideas to finished writing. We have not distinguished in most instances between narrative (fiction) and expository (nonfiction) writing, but have frequently referred to both "stories" and "pieces." Much of the time, especially when we are dealing with issues facing beginning writers, we have discussed writing as it relates to personal expression and creation.

But as students progress through the grades, school writing requires them to be effective communicators of ideas and information. Much of the writing that students do in school—and that adults do—is nonfiction writing. In this chapter, we turn our attention to the special demands and rewards of nonfiction writing: *personal writing*, which includes various kinds of journals and letters; and *subject-area writing*, which includes informational reports, book reports, directions, summaries, and journalism.

THE MANY FACES OF JOURNALS

Journals are so widely used that whole books have been written about them. A journal is simply a vehicle for personal writing, for rereading and reflection, and/or for sharing with and responding to others. Used effectively, journal writing . . .

- Helps students of all ages create a record of thoughts, observations, ideas, and opinions.
- Encourages the process of putting thoughts into words.
- Allows writers to revisit past thinking.
- Fosters reflection and self-awareness.
- Provides a means of documenting writing growth over time.
- Enables teachers and students to integrate personal response with subject-area learning.
- Allows writers to participate in dialogue with others.

Journals can be powerful writing tools, but in our experience they are often vastly underutilized. When journals are mentioned, many teachers think only of notebooks used for unstructured free writing, used mostly to ensure that students write for a few minutes every day. To many students, journal time means getting out that notebook, writing without purpose or reflection, and putting it away unread when the time is up. They rarely revisit their journals or use them for any reflective or self-evaluative purposes.

In the following sections, we describe more productive ways to use journals in the classroom. A bibliography of children's books featuring journal writing is also included in Appendix B.

BOX 7.1. Types of Journal Writing

- Personal
- Response
- Dialogue
- Subject-area

Personal Journals

Many teachers have students keep journals to record their personal lives. This is probably the best-known purpose of a journal. Such journals are first-person records of daily life, feelings, ideas, reflections, and memories. Adults who enjoy writing in journals usually keep this kind. In the classroom, personal journals can serve several purposes: They can help students develop writing fluency, help students find their own individual voices, and provide a safe place to experiment with different kinds of writing.

Most of the time, students' writing in personal journals is innocuous, and students may enjoy sharing their writing with the teacher or each other. But sometimes students use their personal journals to deal with very private feelings or events. It is important to make reasonable efforts to protect students' privacy when we ask them to keep personal journals at school. Some guidelines to keep in mind are the following:

- Warn students that complete privacy cannot be ensured in a classroom.
- Caution students against writing anything they don't want others to see.
- Remind students that there may be better ways to deal with difficult personal issues than journal writing—for example, talking privately with the teacher, counselor, or school nurse.
- Avoid *requiring* students to write about events or feelings they may wish to keep private.
- If students will be expected to share particular entries, tell them so beforehand, or allow them to select an entry to share.
- Encourage students to write about a diversity of topics, not just very personal or negative ones.

Personal writing that is not reread or reflected upon is largely meaningless to writers. It is important to encourage students to periodically reread and rethink what they have already written. Often ideas for stories, poems, songs, and other writings may be gleaned from it. Also, reexamining what they once

---

**BOX 7.2. Guidelines for Protecting
the Privacy of Journal Writers**

- Writers should not expect complete privacy.
- Writers should not write what others shouldn't see.
- Encourage writers to discuss personal difficulties with responsible adults.
- Don't require writing about private matters.
- Tell writers beforehand if they are expected to share.
- Allow writers to choose what they will share.
- Encourage writing about many things, not just personal or negative topics.

---

thought or felt allows students to see the ways in which they are changing and maturing. Dating entries as they are written helps writers see what their concerns and issues were at different points in time. Journal writing accompanied by reflection can be an opportunity for personal growth. This is perhaps the most common reason for adults to keep private journals.

Many teachers mistakenly believe that any interest in or response to students' personal writing is an invasion of their privacy. However, since this writing is an instructional activity, it is teachers' responsibility to monitor and respond to writers and their work in such a way that both teachers and writers feel comfortable. Certainly it is unnecessary for a teacher to routinely read each child's journal, and in fact such close scrutiny would be likely to inhibit many older students. But when teachers show little interest in their journals, and make no attempt to monitor or use them, students often devalue their own efforts. A teacher's response to the writing often helps keep interest and involvement high and helps writers be more reflective.

TEACHER'S TIP: Read and reread your students' journals, and encourage them to do so as well.

Many teachers peruse students' journals occasionally, as a way to monitor students' writing development and the issues with which they are dealing. Checks, stars, stickers, or occasional written comments or questions let writers know that their teachers are periodically in touch with what they're writing.

Many problems (such as copying the same entry over and over, or writing hurtful things about others) can be headed off when students know a teacher will read their journals.

Occasionally, however, serious issues surface that require intervention by a teacher or other school personnel. Violent threats against people or property, incidents of sexual or other harassment, violence or danger in the home, or suicidal thoughts are sometimes disclosed in a journal by a student who needs an adult to confide in, but is afraid or unwilling to speak of these issues directly. Common sense (and in many places the law) requires a teacher to confront such issues first with the student, and then with school supervisory personnel. In such incidents, *concern for safety may overrule privacy*.

When students do the same things day after day, boredom often results. You can help keep interest high by occasionally varying the format of personal writing. Instead of always letting students freewrite, occasionally provide a general topic: a holiday, family celebration, or tradition; memoirs of early childhood; or descriptions of a favorite relative, food, movie, season, or place. Encourage students to keep a topic list in their journals for times when they are stuck, or to make lists as an occasional alternative to narrative writing.

Sometimes just varying the writing materials can give writers a lift. Allow them to write occasionally with markers or colored pencils, or on special papers that can be glued into the journal. Younger students especially enjoy such simple variations in the usual routine.

Response Journals

A *response journal* provides a forum for personal reflection and written response to literature and/or to subject-area learning. These journals are sometimes called *learning logs* or *literature logs*. Writing in a response journal is still personal, but has a different focus than the personal journals described previously: Students write about their responses to things they are reading and learning about, rather than their own personal lives.

Response journals encourage students to respond emotionally, critically, and cognitively to what they read and learn. They can also help students develop higher-order thinking skills and a deeper understanding of subject-area issues. Responses go farther than simple summaries or main-idea statements; these are often included in written responses, but a deeper, more complex response is required—that of criticism, evaluation, and personal reflection. Responding requires students to think with their hearts as well as with their brains.

How can students respond reflectively or critically to what they are reading or learning? Students generally write better responses if they are given *a type of question* or *a kind of response* to use, rather than being told to "Respond to . . ." In response journals, students are encouraged to wonder, speculate, predict, question, and explore their feelings and reactions to literature and subject-area content.

Figure 7.1 lists some typical ways that children in elementary and middle school can be expected to ponder and respond in writing. We make sure students have had lots of opportunities to discuss stories and topics in these ways before we expect them to write such responses. Figure 7.2 is a list of suggestions for response writing; these can be posted in the classroom, to remind students of the many different ways they can choose to respond to a topic or reading selection.

It is most helpful to review periodically with students what *response* is and what it is not. Response is *personal reaction and reasoned evaluation*, and is unique to each individual. It is not merely a factual summary, a sequential list of steps or events, or an opinion without reasoning or supporting argument. The sugges-

Monitoring my own understanding:

Summarizing
Telling about characters
"This reminds me of . . ."

Making inferences or predictions:

"I think . . ."
"It sounds like . . ."
"He probably will . . ."
"She might . . ."

Interacting with characters:

"I know how she feels . . ."
"I feel sorry for . . ."
"_____ is so much like my brother. He should . . ."

Assessing characters:

"She was brave when she . . ."
"He is stupid to . . ."
"It's really mean of them to . . ."

Literary criticism (beyond "I like," if possible)

"I loved this part of the book because . . ."
"The strongest part of this book was . . ."
"This part was boring (or exciting, scary, sad, etc.) because . . ."
"I don't think the author should have them . . ."

FIGURE 7.1. Typical responses by children and preadolescents to their reading.
From Temple and Gillet (1996, p. 285). Copyright 1996. Reprinted by permission of Allyn & Bacon.

tions for response writing shown in Figure 7.2 can be helpful in teaching students how to write responses.

Even when learners are in agreement about an issue, each one's response will be unique. At any grade, you can expect great divergence in students' willingness and ability to respond critically, aesthetically, and emotionally. It may take months or longer for students to adapt their thinking and ways of responding to what they are learning. But we believe it's worth it, because true learning requires an emotional investment as well as a cognitive one. Learning that is purely cognitive rarely leaves a lasting impression on the learner.

□□□

TEACHER'S TIP: Periodically review with students what response
is and is not.

□□□

Figure 7.3 shows a very simple response written by a first grader to a short unit on spiders. Although Shanice did not appear to hold spiders in great esteem in spite of learning a body of facts about them, she demonstrated that she now knew the names of several kinds of spiders, which was more than she knew at the beginning of the unit. Figure 7.4 shows entries from some fourth graders' literature response journals; the titles indicate the books these students were writing about. The entries in italics are queries written by the teacher, to encourage each writer to move away from simple summaries toward more reflective re-

1. What you liked or disliked, and why.

2. What you wish had happened differently.

3. What you wish the author had included.

4. Your opinion of the character(s).

5. Your opinion of the illustrations or other visuals.

6. What you were reminded of as you read.

7. What you felt as you read.

8. What you noticed about *how* you read.

9. What you wondered about as you read.

10. Questions you have after reading.

FIGURE 7.2. Response writing: Suggestions for students.
From Gillet (1999). Reprinted by permission of the author.

I DOt LiKe

SPIDERS bo keks

they Ar UgLY

ANd I DOt

LiKe BICK wido

ANd Tarantula ANd
w6lf spider.

FIGURE 7.3. Shanice's response to spiders.

sponses. (Journal entries that also develop a teacher–student *dialogue* are discussed in greater detail in the section that follows.)

Dialogue Journals

Whereas personal and response journals are intended primarily for private dialogue with oneself, another way of using a journal is to converse in writing with another. Dialogue journals can be used to create written conversations between a student and teacher.

When writers are finished with their journal entries for a particular day, they place their journals in a box or tray to be read by the teacher. After each entry, the teacher writes a comment or a question, or in some other way responds to the writing. These comments or questions are part of a *written conversation*—not criticism or correction of the writing. (Such correction can be given face to face, or in another context, unless the writing is illegible.) Nor is the teacher supposed to serve as an expert, solve problems, or tell students what to do next. Friendly, interested, noncritical responses to writers' message help the writers expand on their topics, explore what they know and feel, and value their communication skills.

Figure 7.5 is an example taken from a fourth grader's journal. In this example the teacher responded with interest to the topic, asked questions that might help the writer add more information, and was an encouraging reader. She refrained from correcting, directing, or challenging the writer. The student wrote

---

The Enormous Crocodile

I like the trick when he was triying to acted like a woodend corcodile trieing to make the girl get on his back but the bird came and said do not git on his back and that's what I like about the 3rd trick.

I like that trick too; I liked how he tucked his head and tail under him to look more like a bench.

He had a hard time tucking his head but he did it.

Do you think he deserved to get "burned up like a sausage" in the sun?

Yes because he was bad. He was going to eat the children. I feel a littel sorry for him thogh.

Pioneer Cat

Duffy said when can we see some buffalos? And then Rosie came over and play with each other. Sometimes like Rosie come to Kates wagen and Kate go over to Rosies wagen. Kate said I fell sick from the buffalos blud. Kate Pa and brother had them a gun so they can eat somethang.

How did you feel as you read the part about the buffalo hunt?

It made me feel sad and sick. I did not want them to shoote the buffalos. I would feel sick if I had to see all that blud.

Do you think they should have shot the buffalo?

I think they should have something else to eat not shoot the buffalos.

How else would they get fresh food, fresh meat to eat? Did they need to eat meat?

I gess they did they need to have meat but maybe they could find somethang eles to eat. But they would have to shoot that too. They just had to be tuff about it. I dont think I could be a Pioneer.

FIGURE 7.4. Entries from two fourth graders' literature response journals.
From Temple and Gillet (1996, p. 286). Copyright 1996. Reprinted by permission of Allyn & Bacon.

about the topic of the family hike until a more immediate event caused her to change topics. In each exchange, the student was supported by the teacher's personal interest.

Although this example shows that the teacher read and responded to this student's writing on three consecutive days, this is certainly not the norm or the expectation. Many teachers like the idea of dialogue journals, but wonder how they can find the time to respond so frequently. It is certainly *not* necessary to

May 8

This weekend my mom, dad, sister and me went on a hike along the creek. We all wore our boots so we could walk in the creek. We started at the bridge near our house. We walked for a long way, past where the creek goes under the railroad tracks, until we got to a place where the creek got so deep that we couldn't wade anymore. So we had to turn back. My sister was mad because she wanted to go on. We tried to walk along the bank but the bank was very steep and everywhere there was tons of poison ivy. Only my dad had pants on so he wouldn't get poison ivy, but he was afraid of snakes.

Your hike sounds like a really neat experience! Do you know how far you went before you had to turn back? Did your dad see any snakes?

May 9

On the hike we did not see any snakes, but we saw a lot of little fish, one big fish and some holes in the bank where things lived. My mom climbed up a steep part of the bank to see where we were, but near the top she saw a big hole. It was a den of something. She got scared and came scrambling back down and almost fell in the water! Me and my sister climbed up to see it but we didn't see what was in it but it scared us too. My sister tried to catch some fish with her hands but my mom made her stop because it might make the fish die. They could get a fungus on their skin. because of being touched. On the way back we saw Kate and Cheryl and they said they saw a snake in the path but it probably was just a stick. Cheryl always tells lies.

I wonder what it was that lived in the big hole? How big was it? Maybe it was a muskrat hole. They often live around streams. Have you ever seen a muskrat?

May 10

I saw a muskrat at the duck hatchery and it was not as big as this hole. This was as big as a fox or a groundhog. Did I tell you my mom fell in a deep place? She was scared and we had to pull her out. It was pretty funny. Last night at Brownies we learned three new hopscotch games. They are games from South America, France and England. The one from France is called escargo that means snail. You hop around the shape of a snail shell. Laura and Katie and I were going to play it at recess if the chalk hasn't rubbed off yet.

Can you show some of us how to play it? It sounds like fun. I think there are some other kids in the class who would like to learn it.

FIGURE 7.5. A teacher–student dialogue journal.

From Temple and Gillet (1996, p. 282). Copyright 1996. Reprinted by permission of Allyn & Bacon.

respond to each entry. Some teachers read and check off each writer's entries, but respond to each writer only once or twice weekly. Others have students turn in their journals on a staggered or rotating schedule—each group on a different day of the week, or half the class Mondays and the other half on Wednesdays, or the like. Another way is to put everyone's name in a hat, draw out five or six at a time, and write responses only in those journals, continuing in this way until every name has been drawn. Yet another way is to require that each student turn in a journal for response once weekly, but let each writer decide on what day that will occur. Whatever the system, it helps to keep responses short. The writers' voices are what we want to hear, not our own.

☐☐

> **TEACHER'S TIP:** When writing in a student's dialogue journal, keep your responses short, encouraging, and noncritical.

☐☐

Subject-Area Journals

Journals are most often thought of as part of the language arts writing program, but they can be very effectively used in subject areas outside of language arts, such as social studies, science, math, music, and foreign languages. Teachers of these subjects have come up with novel and thoughtful ways of integrating journal writing into their classes. They do so for several reasons:

- To integrate reading and writing into traditionally "nonliterary" subjects.
- To deepen students' understanding of subject matter.
- To encourage students to reflect upon what they are learning.

For example, in *social studies* students can keep a history log or journal to accompany their reading and discussion of their textbook. Instead of (or in addition to) traditional outlining and summarizing, students can respond to their reading assignments by writing about the new information or insights they may acquire, their opinions and reactions to it, and questions they have as they read. Students can refer to their responses and questions when they participate in group discussions, and can share and discuss them with peers. In this way their journals serve as a repository for students' thoughts and discoveries that may be forgotten during oral discussions. They help students learn the subject matter more effectively, because they help students clarify what they don't understand as well as what they do, and help students think critically about issues as well as learning facts (Mulholland, 1987).

Art and *music* classes can be enhanced by having students keep journals in which they respond critically and aesthetically to works of art and musical compositions. They can describe in detail what they see or hear, can compare and contrast works by the same artist/composer, can compare their reactions to a particular genre before and after a unit of study, and can create scenes and stories to fit pieces of music or art. For example, a fourth grader listening to a portion of *In the Hall of the Mountain King* wrote a description of what he heard, then created a story line to fit the music:

> The rhythum is slow. It is starting to get faster and louder. Now it is Loud! and very, very fast. I feel excited. This is neat. I hear an orchestra. Someone is sad. Someone is walking down a dark road. they get scared and start to run suddenly gosts appear. They run fast fast they catch him. He's fighting. He's dead. (Larson and Merrion, 1987, p. 257)

A sixth-grade art student in one of our classes wrote this interpretation of George Caleb Bingham's painting *Fur Traders on the Missouri*, including both factual and imaginative details, as part of a study of landscape artists:

> The two traders have been on the Missouri River for weeks. They stop at Indian villages and trade with the Indians, giving them knives, guns, pans, jewelry, and blankets for their furs. Then they sell the furs at trading posts for money and goods they need to live. They have just come through a long stretch of white water, and they are exhausted as they lean on the boxes and let their paddles drag in the water. Their canoe is heavily loaded and sits low in the water. They have to be careful not to get snagged on submerged logs like the one they have just pushed away. In the bow of their canoe, a black cat is chained. They found the cat wandering on the shore, and the man in the hat is taking the cat home to his little girl.

Math journals can help students understand and verbalize their understanding of math concepts and operations. Writing about math often helps students know what they understand and what is confusing to them, see their own progress, help others understand, and avoid "math anxiety." Students can use drawings and diagrams to help them explain concepts and operations they have difficulty verbalizing, and to elaborate on their written descriptions. Reading students' math journals can also help us see which students understand a concept or operation clearly, which ones have a rudimentary understanding, and which ones need more help to understand it. For example, consider these second graders' journal entries on fractions:

> **Talissa:** *A fraction is a part of somthing. If you cut somthing in to parts it has fractions. They are the sam size. Like a pese of pizza can be a fraction.*

> **Cory:** *A fraction has to nubers one on top and one on the botum like ½ its one out of to or 2/5 its to out of five.*

> **Donnell:** *A fraction is like one haf tow haf three haf.*

In these examples, Talissa can articulate an age-appropriate definition of a fraction, and showed an understanding that fractions are equal parts of the whole. Cory's description was directed toward how to write fractions rather than what they are, although his idea of *one out of to* and *to out of five* hinted at a concept of parts. Donnell, however, seemed to lack the basic concept, and needed further explanation and demonstration.

⊡⊡⊡

TEACHER'S TIP: Integrate journal response writing into subject areas like math, science, social studies, and the arts.

⊡⊡⊡

LETTERS

A kind of personal writing that adults use in everyday life is writing letters. For this reason, learning to write both informal and formal letters, or so-called "friendly" and "business" letters, is useful.

Informal or Friendly Letters

Informal letters are a good place to start, since students have more opportunities to write these than they do formal letters. Most grammar or composition books have sections on how to set up informal letters and address envelopes, and suggestions for things to include in such letters. These guidelines can be helpful to students, and are easy to put on a poster or bulletin board for easy reference. However, many English books direct students to practice writing letters as exercises rather than as real communication. Writing a letter that will not be sent, only turned in to the teacher, is the kind of inauthentic writing exercise we want to avoid. Such practice does nothing to encourage our students ever to use what they learn.

There are several ways students can learn to write letters in authentic situations. Teachers commonly have students write thank-you notes to classroom volunteers or speakers, or letters to students in a lower grade. In some schools it's traditional for students to write end-of-year letters describing what to expect in that grade to students in the grade behind them. But these occasions rarely result in students' writing more than a single letter, and they don't get any response to their letters.

A fun way to make letter writing an ongoing activity is to help your students become pen pals with students in another classroom, school, or community. You can get together with another teacher in your school, or can contact the principal of another school to help you connect with other teachers who are interested in such a venture. You may have a friend or relative in another town or state whose students would enjoy having pen pals, or who can refer you to an interested colleague.

Class lists can be exchanged and students can be paired for a period of several weeks, during which time they learn to craft interesting, readable letters in the same ways that they have written other kinds of pieces. Too much emphasis on revision and editing may make letter writing onerous, which we want to avoid; however, some attention to clarity and correctness will make letters more interesting to their readers and elicit a more enthusiastic response. If students receive poorly written or illegible letters, they will quickly see the importance of some revision and editing.

TEACHER'S TIP: Corresponding with pen pals may help students see the importance of legible, correct writing.

When writing to pen pals, students may need help deciding what to include and organizing their letters. In general, writers should tell about themselves and show interest in the other person by asking questions and commenting on things the other person has written. If they receive a letter that asks them questions, they should answer the questions in their next letter. Students can develop topic lists to assist them in thinking of things to write about, including their families, school, sports, hobbies, pets, holidays and celebrations, birthdays, vacations, school trips, jokes, good books and movies, favorite things to do, and so forth.

It's also fun to exchange small objects like photos, drawings, postcards, stickers, unusual stamps, and so forth with pen pals. Students may enjoy using a computer to create unique stationery with clip art.

Formal or Business Letters

Students don't usually have many real opportunities to write formal or business letters, so we may have to create opportunities for them to practice these skills. But as adults, they will need to know how to produce a correctly written business letter that can make a good impression and get results.

TEACHER'S TIP: Avoid having students write letters just for practice. Have them write real letters for real purposes, and send them.

Business letters are often written to request something; to address a problem with a product or service; or to express an opinion to a public official, newspaper editor, or the like. They have a more formal appearance and tone than informal letters, and format requirements are quite strict. As they do for friendly letters, most grammar and composition books contain directions for setting up business letters, with examples. Figure 7.6 is an example of a business letter written by a student to a Career Day guest speaker.

Students can find many real purposes for writing business letters once they begin to look for them. Here are some suggestions you can give your class:

- Write to a *local public official* expressing your opinion on a current situation or controversy in your community.
- Write to *members of your state or federal legislature,* your *state governor,* or *the President* expressing your opinion on an issue.

April 16, 199__

Dr. Brigid Sullivan, DVM
Albemarle Veterinary Hospital
1456 Westfield Road
Charlottesville, VA 22901

Dear Dr. Sullivan,

I enjoyed hearing your presentation at Career Day last week at Walker School. I am interested in applying for one of the volunteer positions at the hospital this summer.

I am 12 years old and a sixth grader at Walker School. I love animals and I hope to be a veterinarian someday. I would like to work at the animal hospital because it would be good experience for me. It would help me to find out if I want to go to veterinarian school after college. I have lots of experience taking care of animals and am a hard worker. I am willing to do whatever jobs need to be done at the hospital.

I will be available for work beginning the week of June 20th. I can come to the hospital every afternoon except when we are on vacation or when I go to camp. Please call me any day after school to tell me if you want me to work with you this summer. I hope to hear from you soon. Thank you for your consideration.

Sincerely,

FIGURE 7.6. A student-written business letter.
From Temple and Gillet (1996, p. 292). Copyright 1996. Reprinted by permission of Allyn & Bacon.

- Write a letter to *the editor of your local newspaper* to express your opinion on a local issue or publicly acknowledge a contribution to the public good.
- Write to *your school principal, superintendent, or school board members* to express your opinion on an important issue concerning your school.
- Write to a *local or state travel or tourism department* requesting travel information about a locality.
- Write to *local businesses* requesting sample job applications, information about public tours, or the like.
- Write to *professional associations or organizations* requesting informational literature.

Many such requests can be worked into science and social studies units. For example, in a fifth-grade social studies class studying the 50 states, the teacher located the address of each state tourism bureau as well as addresses for a number of major cities and tourist attractions. The social studies and language arts teachers collaborated on a series of lessons in which business letters were taught. Then each student wrote letters to at least two addresses requesting travel information. As the responses began to arrive at the school, the teachers collected the form letters that accompanied the responses to use as further examples.

Similarly, science students can write to professional scientific organizations and college science departments requesting information about careers in science. Most college and public libraries have encyclopedias or similar reference books listing the addresses of professional organizations, nonprofit groups, state and national bureaus, and other organizations. Such information is also widely available on the Internet.

INFORMATIONAL REPORTS

Reports on various subjects are probably the most common examples of informational writing in school. Unfortunately, many students think that report writing is boring and approach it with dread. Many reports are dull because students often copy or paraphrase from encyclopedias instead of writing with their own voices.

The topic is perhaps the key to good report writing. It is nearly impossible for any of us to write an interesting report about a topic we care nothing about. Therefore, it is vital that students choose topics in which they have some interest. Even when the general topic is mandated by the curriculum or by the teacher (e.g., the state history report required of all fourth or fifth graders in some states), students should be shown how to choose a specific topic or an angle on a topic that they care about.

□□□

TEACHER'S TIP: Make sure students choose report topics in which they
have real interest.

□□□

The I-Search Technique

An approach for guiding students through the process of investigative writing is
called an *I-Search* (Macrorie, 1980). The I-Search technique helps students learn
to do their own real investigation, write reports they care about, and produce
lively informational writing (Temple and Gillet, 1996). The steps in an I-Search
are shown in Figure 7.7.

   Traditionally, students have chosen (or been assigned) a report topic, then
gone to the library to look up their topic in encyclopedias or similar references
and on the Internet. In contrast, an I-Search emphasizes having students start

1. Choose a Topic

   A. Freewrite or list potential topics you want or need to know about.

   B. Discuss your ideas with a group of four or five others. Explain what you want
   to know and why.

   C. Ask the others who you can talk to about your subject.

   D. Help the others get started with their topics.

2. Get Information

   A. Go to a person who knows something about your topic.

   B. Treat the person and what he or she knows with respect.

   C. Ask the person to recommend others, or books or other sources, to help you
   gather information.

3. Write Up Your Topic

   A. Write what you knew about the topic before you started your search.

   B. Write about why you chose the topic.

   C. Write about your journey to find your information.

   D. Write about what you learned.

FIGURE 7.7. I-Search procedures.
From Temple and Gillet (1996, p. 294). Copyright 1996. Reprinted by permission of Allyn & Bacon.

learning about their topics by going to real people instead of books or other research tools. The rationale is that by talking to others, students are better prepared to assimilate information and to use their own ideas and words in their
writing. After gathering information from someone who knows more than they
do, writers are less likely to copy from books and other references. The I-Search
technique also emphasizes using a variety of sources of information during the
research phase of the project.

Subject-Area Reports

Informational reports are often required as part of a thematic unit. They are opportunities to teach students how to research and write about a topic they are
studying. For example, a third-grade teacher was teaching a science unit on
threatened and endangered North American animals. She wanted to work on
principles of report writing within this unit. So the general topic was given, but
students were responsible for choosing specific examples of wildlife about
which to conduct research.

The teacher began by helping students create a *list* of all the endangered animals, fish, and birds they could think of (regardless of their habitat), as well as a
web to distinguish North American animals from others. Lists, webs, and clus-
ters are effective ways to help students generate possible topics and organize
them into categories. Students then used a modified I-Search approach to
choosing a topic. They wrote and talked in small groups about what they already knew about the animals listed, and looked at magazine articles and pictures to help them choose a specific animal. This helped them recall and share
what they already knew, and ensured that several students didn't choose the
same animal to study.

After students had chosen particular animals to write about, they worked
with partners to generate lists of questions about the animal to be answered in
the reports. The questions served as a sort of outline or organizing scheme as
they used a variety of resources, including other knowledgeable people, to
gather information. Leslie chose the Florida manatee as her topic, and generated
these questions to answer in her report:

> *What kind of animals are they?*
> *Where do they live?*
> *What do they eat?*
> *What are their babies like?*
> *Why are they endangered?*
> *What can we do to help the manatees?*

After generating questions, students listed all the sources they could think
of to help them find the information they needed. They were encouraged to list

people they thought knew something about their subject first. Leslie listed her mother, a friend's mother who was a science teacher, a marine museum she'd visited on vacation, the Florida Department of Wildlife Management, *Ranger Rick* and *National Geographic World* magazines, library books, encyclopedias, and the Internet as possible resources. Students then used their collected resources to gather information about their topics. They took notes as they read and talked to others, and organized their notes on index cards. Finally they were ready to begin writing their reports.

Leslie organized her information into a first draft, shown in Figure 7.8. Because she was most interested in the dangers to manatees, she began her report with this information. After developing their first drafts, students read their initial efforts to partners and small groups and got input on what they might have omitted and where they might include other information. With the help of others, Leslie realized that she actually had a great deal more information that she

Florida   Manatee By: Leslie

Manatee's are endangered becuase of man kind.

Manatees live in the ocean where people sail their ships.

Manatees don't have good eye sight, so the can't see

the boats and the boats bump into the manatees and

sometimes they can get killed. People don't mean to

hert them, but the Manatees can't see the ships.

Manatees are mamals. When their babies are born

the mother has to take the baby up to the sur-

fis for the babie's first breath. Manatees have

little bits of hair on it's nose and mouth. The Man-

atee lives near the coastal warm areas of the

Atlantic Ocean.

FIGURE 7.8. The first draft of Leslie's third-grade class report on manatees.
From Temple and Gillet (1996, p. 296). Copyright 1996. Reprinted by permission of Allyn & Bacon.

had not included in her first draft. This included more about where manatees live, what they look like, information about their young, and what they eat. She added more information and reorganized some parts to create her final draft, shown in Figure 7.9.

Students read their finished reports aloud, presented pictures or other visual aids, and shared some of the most interesting or surprising things they had learned about their topics. Reports were displayed, and copies were bound into a class book on endangered and threatened species for other classes to read.

Another way of creating an informational report is to clothe expository writing in the form of a story, diary, letter, or conversation. These are sometimes called *narrative reports*. To undertake this form of writing, students must do more than gather facts and information; they must also create the role of real or imaginary *participants* in the events. To do so, they must transform the factual information they have into narratives.

In the three examples provided here, students used different means to convey the factual information they gathered. In Figure 7.10, the sixth-grade writer created a character she named Scarlett Banks, writing a letter to a friend describing the conditions under which she was living during the Reconstruction period. In Figure 7.11, a fourth grader created a short informational story entitled "The New West" in which the writer took the role of a member of a pioneer family. In Figure 7.12, second and third graders took roles as children of the Roanoke Island colonists and conveyed factual information through fictionalized letters to grandparents back in England.

Biographies

A biography is a special kind of classroom report, the topic of which is a person's life or accomplishments. Biographies are particularly suited to showing students that good researchers use more than one source to gather information about a topic. When a student is writing a biography, using only one source can result in a biased view of the subject.

Again, students should be encouraged to choose a subject they care something about or have some interest in. If you have a list of possible biography subjects, it's a good idea to provide some background information about each one in order for students to choose. Keep in mind, too, that some subjects are harder than others to find information about. An enterprising teacher we know offers extra points to students who choose the more obscure biography subjects, knowing they'll have a harder time researching these subjects.

A biography is least interesting when it is little more than a chronology of the person's life from birth to death. An interesting biography contains enough chronological information to place the subject in a historical context, but focuses on one or more important events or facts that make the subject memorable to readers. In Figure 7.13, the writers provided some obligatory information

FLORIDA MANATEES

Manatees are aquatic mammals. They live in water all the time. They live near the coastal warm areas of the Atlantic Ocean. They are quite common in Florida. Manatees eat plants that grow under the water. Sometimes they live in large rivers.

Manatees are sometimes called sea cows. They are large grey animals that are shaped like a torpedo. They have two flippers in the front and a flat tail. They use their tails to push them through the water. They have whiskers around their nose and mouth. They have small eyes. They cannot see very well. They move slowly.

Manatees are mammals. That means their babies are born alive and they nurse their babies. Mother manatees have one baby. It is called a calf. They have to take the calf up to the surface when it is born for the baby's first breath.

Manatees are endangered because of mankind. Manatees live in the ocean where people sail their ships. They also live in big rivers where people have boats. Manatees don't have good eyesight, so they can't see the boats and the boats bump into the manatees and sometimes they can get killed. Sometimes they get badly cut by boat propellers. People don't mean to hurt them, but the manatees can't see the ships. In many places in Florida it is against the law to go fast in a boat. If boats go slower they will not hit so many manatees.

by Leslie

FIGURE 7.9. The final draft of Leslie's report on manatees.

From Temple and Gillet (1996, p. 297). Copyright 1996. Reprinted by permission of Allyn & Bacon.

Dear Katie,

    I have wanted to write to you for a long time. So far during Reconstruction it's been hard. People have been tormenting the people who support the blacks. The new gang that's out is the Klu Klux Klan. They have been burning down homes and killing blacks and people who support them. There have been a lot of lynchings around these parts. They have also made new laws like the literacy test to be able to vote. Then there was the Grandfather Clause, a law that says you could vote with out taking the test if your father or Grandfather had voted before. I think that Reconstruction is the worst of things. Our house and the rest of the houses got burned down by angry Union soldiers. My father was killed and one of my brothers died too. Well what's going on in Reconstruction for you? I hope you have not had as much trouble as I have. I've missed you! How is your family doing? I hope to see you soon!

            Your friend,
            Scarlett Banks

FIGURE 7.10. Narrative report in letter form about the Reconstruction era.
From Temple and Gillet (1996, p. 300). Copyright 1996. Reprinted by permission of Allyn & Bacon.

about Amelia Earhart's early life, but focused on her fateful flight and disappearance. In Figure 7.14, the writer built the body of a report on John Adams around a single event in his legal career.

□□

TEACHER'S TIP: Help students focus their biographical writing on one or two key events or issues in the subject's life.

□□

The New West
By Jenny

Once when I was young we lived in the city, Boston. My dad had heard that there were a lot of plains out in the West. So one day he went out to the West to look at it and build a house. He said, "When I come home I will get you and your mama and bring you out to see it." A couple months later my pa came and got us. I was so excited! We started out in a wagon with all of our belongings. It took about two months to get there. When we got about a mile away from our new house we stopped. My father pointed to the hills "Just behind those," he said. I could hardly wait. It was very hot there! We made it there in 15 min. We saw a house that looked like it was made of grass set back in the hill. I thought it was going to be a house like the one that we had in Boston. I was very disappointed. We stayed there for about 5 years and it was hard!
The End

FIGURE 7.11. Narrative report in story form about the New West.
From Temple and Gillet (1996, p. 301). Copyright 1996. Reprinted by permission of Allyn & Bacon.

BOOK REPORTS

Book reports probably rank among students' most despised forms of writing. That may be because they have written and heard too many boring, lifeless summaries written only to prove to the teacher that the books were read. But book reports don't need to be drudgery to write or read.

Written Book Reports

Providing these guidelines for students may help them write more interesting book reports:

January the 17th, 1587

Dear Grampa and Granma,

I eat mostly deer; it is cold in the winter. I hope we see you soon. The people who were here before us which our people call savages stole the deer meat so we had to go without anything except for water for two days. Micah and I have to go almost every night to the neighbor's hut to borrow some fire. We only have one more rag for the tinderbox. Grandma please send me some of Grampa's rags. We send you two wolf skins and five fox skins when a ship comes. Our next door neighbor's house burned down. It caught on to ours so we had to build another one. Micah and I found ten nails. One Indian girl named Pomawak is my friend. I go meet her every day in the woods in a clearing. Three days we pick berries together. We taught each other our languages with our hands, so we can talk to each other a little bit.

Love,

Your granddaughter Elizabeth (Age 8)

Dear Granny,

I made a goose trap and my friend and I caught five geese. Every thing is going fine except for the weather.

Your grandchild Micah (Age 7)

Dear Grampa,

I am freezing to death but I don't die. Orion (Age 7)

Dear Grampa,

Things are getting worse. First I thought the savages were bad, but now I have to go over to chief Okracoke for medicine and food. My mother is getting scurvy but she's lucky her teeth aren't falling out. We are lucky to have the savages. They give us crab, duck, geese and mush, but now they don't have that much so we are starving. The Indians say that in forty-one more days the weather will be warmer. If it wasn't for the Indians we would be dead.

Your Grandchild Andrew (Age 9)

FIGURE 7.12. Narrative reports in letter form about the Roanoke Island colony.
From Temple, Nathan, Burris, and Temple, *The Beginnings of Writing*, 3rd ed. (p. 200). Copyright 1993 by Allyn & Bacon. Reprinted by permission.

- Choose a book you really enjoyed.
- Start with the title, the author, the illustrator (if the book is illustrated), and the year the book was published.
- Prepare by thinking about what the book is about, what the author might want readers to learn from it, and what you like about it.

Amelia Earhart By heslie + Brian
Amelia Earhart was born in 1897, on July 24.
Amelia was nine years old when she saw her first
airplane. Her parents seperated and Mrs. Earhart
took Amelia and her sister to Chicago to live with
friends. In 1937, She and copilot, Luetenent Comand-
er Fred J. Noonan, left Miami Fla. on an around the
world trip. On July 2, 1937, her plane disappeard in
Howland Island in the South Pacific. Search teams
from the U.S. army and navey and from the Japanese
army looked for the missing plane and pilots. Amelia
Earhart was the first woman pilot to fly around
the world.

FIGURE 7.13. A biography of Amelia Earhart by two third graders.
From Temple and Gillet (1996, p. 298). Copyright 1996. Reprinted by permission of Allyn & Bacon.

- Include short quotations from the book, like a colorful description of a character or a portion of dialogue.
- Try writing your report as a news article, a journal entry, or a letter from a character in the book.
- Don't tell the whole story; readers should want to read the book after they've heard your report.

A *book review* is a special kind of book report. In a book review, the writer writes more critically about how the story unfolds, how the author conveyed information, and how the book made the writer think or feel. What happens in the story is less important than how the writer feels about the story and how it was written. Book reviews offer students opportunities to think and respond critically to a book. They can be an outcome of using a literature response journal, as described in a previous section. Reading some book and movie reviews in newspapers and magazines will help students understand the difference between a book report and a book review.

JOHN ADAMS

John Adams was born October 30, 1735 in Braintree, Massachusetts. Braintree is now Quincy, Massachusetts. He was the first vice-president and the second U.S. President.

John Adams lived in Boston, Massachusetts. He was a lawyer. He defended the British soldiers' trials that followed the shootings on March 5, 1770. That event is known as the Boston Massacre.

Adams first went looking for proof of what happened that night. Then he went and talked to people who had seen the shooting. He heard two different stories and did not know which one to believe.

A man named Calef said that he heard the British commander telling the soldiers to fire. He said that he looked at the commander's face and saw his mouth move.

Another man named Hickling said that the commander did not say that because he did not hear him and he was standing a yard away from him.

Adams beat Jefferson in the 1796 presidential election, to become the second President. He was 61 years old when he became President. He was the first President to live in the White House. He was the person who stopped the U.S. from having a war with France in 1800. He ran again for president in 1800, but lost to Thomas Jefferson.

He died on July 4, 1826.

FIGURE 7.14. A biography of John Adams by a sixth grader.
From Temple and Gillet (1996, p. 299). Copyright 1996. Reprinted by permission of Allyn & Bacon.

BOX 7.3. Writing Book Reports: Guidelines for Students

- Choose a book you enjoyed reading.
- Include the title, author, illustrator, and date of publication.
- Write what the book is about, what the author might want readers to learn, and why you like it.
- Include some short quotations.
- Don't tell the whole story.
- Try a different form instead of a summary.

Alternatives to Book Reports

There are many other ways to share a book with others and to demonstrate understanding of it. Students can share what they are reading by using a variety of art, dramatics, and writing activities. Figure 7.15 presents various suggestions for alternatives to traditional written book reports.

▣▣

TEACHER'S TIP: Encourage students to try alternatives to traditional
written book reports.

▣▣

DIRECTIONS

Learning to write clear, precise directions that others can understand and follow is another important nonfiction writing operation. Both in school and out, students need to be able to write down precisely how to do something or get somewhere, so that others can follow the same steps successfully. To write clear directions, students should follow these steps:

1. Select a subject. Choose something you know how to do or make, or something you are interested in learning more about.
2. List all the steps involved. Begin at the very beginning of the procedure, and write down each thing you have to do to complete it.
3. Review your steps to make sure you explained exactly what to do at each step. Use words like *first, second, next,* and *finally,* or number the steps in order.
4. Try out your directions, or have someone else try them. Are there any steps left out? Are there parts that are confusing?
5. Make any changes needed to make your directions clear, precise, and correct.

Figures 7.16 and 7.17 present shows two examples of directions written by students. Figure 7.17 shows how effective drawings or diagrams can be when writing directions.

SUMMARIES

Writing summaries is an excellent strategy for helping students understand and remember the most important information or parts of what they read. Con-

Art-Based Alternatives to Book Reports

1. Create a large, colorful poster "advertising" your book. Include the title, author, and illustrator and a few sentences describing the story or what you liked the best about it. Illustrate your poster with drawing, painting, glued-on real materials, cut-out magazine pictures, or fancy lettering. The posters can be hung in the classroom or library.

2. Using paper or tagboard strips about 2" × 6", make colorful bookmarks and leave them on the library table or circulation desk for others to pick up . . .

3. Create a bulletin board illustrating or describing your book. Make a dimensional display by using inflated balloons with felt-pen faces or features glued on, each one representing characters. Tape the tied-off base of the balloon securely to the board, then make bodies and costumes to scale from paper, cloth, cotton, or whatever. You can even add dialogue in cartoon-style "bubbles" from the characters' mouths. Balloon heads can be made more durable by covering inflated balloons with a layer of papier-mâché (newspaper strips, wallpaper paste, and water), then painting and decorating them after they have dried completely.

4. For historical tales, science fiction, or stories from other lands, create a display of costumes. Use scraps of fabric and other materials to make authentic costumes for clay or wire models or . . . action figures.

5. Make an advertisement "selling" your book just as magazine and TV ads sell cars, cosmetics, and other products. Make up "testimonials" by famous people, catchy slogans, and colorful descriptions.

6. Make a display of masks representing characters, accompanied by written descriptions, or use the masks to role-play part of a story. Masks can be made with sheets of duplicator paper, paper plates, papier-mâché, grocery bags, or similar materials. (Teachers: Be sure eyeholes are large if masks are to be worn.)

7. Use blank transparencies or a continuous roll of overhead projector film to create a "filmstrip" about your book. (Divide the continuous film into frames.) Use china markers, wax pencils, or other markers to draw and color scenes. Project the film or transparencies in order on an overhead projector, with narration.

8. Create a set of puppets you can use to act out scenes from, or a summary of, your book. Puppets can be as simple as paper circles or small paper plates glued to tongue depressors, or much more elaborate hand puppets with stuffed heads, sock or bag puppets, or even simple marionettes. (If you have puppets at home, dress them differently or disguise their original appearance for this activity.)

FIGURE 7.15. Art-based, drama, and writing alternatives to book reports: Suggestions for students.

From Temple and Gillet (1996, pp. 304–306). Copyright 1996. Reprinted by permission of Allyn & Bacon.

Drama Alternatives to Book Reports

1. Dress up in a costume worn by a major character in your book. Improvise with pieces of clothing, hats, wigs, or masks, and include small hand props that your character would carry or use. Tell your classmates about your experiences in the book, your life before or after the book's events, or your feelings about the way you were characterized in the story. If someone were to write another story about you, what would you like to have happen in it?

2. Write a script for a radio play describing parts of your book and summarizing it or describing your feelings about it. Include dialogue between characters as well as your narration. Experiment with different voices or ask friends to read different parts. Experiment with sound effects and/or music too. Tape-record your script or ask if you can read it to your class over the PA system.

3. If you read a book that taught you how to do something, collect materials or make models of them, give a demonstration showing others how to do it too, or show how a character made, discovered, or invented something in a story.

4. Role-play a part of your story, with friends playing other parts. Write a script and read from it while acting (as in readers' theater) rather than trying to memorize lines.

5. Make some puppets and a simple puppet theater from a large carton or movable screen. Write a script and put on a puppet show, reading your script from behind the scenes and using different voices.

6. With some friends (especially others who read the same book), put on a mock trial. This is especially good for mysteries and suspense stories. Create characters (defendants, prosecutors, defense lawyers, judge, witnesses, and jury) and a script showing how events unfolded through testimony, evidence, and arguments. Poll the jury to see who wins the trial. "Reporters" can write news stories about the trial for the class newspaper.

Writing Alternatives to Book Reports

1. By yourself or with others, produce a classroom newspaper in which story events are treated as news stories. Duplicator masters can be used if the newspaper will be distributed; large newsprint sheets can be used for a display or bulletin board. Rule your paper into columns, with room for headlines and illustrations (use a real front page as an example). Mix types of articles: news items, interviews with the author or characters, a travel item about the setting, even a weather forecast. Write or type your stories in narrow columns, draw pictures for illustrations, and write eye-catching headlines in large print.

2. Write a telegram summarizing story events in short sentences. You can make up realistic telegram forms and run them off on a duplicator. For #1 above, reporters can send details of news items to the editor before they write their stories.

3. Write a letter to a friend or pen pal describing your book, or to a story character describing your reactions to a story, or write a real letter to an author or

FIGURE 7.15. *(cont.)*

illustrator, if living, reacting to his or her work. Send your letter to the publishing company and see if you get a letter back!

4. Imagine that you are a character in a story. Keep a diary to record events your feelings about them, and your hopes and plans for the future. Date your entries from the beginning to the end of the story.

5. Select one or two quotations from a book that represents the feelings, attitudes, or personality of a character. Copy the quotations, write a short essay telling why those quotes represent that character, and then write a short summary of how the character's actions showed what kind of person he or she was. You might include a drawing of the character or some important story action.

6. If you read a biography or a historical fiction story about a famous person or historical figure, try the Who Am I? game. Using information from what you read, write clues to the person's identity such as place and date of birth, a description of some physical characteristics, likes and dislikes, hobbies, and important things the person did during his or her lifetime. Make your clues clear and accurate but don't give away too much information—make your classmates guess who the person might be.

7. Try writing a summary of a book or story as a song or poem. Look at some examples of poems that tell a story, such as Robert Nathan's *Dunkirk*, James Tippett's *I Spend the Summer*, or songs like "The Ballad of John Henry."

8. Think of an object that represents the main action, setting, or character of a book you've read. Draw and cut out a large outline of the object from construction paper. You can use an outline map of the country where a story took place, a spaceship or robot for a science fiction story, an animal shape, an article of clothing, a building, or even an invention.

FIGURE 7.15. *(cont.)*

densing a lot of information into a short summary containing all the key points is a skill students will use often in school. Students can learn to write effective summaries by following these guidelines:

- To write a good summary, *read the material twice*: once quickly, to get the main points, and then carefully to get the details.
- While reading, *pay attention* to devices like bold print, italics, headings, and numbered sequences.
- After a careful reading, *list the main points*.
- *Check your list* with the reading selection.
- *Write your summary in your own words*; include the main topic in the first sentence.
- *Include only the most important information*; don't get bogged down in details.
- *Rearrange parts if needed* to be sure your summary follows a logical order.

How to Make Girl Scout Stew

First, have everyone bring two cans of soup or a can of soup and a can of vegetables. Be sure everyone brings different kinds of soup. Do not bring any kind that nobody likes, like asparagus! Everyone should take the labels off the cans and throw them away.

Next, open all the cans. Put all the stuff in a very large pan. If there is any water or anything on the stuff pour it off first. If there is anything nasty throw it away. Then put in some cans of water, about four cans, and mix it all up with a big spoon. If it is too thick, put in some more water. Wash all the cans and put them in the recycling bin.

Put the pan on the fire. If you are cooking outside you should rub some soap on the bottom of the pan so it doesn't get all black. Or put it on the stove. Cook it until it is hot. Spoon it into bowls and eat it. Have some crackers or bread too. If there is something you don't like like lima beans you don't have to eat that part.

FIGURE 7.16. A third grader's directions for making Girl Scout stew.
From Temple and Gillet (1996, p. 307). Copyright 1996. Reprinted by permission of Allyn & Bacon.

- *Have someone else read your summary* and tell you the most important information.
- See if you can *tell yourself the most important ideas* in order.

A perennial problem students have in writing summaries is deciding what to include and what to omit. They may also have trouble finding the one most important fact or idea. Giving students this list of questions to ask themselves can help:

- *What is the biggest or most important main idea of all?*
- *What's the most important thing to remember from this passage?*
- *How could I tell someone else what this passage is about in one sentence?*
- *What would be a good title for this passage that would tell what it is mainly about?*

Students often need help in developing summaries. This is a good opportunity for students to work together in pairs or threes to discuss what each person thinks the main idea is, what key information should be included, what details may be omitted, and in what order the information should be presented. Writing summaries is an excellent cooperative learning activity.

TEACHER'S TIP: Writing summaries is a good opportunity
for cooperative learning.

How to Make a Cornhusk Doll by Marissa

School is fun. Today we made cornhusk dolls. I made the one you see.

First you take a piece of cream-colored cornhusk and take two cotton balls and put the cotton balls inside the cornhusk, and bunch the cornhusk and tie a piece of thin cornhusk. Wrap it around the neck of the head you just made. The head should look like this:

Make one long arm by rolling a piece of cornhusk up in a scroll and trying it at both ends, and then you have made arms.

Then take a piece of blue or red cornhusk; take a piece that looks like this:

and make a diamond hole in the same one and put it on the head of the body.

Then take five pieces of blue or red cornhusk that look like this, tie them around (the middle of the body) and bend them around.

FIGURE 7.17. A second grader's directions for making a cornhusk doll.
From Temple, Nathan, Burris, and Temple, *The Beginnings of Writing*, 3rd ed. (p. 199). Copyright 1993 by Allyn & Bacon. Reprinted by permission.

Students should practice writing summaries of short passages before they attempt longer, more detailed pieces. For example, they can practice summarizing a filmstrip or short video presentation, a short newspaper or magazine article, a letter to the editor, a science experiment, or shorter portions of longer passages. As their summarizing skill develops, they can move toward writing summaries of longer passages, textbook chapters, movies, novels, and so forth.

JOURNALISM

When we were in school, our teachers sometimes tried to teach us how to write nonfiction by having us write newspaper articles. As we have noted in Chapter 3, they taught us the tried-and-true "Five W's" of reporting: *who? what? when? where?* and *why.* Then we'd write about some event as though we were newspaper reporters, and sometimes create a classroom newspaper. It was fun, and we learned to write short, information-filled articles. But it was basically a contrived activity, and we rarely used the skills we learned in any other kind of writing.

We think that two other approaches to journalistic writing are more interesting, and have more lasting impact on students' writing ability, than learning to write the Five W's. These are called *cultural journalism* and *immersion journalism.* Each is a relatively new approach to teaching nonfiction writing. They are most appropriate for students in middle elementary grades and above.

Cultural Journalism

In *cultural journalism*, students write about people, places, and events in their cultural community. They learn from other people, which is also the underlying tenet of the I-Search technique. They talk to and interview people rather than primarily doing library research, although they use text sources to fill in the gaps. The basic tenets of cultural journalism are *using people as primary resources for learning* and *writing about one's own culture.*

The parent of all cultural journalism efforts is *Foxfire*, a magazine that was published for some years by high school students in rural Georgia about the "old ways" of southern Appalachia. Students interviewed older members of their communities about topics like making musical instruments, building houses, mining coal, and spinning yarn, and wrote articles that were produced in magazine form and sold throughout their communities. The magazines proved so popular that they were published as books, became best-sellers, and inspired cultural journalism projects all over the country.

Although the elaborate publishing projects undertaken by high schoolers are too complex for elementary students, these kinds of writing can be adapted and simplified for younger students. With elementary students, the best place to begin is with their own families. For today's children, the 1950s, 1960s, and 1970s are ancient history, and World War II, the civil rights movement, the Cold War, and Vietnam seem (to them) unimaginably distant. But they happened "just yesterday" to their older relatives, who have lots to tell about.

When your students start asking questions and really listening, they will uncover a whole world of things these older folks know: how to build boats, identify animal footprints, carve, weave baskets, score a baseball game, throw pots, bake bread, fix cars, make lamps, play bocce, restore furniture, hunt, and develop photographs. They can make history live through their own experiences and stories: hurricanes, wars, emigration, unemployment, revivals, holidays, and ethnic customs.

🔲🔲🔲

TEACHER'S TIP: Have students interview family members and neighbors
about their own lives and skills.

🔲🔲🔲

Brainstorm with your students about people they know, especially relatives, who might have an interesting story to tell or an interesting skill or hobby: grandparents and great-grandparents, uncles and aunts, and older relatives or friends. Brainstorming helps students recall stories they were told by relatives, and other things they remember older people reminiscing about. Some "olden days" topics to explore might include the following:

- What school was like when they were kids.
- Any of "the firsts" (first day of school, car, date, job, best friend, etc.).
- Dating, courtship, and weddings.
- Long-ago family reunions, celebrations, holidays, and funerals.
- A terrifying experience (flood, mine cave-in, epidemic, hurricane, fire, etc.).
- What they liked when they were the same age as the student interviewing them.
- What work was like (factory, farm, shop, office, school, store, etc.).
- How something was done before modern conveniences became available (farming, home remedies, cooking, sewing, building, furniture making, travel, games, etc.).

One format students can use is *direct transcription* of interviews with their subjects, which will be easier if students can tape-record the interviews and later transcribe them into print. This format may be easier for some students than creating a narrative or expository article may be, but it involves being able to cut and condense parts as necessary. Transcription works best when someone is describing a long-ago event or telling a story. It may not work with demonstrations of how to do something, because these are often filled with ambiguous statements (e.g., "You take this and put it under here, and then you turn it like so . . .").

Another general format is *narrative written about the interview subject.* This is the type of writing we see most often in magazines and newspapers (e.g., "Bert Herring is 95 years old. He began picking out hymns on his mother's dulcimer at the age of five . . ."). Students can use as models news articles and descriptive passages without dialogue, such as those in travel articles, biographies, and how-to articles. This kind of writing is also called *immersion journalism,* the topic of the next section.

Immersion Journalism

One of the few joys of long airport layovers and sporting events one doesn't understand is the opportunity for people watching. Who has not sat in a waiting room somewhere, eyeing the people nearby, eavesdropping on their conversations, and hypothesizing about their lives? That's the stuff of *immersion journalism*: finding a place and becoming a "fly on the wall"; watching and listening to people; trying to figure out what they're thinking, why they're there, what they were doing just before they got here, and what they're going to do next.

Immersion journalism is not centered in learning about one's own culture, as cultural journalism is. It involves not reporting of events, but developing "slice-of-life" nonfiction essays that arise out of total awareness of a scene, a place, or an episode. The writer attempts not to *tell* the reader about the subject, but to *show* it. "Immersion journalists," wrote Lee Gutkind (1996), "immerse or involve themselves in the lives of the people about whom they are writing in ways that will provide readers with a rare and special intimacy" (p. 9).

This style of writing is sometimes referred to as *creative nonfiction.* The work of such well-known writers as Tom Wolfe (*The Right Stuff*), Annie Dillard (*Pilgrim at Tinker Creek*), John McPhee (*Coming into the Country*), and Doris Kearns Goodwin (*Wait till Next Year*) are representative of this genre. It is simultaneously poetic and journalistic. This "literature of reality" is anchored in factual information and framed by the writer's feelings and responses to the subject (Gutkind, 1996).

Often a creative nonfiction piece begins not with an event or a person, as traditional reporting does, but with a real place: a shopping mall, a restaurant, an emergency room, or a school office. The writer describes the scene so that readers feel they are there, observing the people and events that occur. Writers have to develop attention to detail, and sharp eyes and ears, to notice and record the small details that make the scene come alive for the reader—what Kelly Wright and Carol Barry (1996), sixth-grade teachers, called "close encounters" with the community (p. 38).

For students, this means that much of their writing, and preparation for writing, must be done outside the classroom. Teachers who are taking an immersion journalism workshop can go out and wander in the community, watch and listen to strangers, and come back with a story. As Wright and Barry (1996) wrote, however, "We shuddered to imagine a scene where a sixth grader told his mother, 'My teacher said I have to go to the mall by myself and wait for something to happen, then write about it' " (1996, p. 39). So we take students out of the classroom, to everyday locations nearby—a city park, a local museum, a nursing home, and so forth. These generally aren't big, rent-a-bus field trips;

classes sometimes walk to nearby locations, or use public transportation. Students can also take advantage of places they go with family members, such as the video store, doctor's office, and restaurant.

Students begin by learning how to closely observe the environment they are in—sitting quietly with eyes and ears open; making notes on what they see, hear, and even smell. They listen to people talking and jot down scraps of dialogue. They become immersed in the place. Then they attempt to find a story in what they've observed: to bring to life the sights, sounds, and people; to create a "day in the life" narrative of a character; to write from the point of view of a person or object; to reflect on the meaning of the slice of life they've observed. They write in an attempt to understand, to connect with what they have seen and heard, and to convey that connection to their readers.

Immersion journalism is, for many students, an entirely different kind of writing from any they have done before. Hesitant at first, they often enter into the activity with zest. It is well suited to students in the upper elementary and middle school grades, who particularly enjoy observing and analyzing others. It also provides them with opportunities to explore the genre of creative nonfiction—a body of work they are not usually much interested in—as readers.

REFERENCES

Gillet, Jean Wallace. "Fresh Ideas for Journal Writing." Workshop presented at Virginia State Reading Association Conference, Roanoke, VA, March 1999.

Gutkind, Lee. "The Immersion Journalism/Creative Nonfiction Interplay: Living and Writing the Literature of Reality." In *More Than the Truth: Teaching Nonfiction Writing through Journalism*, eds. Dennie Palmer Wolf and Julie Craven. Portsmouth, NH: Heinemann, 1996.

Larson, Catherine M., and Margaret Merrion. "Documenting the Aesthetic Experience: The Music Journal." In *The Journal Book*, ed. Toby Fulwiler. Portsmouth, NH: Heinemann–Boynton/Cook, 1987.

Macrorie, Ken. *Searching Writing*. Portsmouth, NH: Heinemann-Boynton/Cook, 1980.

Mulholland, Bernadette Marie. "It's Not Just the Writing." In *The Journal Book*, ed. Toby Fulwiler. Portsmouth, NH: Heinemann–Boynton/Cook, 1987.

Temple, Charles, and Jean Wallace Gillet. *Language and Literacy*. New York: HarperCollins, 1996.

Temple, Charles, Ruth Nathan, Nancy Burris, and Frances Temple. *The Beginnings of Writing*, 3rd ed. Boston: Allyn & Bacon, 1993.

Wright, Kelly Peacock, and Carol Kuhl Barry. "From the Bones Out: Teaching the Elements of Immersion Journalism." In *More Than the Truth: Teaching Nonfiction Writing through Journalism*, eds. Dennie Palmer Wolf and Julie Craven. Portsmouth, NH: Heinemann, 1996.

APPENDIX A

⬜⬜⬜⬜⬜⬜⬜⬜⬜⬜⬜⬜⬜⬜⬜⬜⬜⬜⬜⬜⬜⬜⬜⬜⬜⬜⬜⬜⬜⬜⬜⬜⬜⬜⬜⬜⬜⬜

Resources for Teaching
Mini-Lessons

SUGGESTED CHILDREN'S LITERATURE FOR MINI-LESSONS

Mini-Lessons on Authentic Dialogue and Punctuating Quotations

Asch, Frank. *Happy Birthday, Moon*. New York: Simon and Schuster, 1982.

Brown, Marcia. *Stone Soup*. New York: Simon and Schuster, 1947.

Brown, Margaret Wise. *The Runaway Bunny*. New York: Harper & Row, 1942.

Bunting, Eve. *Ghosts's Hour, Spook's Hour*. New York: Clarion Books, 1987.

Bunting, Eve. *A Turkey for Thanksgiving*. New York: Scholastic, 1991.

Carle, Eric. *The Very Busy Spider*. New York: Philomel, 1984.

Deedy, Carmen Agra. *Agatha's Feather Bed*. Atlanta, GA: Peachtree, 1991.

Guarino, Deborah: *Is Your Mama a Llama?* New York: Scholastic, 1989.

Kellogg, Steven. *The Three Sillies*. Cambridge, MA: Candlewick Press, 1999.

Lester, Julius. *John Henry*. New York: Penguin Books, 1994.

Martin, Rafe. *The Rough-Face Girl*. New York: Scholastic, 1992.

McKissack, Patricia. *Flossie and the Fox*. New York: Scholastic, 1986.

Pelham, David. *Sam's Snack*. New York: Penguin Books, 1994.

Ringgold, Faith. *If a Bus Could Talk*. New York: Simon and Schuster, 1999.

Trivizas, Eugene. *The Three Little Wolves and the Big Bad Pig*. New York: Scholastic, 1993.

Van Allsburg, Chris. *Just a Dream*. Boston: Houghton Mifflin, 1990.

Waber, Bernard. *Ira Sleeps Over*. Boston: Houghton Mifflin, 1972.

Walsh, Ellen Stoll. *Mouse Paint*. San Diego, CA: Harcourt Brace Jovanovich, 1989.

Wood, Audrey. *Heckedy Peg*. New York: Scholastic, 1987.

Mini-Lessons on Interesting Leads

See also "Mini-Lessons Using Selected Portions of Novels . . . ," below.

Aardema, Verna. *Bringing the Rain to Kapiti Plain*. New York: Penguin Books, 1981.
Barrett, Judy. *Cloudy With a Chance of Meatballs*. New York: Simon and Schuster, 1978.
Bunting, Eve. *Butterfly House*. New York: Scholastic, 1999.
Lester, Helen. *Hooway for Wodney Wat*. Boston: Houghton Mifflin, 1999.
McKissack, Patricia. *Flossie and the Fox*. New York: Scholastic, 1986.
Polacco, Patricia. *Chicken Sunday*. New York: Philomel Books, 1992.
Scieszka, Jon. *The True Story of the Three Little Pigs*. New York: Scholastic, 1989.
Stanley, Diane. *Raising Sweetness*. New York: Putnam, 1996.
Wood, Audrey. *Heckedy Peg*. New York: Scholastic, 1987.

Mini-Lessons on Central Ideas

Carle, Eric. *The Mixed-Up Chameleon*. New York: Crowell, 1975.
DePaola, Tomie. *The Baby Sister*. New York: Penguin Books, 1996.
Feiffer, Jules. *Bark, George*. New York: HarperCollins, 1999.
Kennedy, X. J. *Elympics*. New York: Penguin Books, 1999.
Krauss, Robert. *Leo the Late Bloomer*. New York: Windmill Books, 1971.
Marshall, James. *Miss Nelson Is Missing*. Boston: Houghton Mifflin, 1977.
Martin, Rafe. *The Rough-Face Girl*. New York: Scholastic, 1992.
Morgan, Allen. *Sadie and the Snowman*. New York: Scholastic, 1985.
Munsch, Robert. *Love You Forever*. Toronto: Firefly Press, 1986.
Pienkowski, Jan. *Good Night*. Cambridge, MA: Candlewick Press, 1999.
Schuch, Steve. *A Symphony of Whales*. San Diego, CA: Harcourt Brace, 1999.
Steptoe, John. *Mufaro's Beautiful Daughters*. New York: Morrow, 1987.
Williams, Vera B. *More More More Said the Baby*. New York: Morrow, 1990.

Mini-Lessons on Vivid Vocabulary

The following books use strong verbs, nouns, and/or adjectives.

Bang, Molly. *Ten, Nine, Eight*. New York: Morrow, 1983.
Barrett, Judy. *Cloudy With a Chance of Meatballs*. New York: Simon and Schuster, 1978.
Bunting, Eve. *Ghost's Hour, Spook's Hour*. New York: Clarion Books, 1987.
Carter, David A. *Alphabugs*. New York: Simon and Schuster, 1994.
Chinn, Karen. *Sam and the Lucky Money*. New York: Lee & Low Books, 1995.
Kirk, David. *Miss Spider's Tea Party*. New York: Scholastic, 1997.
Martin, Bill, Jr., and Eric Carle. *Polar Bear, Polar Bear, What Do You Hear?* New York: Holt, 1991.
Martin, Rafe. *The Rough-Face Girl*. New York: Scholastic, 1992.
Matthews, Judith, and Fay Robinson. *Nathaniel Willy, Scared Silly*. New York: Simon and Schuster, 1994.
McKissack, Patricia. *Flossie and the Fox*. New York: Scholastic, 1986.

Polacco, Patricia. *Chicken Sunday*. New York: Philomel Books, 1992.
Shannon, David. *A Bad Case of Stripes*. New York: Scholastic, 1998.
Stanley, Diane. *Raising Sweetness*. New York: Putnam, 1996.
Trivizas, Eugene. *The Three Little Wolves and the Big Bad Pig*. New York: Scholastic, 1993.

Mini-Lessons on Personal Voice

Deedy, Carmen Agra. *Agatha's Feather Bed*. Atlanta, GA: Peachtree, 1991.
Ehlert, Lois. *Top Cat*. San Diego, CA: Harcourt Brace Jovanovich, 1998.
Lester, Julius. *John Henry*. New York: Penguin Books, 1994.
Kellogg, Steven. *Johnny Appleseed*. New York: Scholastic, 1988.
Kellogg, Steven. *The Three Sillies*. Cambridge, MA: Candlewick Press, 1999.
MacLachlan, Patricia. *All the Places to Love*. New York: HarperCollins, 1994.
McKissack, Patricia. *Flossie and the Fox*. New York: Scholastic, 1986.
Polacco, Patricia. *Some Birthday*. New York: Simon and Schuster, 1991.
Polacco, Patricia. *Chicken Sunday*. New York: Philomel Books, 1992.
Scieszka, Jon. *The True Story of the Three Little Pigs*. New York: Scholastic, 1989.
Stanley, Diane. *Raising Sweetness*. New York: Putnam, 1996.
Trivizas, Eugene. *The Three Little Wolves and the Big Bad Pig*. New York: Scholastic, 1993.
Williams, Vera B. *Music Music for Everyone*. New York: Morrow, 1984.
Williams, Vera B. *More More More Said the Baby*. New York: Morrow, 1990.
Yorinks, Arthur. *Hey, Al*. New York: Farrar, Straus & Giroux, 1986.

Mini-Lessons on Organization

The following books follow a logical chronology of events.

Brett, Jan. *Annie and the Wild Animals*. Boston: Houghton Mifflin, 1985.
Brown, Marcia. *Stone Soup*. New York: Simon and Schuster, 1947.
Bunting, Eve. *Butterfly House*. New York: Scholastic, 1999.
Galdone, Paul. *The Gingerbread Boy*. Boston: Houghton Mifflin, 1975.
Hoberman, Mary Ann. *And to Think That We Thought We'd Never Be Friends*. New York: Random House, 1999.
Locker, Thomas. *Where the River Begins*. New York: Penguin Books, 1984.
Munsch, Robert. *Love You Forever*. Toronto: Firefly, 1986.
Numeroff, Laura. *The Best Mouse Cookie*. New York: HarperCollins, 1999.
Perlman, Janet. *Cinderella Penguin*. New York: Penguin Books, 1992.
Say, Allen. *Tea with Milk*. Boston: Houghton Mifflin, 1999.
Scieszka, Jon. *The True Story of the Three Little Pigs*. New York: Scholastic, 1989.
Steptoe, John. *Mufaro's Beautiful Daughters*. New York: Morrow, 1987.
Waber, Bernard. *Ira Sleeps Over*. Boston: Houghton Mifflin, 1972.
Williams, Linda. *The Little Old Lady Who Was Not Afraid of Anything*. New York: HarperCollins, 1986.
Wood, Audrey. *Heckedy Peg*. New York: Scholastic, 1987.

Mini-Lessons on a Variety of Illustrating Styles

Barrett, Judy. *Cloudy with a Chance of Meatballs*. New York: Simon and Schuster, 1978.

Brett, Jan. *Armadillo Rodeo*. New York: Scholastic, 1995.

Brett, Jan. *Annie and the Wild Animals*. Boston: Houghton Mifflin, 1985.

Bunting, Eve. *Butterfly House*. New York: Scholastic, 1999.

Carle, Eric. *The Secret Birthday Message*. New York: Crowell, 1972.

Deedy, Carmen Agra. *Agatha's Feather Bed*. Atlanta, GA: Peachtree, 1991.

Fleischman, Paul. *Weslandia*. Cambridge, MA: Candlewick Press, 1999.

Joyce, William. *George Shrinks*. New York: Harper & Row, 1985.

Keats, Ezra Jack. *Whistle for Willie*. New York: Viking Press, 1964.

Kirk, David. *Miss Spider's Tea Party*. New York: Scholastic, 1997.

Kirk, David. *Miss Spider's New Car*. New York: Scholastic, 1999.

Martin, Jacqueline Briggs. *Snowflake Bentley*. Boston: Houghton Mifflin, 1998.

Pelham, David. *Sam's Sandwich*. New York: Penguin Books, 1990.

Pelham, David. *Sam's Snack*. New York: Penguin Books, 1994.

Pelham, David. *Sam's Pizza*. New York: Penguin Books, 1996.

Ringgold, Faith. *If a Bus Could Talk*. New York: Simon and Schuster, 1999.

Say, Allen. *Tea with Milk*. Boston: Houghton Mifflin, 1999.

Scieszca, Jon. *The True Story of the Three Little Pigs*. New York: Scholastic, 1989.

Van Allsburg, Chris. *Just a Dream*. Boston: Houghton Mifflin, 1990.

Wood, Audrey. *Heckedy Peg*. New York: Scholastic, 1987.

Mini-Lessons on Complete Sentences

The following books contain clear examples of complete sentences, without taking poetic license to use fragments and run-ons.

Anderson, Laurie Halse. *Turkey Pox*. Morton Grove, IL: Whitman, 1996.

Carle, Eric. *Have You Seen My Cat?* New York: Simon and Schuster, 1987.

Fleischman, Paul. *Weslandia*. Cambridge, MA: Candlewick Press, 1999.

Guarino, Deborah. *Is Your Mama a Llama?* New York: Scholastic, 1989.

Krauss, Robert. *Leo the Late Bloomer*. New York: Windmill Books, 1971.

Lester, Helen. *A Porcupine Named Fluffy*. Boston: Houghton Mifflin, 1986.

Meddaugh, Susan. *The Best Place*. Boston: Houghton Mifflin, 1999.

Morgan, Allen. *Sadie and the Snowman*. New York: Scholastic, 1985.

Trivizas, Eugene. *The Three Little Wolves and the Big Bad Pig*. New York: Scholastic, 1993.

Van Allsburg, Chris. *Just a Dream*. Boston: Houghton Mifflin, 1990.

Whitcomb, Mary E. *Odd Velvet*. San Francisco: Chronicle Books, 1998.

Zelinski, Paul O. *Rumpelstiltskin*. New York: Penguin Books, 1986.

Mini-Lessons on "Show, Don't Tell"

Blume, Judy. *The Pain and the Great One*. Scarsdale, NY: Bradbury Press, 1984. (Original work published 1974)

Martin, Rafe. *The Rough-Face Girl*. New York: Scholastic, 1992.
Munsch, Robert. *Love You Forever*. Toronto: Firefly Press, 1986.
Pelham, David: *Sam's Sandwich*. New York: Penguin Books, 1990.
Shannon, David. *A Bad Case of Stripes*. New York: Scholastic, 1998.
Stanley, Diane. *Raising Sweetness*. New York: Putnam, 1996.
Steptoe, John. *Mufaro's Beautiful Daughters*. New York: Morrow, 1987.
Thaler, Mike. *The Teacher From the Black Lagoon*. New York: Scholastic, 1989.
Van Allsburg, Chris. *Just a Dream*. Boston: Houghton Mifflin, 1990.
Waber, Bernard. *Ira Sleeps Over*. Boston: Houghton Mifflin, 1972
Williams, Vera B. *Cherries and Cherry Pits*. New York: Morrow, 1986.
Wood, Don, and Audrey Wood. *The Little Mouse, the Red Ripe Strawberry, and the Big Hungry Bear*. New York: Child's Play, 1990.

Mini-Lessons on Setting and Time

Aardema, Verne. *Borreguita and the Coyote*. New York: Knopf, 1991.
Brett, Jan. *The First Dog*. San Diego, CA: Harcourt Brace Jovanovich, 1988.
Bunting, Eve. *The Wall*. New York: Clarion Books, 1990.
George, Jean Craighead. *Morning, Noon, and Night*. New York: HarperCollins, 1999.
Lester, Julius. *John Henry*. New York: Penguin Books, 1994.
Locker, Thomas. *Where the River Begins*. New York: Penguin Books, 1984.
MacLachlan, Patricia. *All the Places to Love*. New York: HarperCollins, 1994.
Martin, Jacqueline Briggs. *Snowflake Bentley*. Boston: Houghton Mifflin, 1998.
McKissack, Patricia. *Ma Dear's Aprons*. New York: Simon and Schuster, 1997.
Schuch, Steve. *A Symphony of Whales*. San Diego, CA: Harcourt Brace Jovanovich, 1999.
Steptoe, John. *Mufaro's Beautiful Daughters*. New York: Morrow, 1987.
Wilder, Laura Ingalls (adaptation). *My First Little House Books: Going to Town*. New York: HarperCollins, 1994. (Original work published 1932)
Wood, Audrey. *The Tickleoctopus*. San Diego, CA: Harcourt Brace Jovanovich, 1994.
Yolen, Jane. *Merlin and the Dragons*. New York: Penguin Books, 1995.

Mini-Lessons on Repetition and Patterns

Aardema, Verna. *Bringing the Rain to Kapiti Plain*. New York: Penguin Books, 1981.
Brown, Margaret Wise. *The Runaway Bunny*. New York: Harper & Row, 1942.
Campbell, Rod. *Dear Zoo*. New York: Simon and Schuster, 1982.
Carle, Eric. *Have You Seen My Cat?* New York: Simon and Schuster, 1987.
Carle, Eric. *The Very Quiet Cricket*. New York: Philomel Books, 1990.
Fox, Mem. *Time for Bed*. San Diego, CA: Harcourt Brace Jovanovich, 1993.
Guarino, Deborah. *Is Your Mama a Llama?* New York: Scholastic, 1989.
Hoberman, Mary Ann. *And to Think That We Thought We'd Never Be Friends*. New York: Random House, 1999.
Martin, Bill, Jr., & Eric Carle. *Polar Bear, Polar Bear, What Do You Hear?* New York: Holt, 1991.
Morgan, Allen. *Sadie and the Snowman*. New York: Scholastic, 1985.

Munsch, Robert. *Love You Forever.* Toronto: Firefly, 1986.
Williams, Linda. *The Little Old Lady Who Was Not Afraid of Anything.* New York: HarperCollins, 1986.
Williams, Vera B. *Cherries and Cherry Pits.* New York: Morrow, 1986.
Williams, Vera B. *More More More Said the Baby.* New York: Morrow, 1990.
Wood, Audrey. *Heckedy Peg.* New York: Scholastic, 1987.

Mini-Lessons on Personification

Asch, Frank. *Happy Birthday, Moon.* New York: Simon and Schuster, 1982.
Barrett, Judi. *Animals Should Definitely Not Wear Clothing.* New York: Simon and Schuster, 1970.
Bunting, Eve. *A Turkey for Thanksgiving.* New York: Scholastic, 1991.
Carle, Eric. *The Mixed-Up Chameleon.* New York: Crowell, 1975.
Deedy, Carmen Agra. *Agatha's Feather Bed.* Atlanta, GA: Peachtree, 1991.
Feiffer, Jules. *Bark, George.* New York: HarperCollins, 1999.
Fox, Mem. *Koala Lou.* San Diego, CA: Harcourt Brace Jovanovich, 1988.
Kilborne, Sarah S. *Peach and Blue.* New York: Knopf, 1994.
Krauss, Robert. *Leo the Late Bloomer.* New York: Windmill Books, 1971.
Lester, Helen. *Hooway for Wodney Wat.* Boston: Houghton Mifflin, 1999.
Perlman, Janet. *Cinderella Penguin.* New York: Penguin Books, 1992.
Scieszka, Jon. *The True Story of the Three Little Pigs.* New York: Scholastic, 1989.
Thomas, Patricia. *"Stand Back," Said the Elephant, "I'm Going to Sneeze!"* New York: Morrow, 1971.
Trivizas, Eugene. *The Three Little Wolves and the Big Bad Pig.* New York: Scholastic, 1993.
Williams, Linda. *The Little Old Lady Who Was Not Afraid of Anything.* New York: HarperCollins, 1986.
Wood, Don, and Audrey Wood. *The Little Mouse, The Red Ripe Strawberry, and the Big Hungry Bear.* New York: Child's Play, 1990.

Mini-Lessons on Nonfiction

Aliki. *William Shakespeare and the Globe.* New York: HarperCollins, 1999.
Cline-Ransome, Lesa. *Satchel Paige.* New York: Simon and Schuster, 2000.
Lowery, Linda. *Aunt Clara Brown: Official Pioneer.* Minneapolis, MN: Carolrhoda Books, 1999.
Martin, Jacqueline Briggs. *Snowflake Bentley.* Boston: Houghton Mifflin, 1998.
Poole, Josephine. *Joan of Arc.* New York: Random House, 1998.
Ringgold, Faith. *If a Bus Could Talk.* New York: Simon and Schuster, 1999.
Ryan, Pam Munoz. *Amelia and Eleanor Go for a Ride.* New York: Scholastic, 1999.
Schuch, Steve. *A Symphony of Whales.* San Diego, CA: Harcourt Brace Jovanovich, 1999.
Vaughan, Marcia. *Abbie against the Storm.* Hillsboro, OR: Beyond Words, 1999.

Mini-Lessons on Capitalization

The following books feature many different uses of capitalization (e.g., various proper nouns, quotations).

Carle, Eric. *The Very Busy Spider*. New York: Philomel Books, 1984.
Couvillon, Alice, and Elizabeth Moore. *Mimi's First Mardi Gras*. Gretna, LA: Pelican, 1992.
Isadora, Rachel. *Lili Backstage*. New York: Penguin Books, 1997.
Kellogg, Steven. *Johnny Appleseed*. New York: Scholastic, 1988.
Lester, Helen. *Hooway for Wodney Wat*. Boston: Houghton Mifflin, 1999.
Lester, Julius. *John Henry*. New York: Penguin Books, 1994.
Marshall, James. *Miss Nelson Is Missing*. Boston: Houghton Mifflin, 1977.
Marcellino, Fred. *I, Crocodile*. New York: HarperCollins, 1999.
McKissack, Patricia. *Flossie and the Fox*. New York: Scholastic, 1986.
Poole, Josephine. *Joan of Arc*. New York: Random House, 1998.
Say, Allen. *Tea with Milk*. Boston: Houghton Mifflin, 1999.
Viorst, Judith. *Rosie and Michael*. New York: Simon and Schuster, 1974.
Waber, Bernard. *Do You See a Mouse?* Boston: Houghton Mifflin, 1995.

Mini-Lessons on Inflected Endings

The following books contain many examples of correctly used inflected endings.

Barrett, Judy. *Cloudy with a Chance of Meatballs*. New York: Simon and Schuster, 1978.
Blegvad, Lenore. *Anna Banana and Me*. New York: Simon and Schuster, 1985.
Bunting, Eve. *A Turkey for Thanksgiving*. New York: Scholastic, 1991.
Cannon, Janell. *Verdi*. San Diego, CA: Harcourt Brace Jovanovich, 1997.
Edwards, Pamela Duncan. *The Wacky Wedding: A Book of Alphabet Antics*. New York: Hyperion, 1999.
Fleischman, Paul. *Weslandia*. Cambridge, MA: Candlewick Press, 1999.
Kellogg, Steven. *Johnny Appleseed*. New York: Scholastic, 1988.
Kellogg, Steven. *The Three Sillies*. Cambridge, MA: Candlewick Press, 1999.
Kirk, David. *Little Miss Spider*. New York: Scholastic, 1999.
Shannon, David. *A Bad Case of Stripes*. New York: Scholastic, 1998.

Mini-Lessons on Internal Punctuation—Apostrophes

The following books include apostrophes used in contractions and possessives.

Bunting, Eve. *Ghost's Hour, Spook's Hour*. New York: Clarion Books, 1987.
Bunting, Eve. *A Turkey for Thanksgiving*. New York: Scholastic, 1991.
Crimi, Carolyn. *Don't Need Friends*. New York: Random House, 1999.
Deedy, Carmen Agra. *Agatha's Feather Bed*. Atlanta, GA: Peachtree, 1991.
Feiffer, Jules. *Bark, George*. New York: HarperCollins, 1999.
Fleischman, Paul. *Weslandia*. Cambridge, MA: Candlewick Press, 1999.

Kellogg, Steven. *The Three Sillies*. Cambridge, MA: Candlewick Press, 1999.
Kirk, David. *Miss Spider's Tea Party*. New York: Scholastic, 1997.
Kirk, David. *Miss Spider's New Car*. New York: Scholastic, 1999.
Lester, Helen. *Hooway for Wodney Wat*. Boston: Houghton Mifflin, 1999.
Steptoe, John. *Mufaro's Beautiful Daughters*. New York: Morrow, 1987.
Van Allsburg, Chris. *Just a Dream*. Boston: Houghton Mifflin, 1990.

Mini-Lessons on Internal Punctuation—Commas

The following books contain clear examples of different uses of commas (e.g., interrupters, conjunctions, items in a series).

Albert, Richard E. *Alejandro's Gift*. San Francisco, Chronicle Books, 1994.
Keats, Ezra Jack. *Whistle for Willie*. New York: Viking Press, 1964.
Kellogg, Steven. *Johnny Appleseed*, New York: Scholastic, 1988.
Lester, Helen. *Hooway for Wodney Wat*. Boston: Houghton Mifflin, 1999.
Morgan, Allen. *Sadie and the Snowman*. New York: Scholastic, 1985.
Rathmann, Peggy. *Goodnight, Gorilla*. New York: Putnam, 1994.
Walsh, Ellen Stoll. *Mouse Paint*. San Diego, CA: Harcourt Brace Jovanovich, 1989.
Whitcomb, Mary. *Odd Velvet*. San Francisco: Chronicle Books, 1998.
Weisner, David. *June 29, 1999*. Boston: Houghton Mifflin, 1992.
Wood Audrey. *Heckedy Peg*. New York: Scholastic, 1987.
Wood, Don, and Audrey Wood. *The Little Mouse, The Red Ripe Strawberry, and the Big Hungry Bear*. New York: Child's Play, 1984.

Mini-Lessons on Ending Punctuation

The following books include clear examples of questions, statements, and exclamations.

Bunting, Eve. *Ghost's Hour, Spook's Hour*. New York: Clarion Books, 1987.
Bunting, Eve. *A Turkey for Thanksgiving*. New York: Scholastic, 1991.
Carle, Eric. *Have You Seen My Cat*? New York: Simon and Schuster, 1987.
Campbell, Rod. *Dear Zoo*. New York: Simon and Schuster, 1982.
Crimi, Carolyn. *Don't Need Friends*. New York: Random House, 1999.
Deedy, Carmen Agra. *Agatha's Feather Bed*. Atlanta, GA: Peachtree, 1991.
Edwards, Pamela Duncan. *The Wacky Wedding: A Book of Alphabet Antics*. New York: Hyperion, 1999.
Fox, Mem. *Time for Bed*. San Diego, CA: Harcourt Brace Jovanovich, 1993.
Guarino, Deborah. *Is Your Mama a Llama*? New York: Scholastic, 1989.
Martin, Bill, Jr., and John Archambault. *Chicka Chicka ABC*. New York: Simon and Schuster, 1989.
Martin, Rafe. *The Rough-Face Girl*. New York: Scholastic, 1992.
Numeroff, Laura. *The Best Mouse Cookie*. New York: HarperCollins, 1999.
Ringgold. Faith. *If a Bus Could Talk*. New York: Simon and Schuster, 1999.
Wood, Don and Audrey Wood. *The Little Mouse, The Red Ripe Strawberry, and the Big Hungry Bear*. New York: Child's Play, 1990.

Mini-Lessons on Paragraph Construction

Albert, Richard. E. *Alejandro's Gift*. San Francisco: Chronicle Books, 1994.
Bunting, Eve. *Butterfly House*. New York: Scholastic, 1999.
Fleischman, Paul. *Weslandia*. Cambridge, MA: Candlewick Press, 1999.
Locker, Thomas. *Where the River Begins*. New York: Penguin Books, 1984.
Martin, Rafe. *The Rough-Face Girl*. New York: Scholastic, 1992.
McKissack, Patricia. *Flossie and the Fox*. New York: Scholastic, 1986.
MacLachlan, Patricia. *All the Places to Love*. New York: HarperCollins, 1994.
Poole, Josephine. *Joan of Arc*. New York: Random House, 1998.
Say, Allen. *Tea with Milk*. Boston: Houghton Mifflin, 1999.
Schuch, Steve. *A Symphony of Whales*. San Diego, CA: Harcourt Brace Jovanovich, 1999.
Shannon, David. *A Bad Case of Stripes*. New York: Scholastic, 1998.
Steptoe, John. *Mufaro's Beautiful Daughters*. New York: Morrow, 1987.

Mini-Lessons Using Selected Portions of Novels to Teach Almost Any Skill

These books have especially strong leads and well-developed characters. Even younger students who are not yet ready to read a novel can listen to a few passages of these books when read aloud.

Blume, Judy. *Tales of a Fourth Grade Nothing*. New York: Dutton, 1972.
Dahl, Roald. *The BFG*. New York: Penguin Books, 1982.
Danzinger, Paula. *I, Amber Brown*. New York: Putnam, 1999.
Hansen, Joyce. *Which Way Freedom*? New York: Walker, 1986.
Horvath, Polly. *The Trolls*. New York: Farrar, Straus & Giroux, 1999.
Howe, Deborah, and James Howe. *Bunnicula*. New York: Simon and Schuster, 1979.
L'Engle, Madeleine. *A Wrinkle in Time*. New York: Farrar, Straus & Giroux, 1962.
Lowry, Lois. *The Giver*. Boston: Houghton Mifflin, 1993.
Naylor, Phyllis Reynolds. *Shiloh*. New York: Atheneum, 1991.
Paterson, Katherine. *Bridge to Terebithia*. New York: Crowell, 1977.
Sachar, Louis. *Holes*. New York: Farrar, Straus & Giroux, 1998.
Spinelli, Jerry. *Maniac Magee*. Boston: Little, Brown, 1990.

PROFESSIONAL RESOURCES ON MINI-LESSONS

Areglado, Nancy, & Mary Dill. *Let's Write: A Practical Guide to Teaching Writing in the Early Grades*. New York: Scholastic, 1997.
Calkins, Lucy McCormick. *The Art of Teaching Writing* (new ed.). Portsmouth, NH: Heinemann, 1994.
Dancing with the Pen: The Learner as Writer. Wellington, New Zealand: Learning Media, 1995.
Graves, Donald. *Writing: Teachers and Children at Work*. Portsmouth, NH: Heinemann, 1983.
Hajdusiewicz, Babs Bell. *Words and More Words*. Glenview, IL: Goodyear Books, 1997.

Kieczykowski, Carol. *Developing Process Writing Skills: Primary Writer's Workshop.* Torrance, CA: Frank Schaffer, 1996.

Lane, Barry. *After the End: Teaching and Learning Creating Revision.* Portsmouth, NH: Heinemann, 1993.

Robb, Laura. *Easy to Manage Reading and Writing Conferences.* New York: Scholastic, 1998.

Robb, Laura. *Brighten Up Boring Beginnings and Other Quick Writing Lessons.* New York: Scholastic, 1999.

Schwartz, Susan, and Mindy Pollishuke. *Creating the Child-Centred Classroom.* Toronto: Irwin, 1990.

Temple, Charles, and Jean Wallace Gillet. *Language and Literacy.* New York: HarperCollins, 1996.

APPENDIX B

■□■

Resources on Journal Writing

CHILDREN'S BOOKS FEATURING JOURNAL WRITING

Contemporary Journals

Adler, D. A. *Eaton Stanley and the Mind Control Experiment*. New York: Dutton, 1985.

Byars, Betsy. *The Burning Questions of Bingo Brown*. New York: Penguin Books, 1990.

Cleary, Beverly. *Dear Mr. Henshaw*. New York: Morrow, 1983.

Cleary, Beverly. *The Ramona Quimby Diary*. New York: Morrow, 1984.

Cleary, Beverly. *Strider*. New York: Morrow, 1991.

Colman, H. *Diary of a Frantic Kid Sister*. New York: Archway, 1975.

Cummings, Pat. *Petey Moroni's Camp Runamok Diary*. New York: Bradbury Press, 1992.

Fitzhugh, Louise. *Harriet the Spy*. New York: Dell, 1964.

Glasser, D. *The Diary of Trilby Frost*. New York: Holiday House, 1976.

Hayes, Sarah. *Me and My Mona Lisa Smile*. New York: Lodestar, 1981.

Hooker, R. *Gertrude Kloppenburg (Private)*. Nashville, TN: Abingdon, 1970.

Hunter, Latoya. *The Diary of Latoya Hunter*. New York: Crown, 1992.

Lowry, Lois. *Anastasia Has the Answers*. Boston: Houghton Mifflin, 1984.

Lowry, Lois. *Anastasia, Ask Your Analyst*. Boston: Houghton Mifflin, 1986.

Perl, Lila. *The Secret Diary of Katie Dinkerhof*. New York: Scholastic, 1987.

Pfeffer, S. B. *The Year without Michael*. New York: Bantam, 1988.

Robertson, Keith. *Henry Reed, Inc*. New York: Penguin Books, 1989.

Smith, R. K. *Mostly Michael*. New York: Delacourt Press, 1987.

Tolan, S. S. *The Last of Eden*. New York: Scribner, 1981.

Waber, Bernard. *Nobody Is Perfick*. Boston: Houghton Mifflin, 1970.

Zindel, Paul. *The Amazing and Death Defying Diary of Eugene Dingman*. New York: Harper & Row, 1987.

Fantasy Journals

Jones, R. D. *The Beginning of Unbelief*. New York: Atheneum, 1993.
Oakley, Graham. *The Diary of a Church Mouse*. New York: Atheneum, 1987.
Van Allsburg, Chris. *The Wretched Stone*. Boston: Houghton Mifflin, 1991.

Journals from the Past

Blos, Joan. *A Gathering of Days*. New York: Scribner, 1979.
Ginsburg, Mirra. *The Diary of Nina Kosterina*. New York: Crown, 1968.
Hamm, D. J. *Bunkhouse Journal*. New York: Scribner, 1990.
Hesse, K. *Letters from Rifka*. New York: Holt, 1992.
Johnston, N. *The Keeping Days*. New York: Atheneum, 1973.
McPahil, David. *Farm Boy's Year*. New York: Atheneum, 1992.
Orgel, Doris. *A Certain Magic*. New York: Dial, 1976.
Thaxter, Celia. *Celia's Island Journal*. Boston: Little, Brown, 1992.
Wilder, Laura Ingalls. *On the Way Home*. New York: Harper & Row, 1962.
Wilder, Laura Ingalls. *The First Four Years*. New York: Harper & Row, 1971.
Yezzo, Dominick. *A GI's Vietnam Diary: 1968–1969*. New York: Franklin Watts, 1974.

Travel Journals

Anderson, Joan. *Joshua's Westward Journal*. New York: Morrow, 1987.
Conrad, Pam. *Pedro's Journal*. Honesdale, PA: Caroline House, 1991.
Harvey, Brett. *Cassie's Journey: Going West in the 1880's*. New York: Holiday House, 1992.
Lasky, Katherine. *Beyond the Divide*. New York: Morrow, 1986.
Lowe, S. *The Log of Christopher Columbus*. New York: Philomel Books, 1992.
Turner, Ann. *Nettie's Trip South*. New York: Macmillan, 1987.

Biography Journals

Duncan, Lois. *Chapters: My Growth as a Writer*. Boston: Little, Brown, 1949.
Frank, Anne. *The Diary of a Young Girl*. Philadelphia: Washington Square, 1987. (Original work published 1947)
Keyes, D. *Flowers for Algernon*. New York: Bantam, 1970.
Meigs, Cornelia. *Invincible Louisa*. Boston: Little, Brown, 1933.
Miller, Robin. *Robyn's Book: A True Diary*. New York: Scholastic, 1986.
Yates, Elizabeth. *My Diary—My World*. Philadelphia: Westminster, 1981.
Yates, Elizabeth. *My Widening World: The Continuing Diary of Elizabeth Yates*. Philadelphia: Westminster, 1983.

Science Journals

Brenner, B. *A Snake Lover's Diary*. New York: Young Scott Books, 1970.
Heinrich, B. *An Owl in the House: A Naturalist's Diary*. Boston: Little, Brown, 1990.

PROFESSIONAL RESOURCES ON JOURNAL WRITING

Anderson, Jim. "Journal Writing: The Promise and the Reality." *Journal of Reading*, Vol. 36, No. 4 (April 1993): 304–309.

Bromley, Karen. *Journaling*. New York: Scholastic, 1993.

Calkins, Lucy McCormick, and Shelley Harwayne. *Living Between the Lines*. Portsmouth, NH: Heinemann, 1991.

Dahlstrom, L. M. *Writing Down the Days: 365 Creative Journaling Ideas for Young People*. Minneapolis, MN: Free Spirit, 1990.

Fletcher, Ralph. *Breathing In, Breathing Out: Keeping a Writer's Notebook*. Portsmouth, NH: Heinemann, 1996.

Fulwiler, Toby, ed. *The Journal Book*. Portsmouth, NH: Heinemann, 1987.

Kooy, Mary, & Jan Wells. *Reading Response Logs*. Portsmouth, NH: Heinemann, 1996.

Parsons, Les. *Response Journals*.Portsmouth, NH: Heinemann, 1990.

Senn, J. A. *325 Creative Prompts for Personal Journals*. New York: Scholastic, 1992.

Tchudi, S. *The Young Writer's Handbook*. New York: Aladdin, 1984.

Wollman-Bonilla, Julie. *Response Journals*. New York: Scholastic, 1991.

Index